# the disturbed VIOLENT offender

revised edition

# hans toch

# kenneth adams

American Psychological Association, Washington, DC

First edition published 1989 by Yale University Press. Revised edition
published 1994 by the American Psychological Association.

Copies may be ordered from
APA Order Department
P.O. Box 2710
Hyattsville, MD 20784

In the UK and Europe, copies may be ordered from
American Psychological Association
3 Henrietta Street
Covent Garden, London
WC2E 8LU England

This book was typeset in Palatino by Easton Publishing Services, Inc.,
Easton, MD.

Printer: Princeton Academic Press, Inc., Lawrenceville, NJ
Cover Designer: Michael David Brown
Technical/Production Editor: Paula R. Bronstein

**Library of Congress Cataloging-in-Publication Data**
Toch, Hans.
    The disturbed violent offender / Hans Toch and Kenneth Adams.—
Rev. ed.
        p.    cm.
    Includes bibliographical references and indexes.
    ISBN 1-55798-260-0
    1. Violence.   2. Prisoners—Mental health.   I. Adams, Kenneth,
    1953–   . II. Title.
RC569.5.V55T62   1994
364.3—dc20                                                      94-27951
                                                                    CIP

**British Library Cataloguing-in-Publication Data**
A CIP record is available from the British Library.

*Printed in the United States of America*

*When I first read it this morning, I said to myself I never, never believed it before, notwithstanding my friends kept me under watch so strict, but now I believe I am crazy; and with that I fetched a howl that you might have heard two miles, and started out to kill somebody—because, you know, I knew it would come to that sooner or later, and so I might as well begin. I read one of them paragraphs over again, so as to be certain, and then burned my house down and started. I have crippled several people, and have got one fellow up a tree, where I can get him if I want him.*

—Mark Twain, *Sketches New and Old*

# Contents

# Foreword

Hans Toch occupies a unique niche in contemporary American psychology. A lexicographer seeking an operational definition of the word "integrative" need only point to Toch and his impressive body of research and writing. Toch specializes in synthesizing seemingly separate systems and schemas. A social psychologist, he has spent most of his career studying problems usually claimed by clinicians. His approach to research blends the inductive case study methods used by European comparative criminologists with the multivariate quantitative analyses favored by North American psychologists. Although he has concentrated on violent individuals, Toch has avoided the "fundamental attribution error" by continually calling attention to the situational determinants and precursors of criminal (as well as noncriminal) violence. Throughout his career he has been a member of the academy, but in his writings and research Toch has addressed practitioners, the men and women who must understand and deal with violence and mental illness. Despite his long association with the criminal justice system, which rigidly distinguishes the "good guys" from the "bad guys," Toch has contributed studies of violence on the part of law enforcement officers and correctional personnel, while enlisting prison inmates and criminal offenders as collaborators in his research. Like many of Toch's works, this book will interest, intrigue, and also provoke a broad array of readers who are concerned with mental health, criminal justice and associated problems such as homelessness, unemployment, and substance abuse.

The *Disturbed Violent Offender*, originally published in 1989, is now being reissued in a revised edition by the American Psychological Association as part of a project aimed at bringing Hans Toch's writings to the attention of a broader audience. Coauthored by Kenneth Adams, this book focuses on a problem of vital importance to our mental health, criminal justice, and social service systems: what society should do with, to, or for mentally disturbed citizens who engage in violent behavior. This issue is of enormous practical importance, but its philosophical implications are even broader because they involve fundamental assumptions about human nature, civil rights, and the "social contract" that underlie contemporary systems of government and jurisprudence.

Much of the problem stems from society's ambivalence about the legal status of disturbed violent offenders. At present, the U.S. legal system operates on the premise that criminal defendants are rational. To be subject to criminal sanctions, they must have the cognitive and mental capacity to distinguish right from wrong, foresee the consequences of their behavior, and be able to conform to society's rules if they choose to do so. Although specific rules differ, in theory at least those who are legally insane when they committed their violent act cannot be labeled or treated as criminals if their mental illness was responsible for their illegal behavior.

In addition to those who are "bad but mad" and judged not guilty by reason of insanity, there are also those who are "bad and mad," violent criminal offenders who are legally sane but whose mental disturbance makes it difficult or impossible for conventional correctional institutions to meet their needs. Although their legal status is less ambiguous, the most appropriate way to deal with these unfortunates is far from clear. Their dilemma is epitomized by people who have been sentenced to death but whose mental condition has deteriorated to the point that they are no longer "competent for execution." The mental health system is then expected to restore them to competency so they can understand, and presumably profit from, the penalty that is to be imposed.

Finally, there are those who are "mad but bad," mentally disturbed individuals whose erratic or irrational behavior threatens others. Many such people revolve through the mental health system, various community-based social service agencies, and occasionally the criminal justice system. For many, some act of violence eventually defines their final status; sometimes they are the perpetrators, but often they are the victims. Whether a person is "bad but mad," "mad but bad," or "mad and bad," the current system is poorly equipped to deal with people who have multiple needs and belong to more than one conceptual category.

In ancient times, such labels, if they existed, were irrelevant. Before people developed the notion of "crime," if one person attacked another the victim could suffer in silence, go live somewhere else, or gather family and friends to seek redress, vengeance, or both. Even after the concept of crime evolved, it was limited to offenses against the overall community, such as stealing from the common granary. Individual violence was dealt with by the individuals involved.

Eventually, interpersonal violence became a societal concern, a violation of the "king's peace," subject to collective rather than individual sanctions. Still the mental status of the offender was rarely an important consideration. When guilt or innocence was determined in a trial by combat or a Star Chamber inquisition, the issue of mental health was rarely raised. Nor has it been important in those places and times, past and present, in which individuals' political power, social status, or wealth have determined the outcome.

After the American Revolution, the founding fathers, influenced by the writings of British and French social contract philosophers, rejected the concept of justice based on privilege. Instead they sought to balance the interests of society with the rights of individual citizens, who were assumed to be rational people who understood and agreed to the terms of the social contract. But how should society deal with people who were immature, irrational, or disturbed? Intellectually, society could not accept treating mentally ill people who were incapable of understanding the rules or controlling their behavior as criminals. Emotionally, people could not tolerate a system that failed to protect them from violent individuals, whatever their mental status. Most people did not want such individuals to be regarded as criminals, but nevertheless they wished that someone would arrange things so that disturbed but dangerous people would go away or somehow disappear.

In 1954, Federal Judge David Bazelon thought he had the solution. In *Durham v. United States*, Bazelon broadened the narrow McNaghten test so more violent but disturbed individuals could be adjudicated "not guilty by reason of insanity." If mental illness was responsible for their violence, this ruling would enable them to be diverted from prisons to hospitals where they could be cured of their violent tendencies. Unfortunately psychiatry, having no panaceas for violent behavior, failed to fulfill Judge Bazelon's expectations. By 1972, the disillusioned jurist was accusing the mental health professions of having made promises that they were unable to fulfill.

In recent years, as statutes governing involuntary commitments to mental hospitals have grown more restrictive in many jurisdictions, society has increasingly relied on the criminal justice system to deal with disturbed and violent individuals as well as other social problems, such as driving under the influence, substance abuse, and familial violence, past and present. Since 1970, the number of men and women in America's state and federal prisons has increased more than 400% and the rate of imprisonment has tripled. Although imprisonment segregates many disturbed violent offenders from society for a time, it often does little to meet their needs or to prepare them for their eventual release and return to the community.

How then should society deal with the disturbed violent offender? Often the first step on the path to wisdom is to admit one's ignorance. Before one can prescribe how best to meet the needs of disturbed violent offenders, someone must determine what those needs are. Toch and Adams began by rejecting the seductively convenient conventional wisdom, which differentiated people who were mentally ill (i.e., had problems) from those who were criminals (i.e., caused problems). As Toch notes in his Preface, such "predefinitions force irregularly shaped human pegs into conventional holes." Nothing would be learned if they oversimplified the problems. Instead, they realized they had to understand fully all the complexities involved. How? Through empirical research.

The first steps in any scientific inquiry are empirical observation and classification. By gathering a broad array of information on large samples of disturbed and violent offenders, Toch and Adams hoped they could discover their characteristics, their problems, how these problems manifested themselves over time, and the success of various interventions in meeting these needs.

In scientific inquiries, the methods investigators select are often as important as the questions they pose. The techniques Toch and Adams chose relied on what is now termed "fuzzy" logic. The more traditional and simpler approach would have been to sort their subjects into rigid, mutually exclusive categories (e.g., mentally ill, violent, neither, or both) on the basis of some convenient criterion (e.g., their most recent agency contact). Instead, the authors recognized that the people with multiple problems that they wanted to study at some times would be violent, and at other times disturbed; moreover, sometimes some would be both disturbed and violent and often many would be neither. Although these assumptions sound reasonable enough, their effect was to make the researchers' task enormously more difficult and complex. For example, an extraordinarily broad and detailed array of longitudinal data was necessary for each subject if such an approach was to be implemented.

In order to obtain such information on large samples of violent and disturbed offenders, the investigators had to access and crosstabulate records from the New York State correctional and mental health systems. In many states the relationship between these systems is less than warm and friendly. Unless New York is highly atypical, the investigators had to engage in an extraordinary amount of negotiation and manipulation, coaxing, and cajoling to assemble and integrate such an array of data.

Toch and Adams began with all 8,379 offenders who entered the New York State prison system in 1985 after having been convicted of a statutorily defined violent offense. Crosstabulating this list with the computerized records of the New York State Office of Mental Health, they identified 1,833 offenders who had at some time received psychiatric services. Approximately two thirds, however, had been seen solely for forensic evaluations. Excluding these cases, after further study, the investigators were able to subdivide their offenders into three groups on the basis of their contact with the civil mental health system: those seen for problems stemming from substance abuse ($n = 83$), those seen for psychiatric problems ($n = 540$), and those seen for both ($n = 141$). These cases were contrasted with 543 violent offenders who had apparently never been treated for mental health problems.

Using the other data at their disposal, the investigators were then able to compare the mental health and criminal histories of these groups. They could also formulate career histories for the subjects, concentrating on criminal violence and contacts with the mental health system. By subdividing the offenders' careers into 3 periods, the time of the offense, the 3-year period preceding the offense, and the "remote history" occurring more than 3 years before, the investigators could gauge the chronicity of the observed patterns and assess the sequences of events. These data were then cluster analyzed in an attempt to differentiate subtypes or categories. The investigators' goals are succinctly stated (pp. 44–47):

> The goal of our research was to illuminate sequences of offender behavior in which the advent of criminal acts and of symptoms that are serious enough to justify diagnosis and treatment can be located in time. Such patterns of behavior over time permit us to show when a person is unambiguously disturbed, when he or she is engaging in crime, and when he or she is both. Given a large enough sample, temporal patterning permits the grouping of offenders into types that are characterized by different admixtures and sequences of offenses and symptomatology. . . . By including both offender and offense attributes in the same typology we can develop a composite picture of persons, histories and behavior, and such combinations can provide clues to offense motivation as well as to other psychological processes associated with offending.

Having assembled the database, the technique the investigators selected was hierarchical cluster analysis. The specific methods are described in chapter 2, which specifies how they chose the variables to include in the analyses, how they selected the specific clustering technique, how they assessed the homogeneity of each group, and how they determined the optimal number of clusters to be used in the final solution.

In chapters 4–6, the authors set forth the result of these analyses, delineating 10 types of violent offenders with mental health histories, 5 with substance abuse histories, and 8 without mental health histories. Using longitudinal data they were able to differentiate how different patterns of behavior developed over time. Each type derived is given a descriptive label and richly embellished with excerpts from case histories, including clinical notes and quotations from offender interviews. It remains for further research to determine the validity, generalizability, and heuristic value of these suggested categories.

In chapter 7, the authors shift the focus from the disturbed violent offenders to some of the offenses they committed, offenses in which their psychopathology played a conspicuous role. Ranging from vehicular violence and bungled burglaries to sexual attacks and homicides, these capsule accounts reveal the essential craziness of many of the crimes committed by these disturbed individuals and the fundamental irrationality of their behavior.

This paves the way for chapters 8 and 9. Both address the problem of dealing with the extremely disturbed offender. Chapter 8 addresses the problem of finding an appropriate sentence for the extremely disturbed but minimally violent offender, whereas chapter 9 discusses the problems of programming for the extremely disturbed and extremely violent offender.

The issue in the first case is whether prison is the most appropriate setting for those who are extremely disturbed but minimally violent. The data show that most of these individuals had failed to adjust in the community. Prisons as presently constituted rarely meet their needs, and their presence interferes with correctional institutions' primary task of dealing with "normal" offenders. One solution might be institutions that are similar to the British Special Hospitals for Mentally Abnormal Offenders.

For the extremely disturbed offenders who are also extremely violent, the problem is providing them with the mental health resources they require while they are maintained in a secure setting. The authors note that some of these individuals would be found not guilty by reason of insanity in jurisdictions in which a broader definition than McNaghten was in effect. After discussing the problems posed by these individuals in prisons and in hospitals, the authors describe a program designed to deal with the multiple needs of these offenders in a secure setting.

The question of dealing with such multiproblem offenders is reconsidered in the concluding chapter, which was prepared especially for this edition. Given increasing evidence of an association between certain types of mental disorders and the occurrence of violent offenses (e.g., those described in chapter 7), the issues of risk assessment and treatment assume even more importance. Readers who have read the diverse array of case excerpts presented in the pages leading up to this chapter will share the authors' pessimism regarding nomothetic actuarial predictors.

In this chapter, the authors once again review the problems that are associated with dealing with disturbed violent offenders in ordinary correctional or mental health settings, and the difficulties of providing them with adequate aftercare services following release to the community. It appears that several years after the initial publication of *The Disturbed Violent Offender*, the only improvement in the situation is that more people may now be aware of the problem.

This conclusion is especially discouraging when contrasted with the optimism expressed by Lloyd Ohlin in his Foreword to the first edition of this book. Terming the present report and its companion, "a path-breaking contribution to the study and understanding of violent offenders inside and outside of prison," Ohlin called for, "prospective longitudinal studies that disclose the processes and experiences that lead to the development of these career patterns and provide the data for theoretical analysis of cause and effect sequences [and for analyses of the] policy implications of these findings and their applications in sentencing and correctional decision making." These studies are still needed, as are well-documented programs attempting to implement the authors' proposals for multiservice programs to deal with the multiproblem violent offenders described in this book.

Readers who have followed recent developments in society's approach to criminal justice will not be surprised. Whereas Toch and Adams emphasize the complexity of criminal violence and the variability among offenders, legislators have been jostling each other aside in their eagerness to propose increasingly simplistic solutions. "Getting tough on crime," has given way to, "Three strikes and you're out!" and, emulating 18th century England, extending the death penalty to an ever-increasing array of offenses.

If nothing else, Toch and Adams' research demonstrates that offenders committing the same crime may differ greatly from one another with respect to the chronicity of their offending, the role, if any, played by substance abuse, the danger they pose to themselves and others, and their needs for mental health programming. The logical conclusion is that all these factors should be considered in sentencing and subsequent programming. Instead, however, there has been a proliferation of legislation mandating fixed mandatory sentences for a wide variety of offenses. As a result, from 1986 to 1993 the number of federal prisons increased from 29 to 77, and the number of state prisons grew from 556 to 770. With such massive resources being devoted to prison construction, correctional programming must lag behind. Moreover, when treatment funds and line positions are specifically designated for specialized programs such as classes for drunk drivers and substance abuse treatment, fewer resources are left for treating other offenders.

The first step in coping with a problem such as that posed by disturbed violent offenders is to investigate it empirically. Toch and Adams have begun that task; one hopes other investigators will follow their example and address some of the important questions they have raised.

The second step is to make this information available to the scientific community and the public. That is what the American Psychological Association is doing with this publication project.

The third is for you, the reader, to learn more about the problem so you, too, can help seek solutions. You can begin by turning this page.

EDWIN I. MEGARGEE

# Preface

For both authors this book represents the culmination of a learning experience. In my case this lesson has spanned decades, even though I had the benefit of wise mentors, chief among whom is a one-time colleague, Fritz Redl. Redl often started disquisitions about developmental difficulties by saying, "I want to highlight complexity." He was equally fond of noting that if textbook psychiatric patients had ever existed, they had become extinct—or virtually extinct.

Others to whom I should have listened were offenders and exoffenders I met over the years who offered lessons in complexity that I did not digest. The principal lesson was that offenders can deviate not only from descriptions in criminology textbooks but also from portraits in other textbooks, such as those dealing with mental health problems. The "Sturdy Professional Criminal" is mostly a myth, as is the "Neat Uncompounded Patient."

The culminating lesson I should have learned derives from Redl's studies of aggressive adolescents. These seminal studies had shown (among other things) that personal skills and deficits coexist in delinquents, as do discrepant dispositions and personality structures.[1] A tough predator by day can become a fearful infant by night, and a notorious gang leader can become regressed and anxiety ridden, without disjuncture or discontinuity. Complexity of this sort encompasses the cohabitation of paradoxical elements and requires a view of psychodynamics that links what at first blush looks inconsistent.

Such are lessons I should have assimilated, and I have a great deal of company in not assimilating them, particularly among "forensic mental health" experts, who deal with the overlap between clinical and criminological problems and reliably underestimate it. There is an indication that we share

---

[1] F. Redl and D. Wineman, *Children Who Hate: The Disorganization and Breakdown of Behavior Controls* (New York: Collier Books, 1962).

an aversion to complexity in the shape of combinatory (crime–mental health) problems.

Other observers and I may also have been impatient because as social scientists we have a built-in penchant for cleaning up messes (data are invariably messy) and for trying to make sense of what we find as quickly as we can. My predilection as a psychologist has been for sorting groups of people into homogeneous subgroups that I felt I could understand. This enterprise is best expedited by starting with a neatly defined population, not by increasing heterogeneity (highlighting complexity) first, as Redl advised.

My research experience rests on two enterprises in which I have been involved over the years—one that studied violent offenders and another that focused on mental health problems of prisoners.[2] Both enterprises consumed time and energy, and they were conceptually watertight. I now know that I must have ignored along the way, or brushed aside, evidence suggesting that my subjects in these studies overlapped, that vulnerable persons could and often did victimize other persons as they struggled to adapt.

I owe the change in my general approach to my colleague Ken Adams, who studied prison mental health from the perspective of guards. In the course of his work, Adams noted that prisoners who received mental health services were often the most recalcitrant inmates and sometimes engaged in chronic misbehavior. This observation later inspired our first shared excursion into complexity, which centered on prisoners who had both mental health and behavioral problems in prison.

We decided early on to try to market a combinatory category that we called the Disturbed Disruptive Inmate. Armed with government money, we spent a full week at a motel with 40 mental health and corrections staff, ranging from the head and the clinical director of a hospital and two deputy wardens through eight mental-health-unit chiefs, several clinicians and

---

[2]See especially H. Toch, *Violent Men: An Inquiry Into the Psychology of Violence* (Washington, DC: American Psychological Association, 1992) and H. Toch (*Mosaic of Despair: Human Breakdowns in Prison* (Washington, DC: American Psychological Association, 1992a).

counselors, and a number of prison guards.[3] An illuminated sign at the entrance to the motel read "Welcome DDI Workshop." Passing motorists no doubt wondered whether we were concerned with deductible dental insurance or double-digit inflation. In the motel, however, our fellow-retreatants experienced no ambiguity and accepted (and nowadays widely use) the acronym DDI with no doubt about its referent. These workers bought our concept because they all knew inmates who in their minds unquestionably qualified as both disruptive—posing disciplinary problems—and disturbed—manifesting semicontinuous mental health problems. The sorts of prison inmates who first came to our participants' minds were mostly extremes—legendary and infamous prison figures who were known (at least by reputation) to all staff in the system. These are the kinds of examples that seem to make definitions superfluous.

Consensus at the core of the problem is merciful, because at the outer reaches of the range—particularly when it comes to the question of whether individuals qualify as disturbed—there is a persistent lack of consensus. Whereas extremes require no definition, borderline cases discourage definition. Harmony is maintained by agreeing that where a specific person seems to need contact with mental health staff, or seems likely to benefit from such contact, little is to be gained by quibbling over whether the person's need—his vulnerability or his disequilibrium—transcends or fails to transcend an arbitrary diagnostic boundary.

My colleagues and I felt that if a definition of DDIs was in order, we would like to work up to it rather than start with it. We wanted to begin with shared, plausible personal experiences. To this end, we asked our participants in the workshop to confer in advance with other staff and to enter nominations of disturbed and disruptive inmates. For each inmate

[3]The workshop was supported by Technical Assistance Grant FC-5, "Workshop on Disturbed, Disruptive Offenders" by the National Institute of Corrections, and by the New York State Office of Mental Health and Department of Correctional Services; the state agencies supplied release time and travel assistance to workshop participants.

nominee, we requested mental health and corrections dossiers. We distributed nine such dossiers to four- or five-person interdisciplinary task forces, whose mission it became to characterize their assigned inmates, highlight their motivational patterns, and track their careers through the corrections and mental health system. The sum of these group characterizations became our preliminary "definition"—the shared common ground on which further deliberations were premised.

Our subsequent task was to conduct a study of inmate difficulties in the prison, which we have reported elsewhere.[4] In this study we extended our inquiry, covering the widest possible range of maladaptive behavior among prisoners, with the extremes (DDIs) as the tip of our iceberg. We then grouped inmates according to the problems they seemed to manifest. Our hope was that our groupings now made more sense because we had liberated ourselves from constraints of the mind that resulted from the preclassification of people in terms of whether they have problems (are mental health clients) or produce problems (behave disruptively). Keeping such categories in suspension made the problem of human motivation messier, but we thought it might help to uncover psychological commonalities that we would otherwise miss.

The report that follows extends the logic of this approach from the prison to the community, and from misbehavior to criminal violence. The methodology we use on this occasion is new and different (we shall review it in detail), but our aim is the same: to enhance complexity before reducing it.

What we mean by complexity in this instance is denoted by the title of our book. Our concern is with serious (violent) offenders, but we assume that such offenders can also be persons who suffer from mental health problems (are disturbed). As the other side of the coin we are concerned with persons who have mental health problems (are disturbed), but we shall assume that such persons can also be serious (violent) offenders. The first enterprise is a criminological one and the

---

[4]H. Toch & K. Adams, with J. D. Grant, *Coping: Maladaptation in Prisons* (New Brunswick, NJ: Transaction, 1989).

second is psychological or psychiatric, but the combination allows for interdisciplinary questions.

Definitional issues that we will face are analogous to those in our earlier study. At the extremes, our definitions will come easy but will be superfluous: A murderer is unquestionably a violent offender because he does serious personal harm; a psychotic in full bloom is by the same token "disturbed," given the floridity of his symptoms; a psychotic who commits murder is a "disturbed violent offender," given the consensus we find covering the significance of the person's crime and mental health status. The problem is that as we move from such extremes the definitions sit less easily and hang more loosely. This problem is particularly serious for mental health status, because violent offending is defined by statutes and ratified by courts, whereas mental illness is a seemingly evanescent, arbitrary line clinicians draw which bisects a continuum of behavior that ranges from exemplary adjustment to serious maladjustment.

In the face of this dilemma we opt for inclusiveness, which permits us to define and undefine categories as the facts dictate. We shall at times describe disturbed *violent* offenders, where violence is indisputable and mental health status questionable, and *disturbed* violent offenders where the opposite pertains. Given inclusiveness, we will encounter many persons who combine nonserious offenses with lower order mental health problems, and conceptually we are interested in such combinatory noncoping where we find it. Public policy issues will arise more narrowly, principally revolving around *disturbed violent* extremes and around relatively nonviolent but very disturbed offenders (the *disturbed* violent), who now suffer because they fall between the cracks of the system.

Our self-assigned strategy is to sort or group people as sensibly as we can on the basis of the information available to us. This task is atheoretical, though there are choices to be made about the attributes one considers in grouping. We must obviously admit that *atheoretical* sounds inhospitable to thinking, but we feel that in practice it has the opposite impact, in that descriptive groupings leave a good deal of room for speculation, including speculation from different disciplinary perspectives. This openness is particularly important when the persons we group are of interest to different specialities (e.g., criminology and psychology) in which observers have different concerns. The aim of typologizing hybrid persons as we see it must be to ensure that observers who have interests in different aspects of these persons can think about them more easily and compare them along attributes that are of concern to themselves and to their colleagues. As it happens, this is a necessity for our study, given its clearly cross-disciplinary focus.

Another concern we have is that of public policy, to which we have already alluded. In this realm, we contend that insensitivity to complexity is particularly fateful, because pre-definitions force irregularly shaped human pegs into conventional holes comprising services and institutions that do not accommodate those assigned to them. This matters because the harm reliably done in this way can be serious, not just to persons who are ill-served by settings, but to institutions that cannot accomplish their missions and to society at large.

HANS TOCH

# Acknowledgments

This book is based on research supported by the National
Institute of Justice (NIJ) under Grant Number 85-IJ-CX-
0044. We appreciate the confidence shown us by the Institute
and the patience with which its project monitors (Helen Er-
skine and Richard Laymon) suffered through seemingly endless time extensions. We must emphasize, however, that opin-
ions expressed in the following are ours, not those of the NIJ
staff.

A study such as the one chronicled here requires a great
deal of support from corrections and mental health personnel.
We are fortunate in this regard and feel indebted for the good-
will we enjoyed and the assistance we received from many
persons in the New York State Department of Correctional
Services and Office of Mental Health. Among those who repeatedly facilitated our work are Raymond Broaddus, Joel
Dvoskin, Ronald Greene, Frank Tracy, and Donna Mackey and
her efficient staff.

Data collection and coding would have been a nightmare
without the meticulous contribution of our long-term colleagues Gail Flint and Mary Finn, who dedicated much time
to the agonizing details of this study. Sally Spring bore the
burden of the report, including its numerous revisions, and
preserved both her sanity and ours.

Chapter 8 was published in modified form as "The prison
as dumping ground: Mainlining disturbed offenders," *The Journal of Psychiatry and Law* (Winter 1987). In connection with this
version of the chapter, we are indebted for comments from
Commissioner Thomas Coughlin, Joel Dvoskin, Ronald Greene,
and Scott Christianson.

This edition of *The Disturbed Violent Offender* has undergone
revisions. In addition to other changes, mainly of clarification,
we have added a new, concluding chapter. Joel Dvoskin and
Scott Christianson reviewed drafts of this chapter.

We are grateful to David McDowall, who helped along the
way as consultant, and to Lloyd Ohlin and Gladys Topkis,

who reviewed and improved drafts of the original edition. Professor Emeritus Louis L. McQuitty, whose thinking guided us when we mapped our research, passed away as we began our study. We miss him and regret his passing, and dedicate this book to his memory.

# 1

# Introduction

A crime may capture glaring headlines for a number of reasons. The most obvious has to do with political salience,
which is the reason drug-related violent crimes get consider-
able publicity these days. There are also local concerns that
are mobilized by circumscribed statistical spurts (or "waves")
in certain types of offenses. For example, a community may
see itself as engulfed by intoxicated drivers at one point or
beset by gang members or by serial rapists at another time,
and such perceptions tend to translate into public demands
for action.

There are also types of offenders that consistently stir the
imagination, such as parolees who commit sex-related offenses, terrorists or political assassins, child abusers, citizens
who kill police, and police who are criminally corrupt.

Another type of figure that consistently sparks public concern is the disturbed violent offender. This perpetrator is represented in headlines as an enigmatic person of inscrutable
motives who picks his or her victims for private reasons and
casually maims them or ends their lives. He or she is depicted
as unreachable and unfeeling. Viewed in retrospect, such a
person is described as one who has led a life of fatally accu-
mulating bitterness. If he or she has been seen by mental health
workers, the public wants to know why the system has failed
and why tragedy was not foreseen and prevented.

Headlines that describe the disturbed violent offender (e.g.,

"Fired Janitor Kills School Children," "Gun-Collector Goes on Rampage," "Ex-Patient Shoots Up Hospital," "Sex Killer's Backyard Yields Victims") paint an alarming portrait of a seemingly prevalent problem. This problem is that of offenders who have deep-seated conflicts that make them immensely and promiscuously destructive.

The headlines do both a service and a disservice. They are valid in the sense that the offenders they depict are unquestionably disturbed and indisputably violent. They are helpful in posing a question: How can we protect ourselves from dangerous persons who—some would tell us—belong in hospitals rather than prisons? Where the headlines fail, however, is in conveying the range of behaviors that characterize the "mad" and "bad."

Many crimes committed by disturbed offenders are not headline-grabbing or bizarre and are, in fact, no different, or not very different, from offenses committed by nondisturbed offenders. There are also persons who lead double lives in which chronic psychological problems and chronic offending coexist. Links between mental health problems and violence vary: Some crimes committed by the same person may appear "crazy" and others utterly "sane." Finally, some disturbed offenders may commit serious crimes, but there are many more whose crimes are ineffectual and largely nonserious.

Even such statements, however, must be made with caution. The subject of the disturbed offender is a tantalizing one—though admittedly depressing—but it is largely unexplored. This circumstance does not reflect a lack of interest or of thought. Rather, it is the result of a number of difficulties, many of which are substantial enough to make one refrain from treading where the terrain is unquestionably treacherous.

In the face of discouraging odds, we shall try to present a descriptive overview and typology of disturbed violent offenders and their offenses. This attempt will be tentative and exploratory because the task is indeed inhospitable. Lest the obstacles be underestimated, we begin in the remainder of this chapter by inventorying some of the conceptual and methodological traps that face us as we proceed.

In the next chapters we survey disturbed violent offenders, as we define them at prison intake. We subdivide this universe, and present some case histories to illustrate "typical" offender careers. In the process, we look at offenders with substance abuse problems who may or may not have mental health problems, and vice versa. Throughout, we examine combined offense and mental health histories, because our concern is with the relationship between mental disorder and violence. For the same reason we take a closer look at some offenses committed by disturbed offenders (chapter 7). Chapters 8 and 9 consider dilemmas posed by contrasting types of offenders: One problem person is the basically helpless and ineffectual individual who does not belong in the criminal justice system, but ends up there by default. The second challenge to public policy is the extremely disturbed and violent offender who becomes a mental health client in the prison, where he or she spends a great deal of time. Chapter 10 (the final chapter) raises questions about what can be done for such multiproblem offenders once they return to the community.

## Problems in Studying Disturbed Violent Offenders

When we began studying disturbed violent offenders we knew that we would be vulnerable to criticism, mostly on the grounds that our subject would be deemed illegitimately framed or our coverage indiscriminately inclusive. Such criticism is virtually inevitable, and to consider why, we must delve into the history of the field and into its present-day context.

### Inauspicious Prehistory of the Topic

When criminology and psychiatry were in their infancy, the field was rife with overgeneralizations about possible links between psychological abnormality and crime. To claim such links seemed particularly inviting when considering violent acts (especially murder) because the extremity of the behavior seemed to suggest extremity of motive. Clinical science at its inception also overestimated its reach. Psychiatrists who interviewed (and sometimes tried to treat) exotic offenders often implied that these offenders were, in essential respects, typical. These pioneers also espoused ambitious theories of crime causation, and their form of documentation—freely constructed case histories—made it impossible to disprove enticingly unfolded schemes.

Even in recent times, clinicians have conducted studies of violence that included unverifiable observations. A popular book about murder written in the seventies, for example, detailed a single case that the author supplemented with references to clinical experience, such as

> "having examined hundreds of people who have killed (and I exclude murders committed by organized crime), I have found that homicide usually does not originate because of a clearly defined impulse to murder, but is related to the intensity of inner conflicts,"[1]

and

> "eleven defendants charged with threatening the president or other government officials (of whom I examined eight and studied the records of two others) . . . all showed surprising similarities in their family background, their personality makeup and their pattern of behavior."[2]

Psychoanalytic theorists in particular have traditionally relied on case studies of patients to gain an understanding of their psychological functioning. In the United States this approach was first applied to offenders after the turn of the century under the auspices of the Juvenile Psychopathic Clinic in Chicago and by others, such as Bernard Glueck at Sing Sing Prison. In a seminal work published more than 50 years ago, Franz Alexander and William Healy reviewed the personal histories of delinquent adolescents for "unconscious motives"

---

[1]D. Abrahamson, *The Murdering Mind* (New York: Harper & Row, 1973), p. 10.

[2]D. Abrahamson, 1973, p. 18.

rooted in childhood.[3] In an earlier volume, Healy had tabulated psychological and social variables ("factors") in the case histories of 823 repetitive juvenile offenders referred to his clinic by the Chicago juvenile court. Among other things, he found most of the delinquents to be disturbed.[4] In a more sophisticated book-length study Healy and Augusta Bronner examined paired cases of delinquent and nondelinquent siblings, using a matched experimental-control design. Healy and Bronner interviewed their subjects' parents and teachers and incorporated both these participants' perspectives in describing the interactions leading to the unfolding of delinquency.[5]

The earliest uses of case materials in forensic psychiatry were less disciplined and often reflected prevailing biases and preconceptions. This fact is illustrated by a "disorder" that was invented in the 19th century called *moral idiocy* or *moral insanity* (later dubbed psychopathy, sociopathy, and antisocial personality disturbance). This disease entity, according to an early textbook, was a brain defect leading to "more or less complete moral insensibility and absence of moral judgment and ethic notions" for which "treatment . . . is without prospect of success," so that "these savages in society must be kept in asylums for their own and the safety of society."[6] The case material that documented such pessimistic prognoses suggests to modern readers that the diagnosis offered psychiatrists a way of expressing their disapproval of uninviting clients:

> She was lazy, mendacious, chasing after men, and given to prostitution. . . . She spent, in gourmandizing and amusements, money which her brothers and sister gave her. She did the same thing with what she earned, whether it was in service or by prostitution. . . . On account of her dissolute life she frequently had encounters with the police, for she offended public decency and gave no attention to police

---

[3]F. Alexander & W. Healy, *Roots of Crime* (New York: Knopf, 1935).
[4]W. Healy, *The Individual Delinquent* (Boston: Little, Brown, 1914).
[5]W. Healy & A. Bronner, *New Light on Delinquency and Its Treatment* (New Haven: Yale University Press, 1936).
[6]R. von Krafft-Ebbing, *Textbook of Insanity* (Philadelphia: F. A. Davis, 1904), pp. 623, 626.

regulations. She found nothing improper in her manner of life. . . . She played the injured innocent, paid no attention to the regulations of the house, incited other patients to mischief, had constantly explosions of anger in her great irritability, always about her affair with the police. The police were her enemies, and tried to injure her, though she had never done wrong. Of her moral defect and her inability to direct herself she had no idea. . . . The patient is impossible, coarse to brutality, afraid of work, tries to persuade others not to work, goes about disturbing and scolding others, trying to attract men, and demands her discharge; but she cannot say what she will do when she is put at liberty. The patient was transferred to an institution for chronic insane.[7]

The creation of the concept of moral imbecility proved especially fateful because it was later used by diagnosticians to define reprehensible or obnoxious offenders as clinically different from other offenders, and as less amenable to mental health ministration.[8] The content ascribed to the alleged dis-

---

[7]R. von Krafft-Ebbing, 1904, p. 627.

[8]Millon (1981) has highlighted the continuity of diagnostic labels. He has pointed out that the diagnosis of antisocial personality (the current transmigration) is "but a minor version of earlier ill-considered and deplorable notions such as 'moral imbecility' and 'constitutional psychopathic inferiority'" (p. 181). Both Millon (*Disorders of Personality DSM–III Axis I*, New York: Wiley, 1981) and Wulach ("Diagnosing the *DMS–III* Antisocial Personality Disorder," *Professional Psychology: Research and Practice*, 1983, *14*, 330–340) emphasize that if one applied diagnostic criteria liberally, almost all imprisoned offenders would qualify for sociopathic status. In practice, the diagnosis represents a judgment by the clinician that an offender is reprehensible and less-than-amenable to intervention. Gail Flint Stevens ("Prison Clinicians' Perceptions of Antisocial Personality Disorder as a Formal Diagnosis," *Journal of Offender Rehabilitation*, 1994, *20*, 159–185) has confirmed this in a survey of corrections mental health staff. While some staff dismiss antisocial personality as "a wastebasket diagnosis," others proclaim that "a majority of people (in prison) are antisocial personalities." Those who use the diagnosis assiduously characterize the prisoners as manipulative, hedonistic, and chronically dangerous. The implicit prognosis is pessimistic. A psychiatrist said to Stevens that psychopathic characteristics "are something you're kind of born with." A social worker asserted that when she encountered the label, "what I see people convey to me is 'put a bandage on this guy and let him go back to population.'" Stevens (1994) concludes that "perhaps most disturbingly, the diagnosis antisocial personality is given mainly to convey to others supposed negative characteristics of inmates so

order—a hedonic outlook or a defect of the offender's conscience—invited this usage, making it a euphemism for congenital badness, malevolence, or deviant character. In a recent book on mass murder, for example, the authors conclude:

> The serial killer . . . travels around, sometimes from state to state, searching for victims whom he can rape and sodomize, torture and dismember, stab and strangle. Even these truly sadistic killers are, however, more evil than crazy. Few of them can be said to be driven by delusions or hallucinations; almost none of them talks to demons or hears strange voices in empty rooms. Though their crimes may be sickening, they are not sick in either a medical or a legal sense. Instead, the serial killer is typically a sociopathic personality who lacks internal control—guilt or conscience— to guide his own behavior, but has an excessive need to control and dominate others. He definitely knows right from wrong, definitely realizes he had committed a sinful act, but simply doesn't care about his human prey. The sociopath has never internalized a moral code that prohibits murder. Having fun is all that counts.[9]

Many early psychiatrists (including Benjamin Rush, a signer of the Declaration of Independence)[10] have held an assortment

---

diagnosed and not in the hopes of possible treatment or understanding of the diagnosis" (p. 183), that "the person so diagnosed is generally considered not only a serious, violent offender, but also someone who is fated to continue a life of criminal behavior and hopelessness" (p. 184).

[9]J. Levin & J. A. Fox, *Mass Murder: America's Growing Menace* (New York: Plenum, 1985), pp. 229–230.

[10]The psychology of crime was Rush's long-term avocation. He delivered papers on prison reform in a seminar that ran under Benjamin Franklin's auspices, in which he advocated psychological sorting and differential treatment of prisoners, including medical treatment for offenders whose motives he adjudged to be pathological. Rush felt that all prospective convicts could be classified according to whether their crimes were inspired by "passion, habit, temptation or mental illness" (D. Fogel, *We Are the Living Proof* [Cincinnati: Anderson, 1979], p. 14). An example of Rush's penchant for taxonomy is the following: "When the will becomes the involuntary vehicle of vicious actions, through the instrumentality of the passions, I have called it *moral derangement*. [My prior discussion of] the morbid operations of the will are confined to two acts, viz., murder and theft. I have selected those two

of views that were surprisingly eclectic, and they favored classifying offenders into types, including groups to be treated medically. The evidence used by such alienists to classify offenders as normal or pathological, unfortunately, was often sketchy and prominently centered on the nature and/or severity of the offenders' crimes. At other times the material was a promiscuous assembly of data, permitting emphases to taste.

The historian David Rothman notes that the construction of comprehensive case histories such as those that to this day can be found in the folders of offenders was intended to illuminate causes of personal difficulties so that individualized treatment programs could be designed for them. This approach reflected what Rothman describes as naive faith in science because it assumed that patterns of pathology would somehow emerge from comprehensive inventories of facts.[11] The result, however, has been precisely the opposite, in that biographical accounts contain some presumptive wheat but much chaff and offer no clues to which facts may be most characteristic or informative or causally relevant in individual instances.

More serious problems occurred as a result of high clinical expectations. The overblown claims of mental health experts had annoyed a generation of social scientists, who ended up by condemning the substance of the clinicians' concerns as well as their methods. Most early textbooks in criminology (written by sociologists reared in the hard-nosed positivistic tradition) ridiculed the notion that offenders could be seen as disturbed and took pains to stress the "normalcy" of crime, meaning all crime. This understandably parochial stance created a disjuncture in the field, whereby ruminations about crime causation diverged from clinical thinking, which was thereby denuded of criminological theory. Psychologists and

---

symptoms of the disease (for they are not vices) from its other morbid effects, in order to rescue persons affected by them from the arm of the law, and to render them the subjects of the kind and lenient hand of medicine." This passage dates from an 1812 publication (excerpted in Szasz, *Age of Madness* [Northvale, NJ: Jason Aronson, 1974], p. 25). In the same essay, Rush prescribes "sober houses"—to be established "in every city and town in the United States "—for persons addicted to alcohol (pp. 26–27).

[11]D. Rothman, *Conscience and Convenience* (Boston: Little, Brown, 1980).

psychiatrists who aspired to enter the forensic area were trained without benefit of crime-related expertise, while criminologists routinely dismissed offenders' mental health problems as having nothing to do with their criminal careers.

The reason this developing situation mattered was that clinical practitioners—particularly social workers, who for a time entered corrections in sizable numbers—interfaced blithely with delinquents, addicts, and disturbed offenders, applying their "mainline" clinical thinking, which criminologists had dismissed as not relevant to crime causation or to recidivism. In time, criminologists and their allies—armed with masses of program evaluation data which showed that "nothing [that is, no treatment] works"—brought this activity into disrepute.[12] Clinicians continued to function in reduced numbers in correctional settings but were mostly seen as "mental health staff" who were ameliorators of medical conditions, and no longer as rehabilitators of special groups of offenders.

To be sure, exceptions remained to the rule that mental health staff were not regarded as crime experts. These exceptions, however, were not contributions to clinical criminology. One exception was the demand that clinicians estimate the future probability of violent offenders' recidivism (dangerousness). Another exception involved the requirement that clinicians contribute to judgments as to the "sanity" of (mostly violent) defendants in courts. The former enterprise was in-

---

[12]The phrase derives from R. Martinson's article "What Works?—Questions and Answers About Prison Reform" (*Public Interest*, 1974, 35, 22–54). Martinson's conclusion was that "with few and isolated exceptions, the rehabilitative efforts that have been reported so far have had no appreciable effect on recidivism." A more recent summary of authoritative opinion based on review of the same data concluded that "at the present time, no recommendation about ways of rehabilitating offenders could be made with any warranted confidence, and, therefore, no new major rehabilitative programs should be initiated on a widespread basis. At the same time, neither could one say with justified confidence that rehabilitation cannot be achieved, and, therefore, no drastic cutbacks in rehabilitative effort should be based on that proposition." This conclusion was arrived at by a panel of social scientists convoked by the National Research Council (L. Sechrest, S. O. White, & E. D. Brown, eds., *The Rehabilitation of Criminal Offenders: Problems and Prospects* [Washington, DC: National Academy of Sciences, 1979], pp. 102–03).

auspicious because many experts adjudged it to involve dubious extrapolations.[13] The latter concern was not in fact intended to be one of clinical diagnosis. However, testimony about insanity is an important activity because it lends the illusion of science to a distinction that must be made on unscientific grounds when one wishes to sort disturbed from nondisturbed offenders.[14]

## The Insanity Defense as an Exculpatory Criterion

The insanity defense originated as a way of ensuring that crazed assassins and other transparently demented offenders were not dragged, kicking and screaming, to the scaffold.[15] It is important to keep this goal in mind because it means that the concern was with avoiding farcical displays of punitiveness rather than with excluding disturbed persons in general from punishment. The point of the insanity defense was to define the limits of what one could sensibly call blameworthy conduct. This issue was important to judges, who resolved it by concluding that blame should not attach to any act committed by a person who did not know what he or she was doing

---

[13]Some limitations have to do with the unreliability of clinical judgments, and others relate to the low probability of violent behavior, except among very chronic violent offenders. This low probability creates a problem because "events that have low base rates are very difficult to predict with high levels of accuracy. Moreover, even the accuracy that is achieved comes at the cost of high rates of 'false positives,' that is, persons who are predicted to be dangerous but who will actually not display such behavior" (S. A. Shah, "Dangerousness: Conceptual, Prediction and Public Policy Issues," in J. R. Hays, T. K. Roberts, & K. S. Solway, eds., *Violence and the Violent Individual* [New York: Spectrum, 1981], p. 161).

[14]Though insanity is a purely legal concept, one problem with the term is that colloquial and past technical usage broaden its connotations. The dictionary defines *insanity* as "a deranged state of mind" or "a mental disorder." These lay definitions correspond to vintage clinical definitions, as witnessed by the fact that the earliest house organ of the American Psychiatric Association was the *American Journal of Insanity*, which continued publication for many decades.

[15]H. Weihofen, *Insanity as a Defense in Criminal Law* (New York: The Commonwealth Fund, 1933). A more contemporary perspective is that of Justice Bazelon, who wrote in the well-known *Durham* decision (see note 24) that "our collective conscience does not allow punishment where it cannot impose blame."

while he or she was doing it. The earliest versions of this doctrine were formulated during the reign of Edward I (1272–1307).[16] Later, routine pardons were accorded to murderers classed as "lunaticks" because of "not knowing more than wild beasts"; historians further noted that "madness became a complete defense to a criminal charge" under the liberal auspices of Edward III (1327–1377).[17]

The insanity defense preceded the advent of clinical science by several centuries. By 1843, however, when the contemporary insanity defense was formulated (the action was taken in an uproar over a case reminiscent of that of John Hinckley),[18] medical evidence was introduced in the trial, as in others in which insanity had become an issue. The landmark case that sparked controversy was that of Daniel McNaghten, about whom physicians testified that he "labored under an insane delusion" that he was persecuted by (among others) the prime minister of England. McNaghten was acquitted "on the ground of insanity" of having shot and killed the prime minister's secretary, and the judges of England were challenged by indignant legislators to justify their verdict. The McNaghten doctrine, which defines insanity in many U.S. jurisdictions to this day, is annunciated in the key paragraph of the judges' reply:

> The jury ought to be told in all cases that . . . to establish a defense on the ground of insanity, it must be clearly proved that, at the time of committing the act, the party accused was labouring under such a defect of reason, from disease of the mind, as not to know the nature and quality

---

[16]S. S. Glueck, *Mental Disorder and the Criminal Law: A Study in Medico-Sociological Jurisprudence* (Boston: Little, Brown, 1925).

[17]R. M. Perkins, *Criminal Law* (New York: Foundation Press, 1957), p. 739.

[18]John Hinckley made an assassination attempt on President Reagan in which the president and a member of his entourage were injured. Hinckley was subsequently acquitted by reason of insanity under the American Penal Law Institute standard (see note 25), as adopted by federal courts in *United States v. Brawner* (471 F.2d 969, D.C. Cir., 1972). Hinckley's insanity acquittal sparked a public furor, and in partial reaction Congress tightened the insanity standard (in the Federal Crime Control Act of 1984), requiring "clear and convincing evidence" of incapacity and placing the burden of proof on the defense.

of the act he was doing, or if he did know it, that he did not know he was doing what was wrong.[19]

Obviously, the issue for the judges was not that the offender suffered "from disease of the mind," although he had to be mentally disturbed for the definition to apply. The issue, rather, was that the offender must be oblivious to his actions or their impact as a result of being thus disturbed. This criterion is narrow and describes (a) a purely hypothetical, metaphysical state of mind which (b) is difficult for an observer to ascertain, particularly in retrospect. The criterion is also not spontaneously thought of by psychiatrists when they are left to their devices in dealing with patients. Given the narrowness and diagnostic irrelevance of the rule, it is not surprising that physicians found it uncomfortable almost as soon as it had been formulated. Among others, the American psychiatrist Isaac Ray led a spirited attack on the insanity defense in the 1860s and convinced the courts in his home state of New Hampshire to expand the definition. Ray felt strongly that psychiatrists should be allowed to operate in an unfettered fashion, and should present evidence as they saw it as to the mental condition of the offender and its expected impact on his crime.

Isaac Ray was a founder of the American Psychiatric Association and has been called "by far the most influential American writer on forensic psychiatry during the whole 19th century."[20] Like other psychiatric critics of the McNaghten rule, Ray objected to the premium the rule placed on impairment of knowledge. He wrote,

> The error arises from considering the reason, or to speak more definitely, the intellectual faculties, as exclusively liable to derangement, and entirely overlooking the passions or affective faculties. . . . While the reason may be unimpaired, the passions may be in a state of insanity, impelling a man . . . to the commission of horrible crimes in spite of

---

[19]Weihofen, 1933, p. 28.
[20]W. Overholser, "Isaac Ray, 1807–1881," in H. Mannheim, ed., *Pioneers in Criminology* (Montclair, NJ: Patterson Smith, 1973), p. 177.

all his efforts to resist. . . . The whole mind is seldom affected; it is only one or more faculties, sentiments, or propensities, whose action is increased, diminished or per-
verted, while the rest enjoy their customary soundness and
vigour. . . . True philosophy and strict justice require that
the action of the insane should be considered in reference
. . . to the faculties that are diseased.[21]

More fundamentally, Ray opined that insanity was either a
fact or not a fact, and "properly speaking, there can be no law
on this subject other than the facts themselves."[22] Ray felt that
psychiatrists should be recognized as scientific experts and
dismissed as irrelevant the circumstance that they often disagreed as witnesses (he wrote that "very little evidence of any
sort is completely harmonious").[23] This position has recently
been characterized as cavalier by such incisive critics as Thomas
Szasz, who writes,

It is possible, in virtually any case in which psychiatric testimony is introduced, to secure psychiatric testimony in op-

---

[21]I. Ray, "Lecture on the Criminal Law of Insanity," *The American Jurist*,
1835, *14*, 253. The same point has been made by many psychiatric spokes-
persons, including a committee for the Group for Advancement of Psychiatry, who wrote about the McNaghten standard that "the rules place a premium on intellectual capacity and presuppose that behavior is actuated
exclusively by reason and untrammeled choice. On the one hand, this
overemphasizes the importance of the intellect, reason and common sense;
on the other hand, it underemphasizes the emotional pressures that energize
behavior" (Group for the Advancement of Psychiatry, Committee on Psychiatry and Law, *Criminal Responsibility and Psychiatric Expert Testimony*, report
no. 26 [Topeka, KS, 1954], p. 4). Some psychiatrists disagreed with this
view. Carl Wertham, for instance, wrote that "The distinction between right
and wrong is not a purely intellectual performance, but affects the whole
personality and has definite and important emotional components. . . . So
the rule inherently does include emotion and affect. . . . The law allows the
psychiatrist to lay all the proof of the diagnosis and degree of a mental
disease before the court. According to scientific psychiatry, that includes
necessarily the emotional part of the personality. If the law singles out one
criterion for its own purposes, that does not mean that the psychiatrist has
to seal off that aspect from the rest of the affected personality" (F. Wertham,
*A Sign for Cain* [New York: Paperback Library, Coronet, 1969], p. 245).
[22]Overholser, 1973, p. 194.
[23]Overholser, 1973, p. 192.

position to it. How are we to reconcile this fact? If we compare psychiatric to, say, toxicological testimony, a comparable situation would be one in which the toxicologist for the prosecution testified that a body contained a lethal amount of arsenic, whereas the toxicologist for the defense testified that it did not. This, of course, never happens, because one of the experts could be, and would be, proved guilty of perjury. . . . Mental illness is not the sort of phenomenon whose presence or absence can, at least according to current practices, be easily identified by scientifically impartial methods. Since there are no scientifically accepted ethical and social criteria of mental health—a concept corresponding to the permissible level of arsenic in the human body in our analogy—there can be no scientifically accepted criteria of mental illness.[24]

Notwithstanding such criticisms, experiments with liberalized insanity definitions that gave psychiatrists more elbow room were introduced. For a period of several years, for example, the District of Columbia used a standard (the *Durham* rule) which provided psychiatrists unlimited opportunity for unfettered testimony. The three-judge panel of the U.S. Court of Appeals (headed by J. Bazelon) wrote,

We find that as an exclusive criterion the right–wrong test is inadequate in that (a) it does not take sufficient account of psychic realities and scientific knowledge, and (b) it is based upon one symptom and so cannot validly be applied in all circumstances. . . . We conclude that a broader test should be adopted. . . . The rule we now hold must be applied on the retrial of this case and in future cases is not unlike that followed by the New Hampshire court since 1870. It is simply that an accused is not criminally responsible if his unlawful act was the product of mental disease or defect. . . . The legal and moral traditions of the Western world require that those who, of their own free will and with evil intent, commit acts which violate the law shall be

---

[24]T. Szasz, "Criminal Responsibility and Psychiatry," in H. Toch, ed., *Legal and Criminal Psychology* (New York: Holt, Rinehart & Winston, 1961), pp. 162–163.

criminally responsible for those acts. Our traditions also require that where such acts stem from and are the product of a mental disease or defect as those terms are used herein moral blame shall not attach and hence there will not be criminal responsibility. The rule we state in this opinion is designed to meet these requirements.[25]

More recently the federal courts and a number of states adopted a modified McNaghten rule which incorporated moderately liberalizing recommendations of the American Law Institute's *Model Penal Code*. This definition read,

A person is not responsible for criminal conduct if at the time of such conduct as a result of mental disease or defect he lacks substantial capacity either to appreciate the wrongfulness of his conduct or to conform his conduct to the requirements of the law.[26]

The post-Hinckley backlash has changed the direction of reform. Several states have taken the insanity defense off the books. Elsewhere, it has become an increasingly circumscribed defense. It offers a legal—not a clinical—criterion designed to apply (and applied) to a small minority of very seriously disturbed offenders.[27] The existence of the rule helps make salient the question of whether these offenders are disturbed but otherwise creates a problem because it invites the presumption that the law distinguishes between disturbed offenders and nondisturbed offenders, as it largely does not. The critical fact is that the overwhelming majority of disturbed offenders are processed without the question of their sanity being raised. This does not mean that these persons' mental states are criminologically irrelevant or that their offenses are untainted by their conditions. The fact that some offenders are adjudged

---

[25]*Monte W. Durham v. United States,* 214, F.2d 862 (D.C. Cir., 1954).

[26]See note 17. The ALI proposal was first published in the American Law Institute's *Model Penal Code,* Proposed Official Draft (Philadelphia: Author, 1962).

[27]H. J. Steadman et al., *Before and After Hinckley: Evaluating Insanity Defense Reform* (New York: Guilford Press, 1993).

"insane," however, creates the implication that all offenders not so adjudged must be "sane" persons who commit "normal" offenses.

## The Problem of Locating and Defining Disturbed Violent Offenders

We can take it for granted that the violent offenders who are adjudicated not guilty by reason of insanity must first be disturbed offenders, but the group is miniscule and presumably quite unrepresentative. Other individuals who could be characterized as disturbed offenders are dispersed in a variety of settings, and, once located, they are apt to present definitional problems in that cross-sectional and historical portraits may yield different admixtures of emotional problems, offenses, and violent behavior, particularly over time.

Mental health varies over a person's life span, and violent offenses take place at particular junctures in time, during which the person may be disturbed or nondisturbed. Even if the person is disturbed and commits an offense, however, this does not mean that the occurrence of the offense, its nature, or its quality is affected by the person's mental condition. Psychological problems, moreover, cover a wide range, and we have noted that a line between disturbed and nondisturbed is very hard to draw. Violence is also a spectrum, ranging from moderate to extreme and from sporadic to habitual.

If we define a disturbed violent offender as a person who is sometimes undeniably disturbed and who sometimes commits offenses involving violence, such a person may be located among mental patients at a given point in his life and among offenders at other points. The former fact has been a matter of concern because the mixture of disturbed violent persons and other disturbed persons may in the public mind stigmatize mental patients as violence-prone.[28] To neutralize this stigma

---

[28]As has been pointed out by Shah (1981), this stigma is increased by involuntary commitment criteria which emphasize "danger to self and others," leaving the impression that persons are hospitalized because they are violence-prone. Shah wrote that "there is the implicit, sometimes even explicit,

some observers in the 1970s stressed that mental patients appeared to be more criminogenic than nonmental patients only statistically because mental patients who had criminal records were included in the calculations.[29] The implication was that these disturbed offenders were in fact mainline offenders who happened to be in hospitals but would look more at home in prisons.

A comparable point could be made for offenders in the criminal justice system—particularly inmates in prisons—who turn out to have mental health problems that require attention. One can demonstrate that such persons have frequently had problems in the community and have received services, including hospital services. This fact invites the charge that prisons have become repositories for the mentally ill and that chronic patients have become inmates because they were prematurely discharged or "dumped," landing in prisons by default.[30]

Neither crime-accentuating nor pathology-accentuating portraits accommodate the third possibility that many persons are both legitimate patients and legitimate offenders and become

---

assumption that by virtue of being mentally ill a person is more likely to engage in dangerous and violent behaviors. . . . Commitment laws for the mentally ill seem to be premised on the assumption (actually a belief) that, as a group, the mentally ill constitute one of the most dangerous groups in our society. Yet there is no sound or convincing empirical evidence to support such a belief" (p. 168).

[29]Actually, the statistic at issue is misleading. Hospitalized ex-offenders have higher arrest rates than the general population, but arrest rates for *violent* crimes of the group are similar to those of the population when both are compared to offenders released from prison (H. J. Steadman, J. J. Cocozza, & M. E. Melick, "Explaining the Increased Arrest Rate Among Mental Patients: The Changing Clientele of State Hospitals," *American Journal of Psychiatry*, 1978, *135*, 816–820).

[30]This charge is premised on another assumption, which is that disturbed persons in prisons have proliferated in proportion to inmate populations. This assumption is universally endorsed by prison administrators but cannot be substantiated given (a) the paucity of trustworthy epidemiological surveys, and (b) disagreement about the definitions of mental illness one would have to agree on for epidemiological research to take place. One stumbling block, for example, is that rates can be inflated or deflated through the inclusion or exclusion of the "antisocial personality" construct (see note 8) as a formal diagnosis. In one prison survey, for example, 78% of male inmates were diagnosed as sociopathic (S. Guze, *Criminality and Psychiatric Disorder* [New York: Oxford University Press, 1976]).

legitimate clients of both systems, or of one or the other system at different points in time.

To be sure, any system may make an effort to exclude inappropriate clients at intake. The insanity defense can be regarded as such an effort by the courts, as can the competency examination, which is designed to avoid criminal trials in which defendants are so handicapped that they do not understand what is happening to them when they are tried.[31] Mental health programs in their turn can exclude offenders with behavior problems as unacceptably "disruptive." There are also more complex and subtle screening procedures, which include rejecting multiproblem clients on the ground that they are better served elsewhere (see chapter 10).

The issue of multiproblem clients is particularly germane to disturbed offenders because such offenders are often disadvantaged persons who manifest a variety of deficits. This observation is familiar to service providers today but could have been advanced decades ago because the sociologists' original case against the clinical approach was buttressed by statistics demonstrating that crime was associated with social disadvantages that were known to produce other undesirable consequences as well.

Shaw and McKay, of the pioneering Chicago Area Study, for example, asked,

> Many other "problem" conditions might be listed, each representing a state of affairs considered undesirable by most citizens. These would include various forms of unemployment, dependency, misconduct, and family disorganization,

---

[31]Halleck pointed out that the doctrine of pretrial competency, which dates to the 17th century, is "fundamental to the integrity and dignity of the legal process" because "trying individuals who may not even understand why they are on trial is inherently absurd, as well as incompatible with the commitment to justice" (S. Halleck, *The Mentally Disordered Offender* [Washington, DC: National Institute of Mental Health, 1986], p. 20). Halleck also noted, however, that competency to plea bargain is rarely at issue. Given that the defendant is in theory a party to the plea bargain, which presupposes his active participation, the failure to raise the "competency" question at this key juncture is mystifying, especially because most criminal cases are resolved through guilty pleas, which presuppose plea bargains.

as well as high rates of sickness and death. It may be asked: Do these other phenomena exhibit any correspondence among themselves and with rates of boys brought into court?[32]

Shaw and McKay answered their own question affirmatively. They reported very high intercorrelations among problems of persons who reside in the most disorganized neighborhoods of metropolitan areas, and concluded that

> any great reduction in the volume of delinquency in large cities probably will not occur except as general changes take place which effect improvements in the economic and social conditions surrounding children in those areas in which delinquency rates are relatively high.[33]

The recognition that social disadvantages can produce multiple handicaps is important because it means not only that the same person can have two or more problems but that these problems can reinforce each other in a variety of ways. This fact has become increasingly obvious to scholars and is illustrated by changes in their perspective about causal links such as those between family problems, educational deficits, unemployability, and addiction, on the one hand, and delinquent careers, on the other.[34] The accommodation of contemporary criminologists to the possibility of increased complexity of causation is especially stimulated by longitudinal studies which permit them to order events in time so that they can trace antecedents and consequences in causal chains and loops.[35]

Such developments are helpful to our own inquiry, but the evolving sociological model does not include mental health problems, and it cannot do so because the proportion of offender populations who have such problems looks small. This

---

[32]C. R. Shaw & H. D. McKay, *Juvenile Delinquency and Urban Areas* (Chicago: University of Chicago Press, 1942/1972), p. 90.

[33]Shaw & McKay, 1972, p. 321.

[34]T. P. Thornberry, "Toward an Interactional Theory of Delinquency," *Criminology*, 1987, *25*, 863–891.

[35]D. P. Farrington, L. E. Ohlin, & J. Q. Wilson, *Understanding and Controlling Crime* (New York: Springer, 1986).

means that whereas more prevalent deficits (such as drug addiction and school failure) can be plugged into criminological equations, emotional problems are likely to remain as noise in such equations, as long as they are narrowly defined.

Violence as a variable suffers from the opposite problem in that a good deal of the offense spectrum includes violence, which complicates the task of disentangling violent crime from nonviolent crime, except at extremes. Long careers are apt to be heterogeneous in the sense that they include both violent and nonviolent offenses.[36] The specialized "violent offender" is a rarity, and definitions of violent offenders must accommodate mixed careers that include repeated violent involvements. Even when this is done, however, the dependent variable in studies that use such definitions is more saliently the chronicity of crime than the violence of the offenses committed.

## The Juxtaposition of Illness and Malevolence

We have implied that the insanity defense has become unpopular and has been controversial since its inception. One reason is that where harm is salient, the notion of exculpation (and escape from punishment) is uncongenial to the public. A second reason has to do with the connotations of crime and mental illness, which make these concepts hard to reconcile and combine.

One generally tends to equate crime with malevolence and illness with helplessness. Crime, therefore, invites resentment, illness, and sympathy. It is hard to summon up sentiments that contrast so sharply, assuming it were possible to envision malevolent helplessness (or helpless malevolence) as a target of feelings.

Combinations of "madness" and badness are also puzzling, and the mind rejects them. Fortunately, badness tends to be documented in most instances, whereas madness is at best postulated. The harm crime does is a tangible fact, whereas the offender's hypothesized disability is an issue that is often

---

[36]M. E. Wolfgang, R. M. Figlio, & T. Sellin, *Delinquency in a Birth Cohort* (Chicago: University of Chicago Press, 1972).

in dispute by experts who assert and deny its existence. This makes it easy to resolve the problem of logical dissonance by classifying mad and bad persons as bad persons who are of somewhat eccentric dispositions and whose badness preempts attention.

The problem is eased by sequencing of conduct. If a person behaves in a disturbed way today and commits violent acts tomorrow he or she is not deemed mad and bad but mad-turned-bad. After the person offends he or she becomes an offender and can be dealt with as such. After the same person breaks down (provided he is not offending at the time) he or she becomes a patient, and can again be treated.

The formula of personal transmutations is convenient, but it must often be applied in strangely compartmentalized ways. If symptoms are destructive or misbehavior is bizarre, different aspects of the same act can invoke disparate responses in tandem. Deadpan punitiveness can precede therapy, or vice versa. This sequential process implies such assumptions as that treatment can restore the person-as-patient to a condition such that the person-as-offender can be punished. The person-as-offender can then become a person-as-patient as soon as his or her medication wears off or his or her punishment commences, as when the offender enters prison where he or she receives mental health services.

## Problems Posed by Early Recidivism Studies

Offenders and patients, and combinations of the two (such as insanity acquittees, defendants judged incompetent, and disturbed offenders adjudicated as "dangerous"), have been tracked in follow-up studies to ascertain their rates of rehospitalization and reoffending.[37] One would think that such investigations

---

[37]The third category includes two "natural experiments," in which courts of appeal ordered the release of disturbed offenders who had been retained in prison hospitals because they had been judged dangerous a number of years earlier. The offenders did relatively well after they had been released into the community. See H. J. Steadman & J. J. Cocozza, *Careers of the Criminally Insane* (Lexington, MA: Heath, 1974); T. P. Thornberry & J. E. Jacoby, *The Criminally Insane* (Chicago: University of Chicago Press, 1979).

would point to linkages between mental illness and crime, but the research had the opposite import, even when the persons studied were clearcut disturbed violent offenders when they became subjects of study.

This outcome of research is a combined effect of the facts that are customarily unearthed in the studies (variables predicting one sort of recidivism or the other) and the approaches to the garnering of these facts (how one goes about recidivism research, which means locating variables that predict and denote recidivism).

Segmentation of the disturbed offender as subject occurred because reoffending was correlated with one set of facts—age, for instance, and type of offense—and rehospitalization with a somewhat different set of facts.[38] Even when unquestionably disturbed offenders were followed into the community, different failures of members of the group could be traced to different predictors, making it appear that the group contained (a) chronic offenders who happened to be disturbed, (b) chronic patients who happened to have offended, and (c) a composite type of offender whose offense behavior and emotional problems existed side by side, responding to different drummers in compartmentalized ways.[39]

---

[38]The three classic variables that predict offender recidivism are age, prior criminal record, and present offense (V. O'Leary & D. Glaser, "The Assessment of Risk in Parole Decision Making," in D. West, ed., *The Future of Parole* [London: Duckworth, 1972] pp. 135–199). Among the variables that predict rehospitalization are age, past mental illness, marital status, and diagnosis (E. Zigler & L. Phillips, "Social Competence and Outcome in Psychiatric Disorder," *Journal of Abnormal and Social Psychology*, 1981, *63*, 254–271; W. Schofield, S. Hathaway, D. Hastings, & D. Bell, "Prognostic Features in Schizophrenia," *Journal of Consulting Psychology*, 1954, *18*, 155–166; W. Morrow & D. Peterson, "Follow Up of Discharged Psychiatric Offender," *Journal of Criminal Law, Criminology and Police Science*, 1966, *57*, 33–34).

[39]Two authors who hold this view wrote that "the correlates of crime among the mentally ill appear to be the same as the correlates of crime among any other group: age, gender, race, social class, and prior criminality. Likewise, the correlates of mental disorder among criminal offenders appear to be the same as the correlates of mental illness among other populations: age, social class, and previous mental illness" (J. Monahan & H. Steadman, "Crime and Mental Illness: An Epidemiological Approach," in N. Morris & M. Tonry, eds., *Crime and Justice: An Annual Review of Research*, vol. 4 [Chicago: University of Chicago Press, 1983], p. 181).

This bifurcated (or trifurcated) view of recidivism persisted in reviews of research trends over time. When some studies were compared with older studies, for example, more recidivism was reported among patients.[40] As we have implied, this trend can be attributed to an influx of diagnosed offenders whose advent among nonoffending patients gives them a bad name. Contemporary prisons can be similarly characterized as increasingly permeated with disturbed individuals, and the past absence of patients could be seen as accounting for the fact that early studies showed no disproportionate pathology among prison inmates.[41] Recidivism statistics as data also posed a special problem for disturbed violent offenders because the form of violence most likely to be associated with pathology

---

[40]Among the earlier studies, which showed lower rearrest rates, were M. C. Ashley, "Outcome of 1,000 Cases Paroled From the Middletown State Homeopathic Hospital," *State Hospital Quarterly*, 1922, *8*, 64–70; H. M. Pollock, "Is the Paroled Patient a Menace to the Community?" *Psychiatric Quarterly*, 1938, *12*, 236–244; H. Brill & B. Malzberg, *Statistical Report of the Arrest Record of Male Ex-Patients, Age 16 and Over, Released From New York State Mental Hospitals During the Period 1946–48* (Albany: New York State Department of Mental Hygiene, 1954); and L. H. Cohen & H. Freeman, "How Dangerous to the Community Are State Hospital Patients?" *Connecticut State Medicine Journal*, 1945, *9*, 697–700. Among later studies, which show higher rearrest rates, are J. R. Rappeport & G. Lassen, "Dangerousness—Arrest Rate comparisons of Discharged Mental Patients and the General Population," *American Journal of Psychiatry*, 1965, *121*, 776–783; J. R. Rappeport & G. Lassen, "The Dangerousness of Female Patients: A Comparison of Arrest Rates of Discharged Psychiatric Patients and the General Population," *American Journal of Psychiatry*, 1966, *123*, 413–419; J. M. Giovannoni & L. Gurel, "Socially Disruptive Behavior of Ex-Mental Patients," *Archives of General Psychiatry*, 1967, *17*, 146–153; A. Zitrin, A. S. Hardesty, & E. T. Burdock, "Crime and Violence Among Mental Patients," *American Journal of Psychiatry*, 1976, *133*, 142–149; and J. R. Durbin, R. A. Pasewark, & D. Alberts, "Criminality and Mental Illness: A Study of Arrest Rates in a Rural State," *American Journal of Psychiatry*, 1977, *134*, 80–83.

[41]One well-informed researcher concluded that "the literature, albeit methodologically flawed, offers at least modest support for the contention that the mentally ill are being processed through the criminal justice system" (L. A. Teplin, "Managing Disorder: Police Handling of the Mentally Ill," in L. A. Teplin, ed., *Mental Health and Criminal Justice* [Sage, 1984b], p. 54). On the other side of the fence, researchers contended that "mental hospitalization is an ever increasing occurrence for those with histories of criminal activity" (J. Cocozza, M. Melick, & H. Steadman, "Trends in Violent Crime Among Ex-Mental Patients," *Criminology*, 1978, *16*, 330).

(non-felony-related) was seen as relatively nonrecidivistic.[42] Pathology, however, was assumed to be an independent cause of violence, which is why psychiatrists were invoked to predict "dangerousness" not illuminated by statistics.

## Failure of Settings to Accurately Classify Client Attributes

One assumes that practitioners cannot avoid facing "mixed" client problems and dealing with them. Schools, for example, must manage students who are not only disruptive and disturbed but obviously disruptively disturbed or crazily disruptive. Although recognition of such problems is inevitable in the front lines, administrative considerations may constrain classifications of problems, which means that perceptions need not translate into veridical labels.

Classifications of people very often become byproducts of resource allocation. In schools, for example, the proportions of students with misbehavior problems as opposed to mental health problems may be adjusted to accord with programmatic emphases such as those in special education programs. In this sort of calibration, adding mental health staff expands the pool of mental health clients and shrinking services reduces the pool. One can also try to ignore one's resources and expand or contract labels of people as one thinks they are needed, as in smoking and nonsmoking sections of airplanes. In some large jails, for example, the numbers of "mental health beds" vary from count to count, with services and facilities remaining roughly the same.

Such taxonomic exercises can be a problem because operational definitions can be enacted that bear no resemblance to the substance of real client needs. In jails, for example, mental health problems are often equated with suicide potential.[43] This

---

[42]See O'Leary and Glaser (1972); also, G. Kassebaum, D. Ward, & D. Wilner, *Prison and Parole Survival: An Empirical Assessment* (New York: Wiley, 1971).

[43]H. J. Steadman, D. W. McCarty, & J. P. Morrissey, *Developing Jail Mental Health Services: Practice and Principles* (Washington, DC: National Institute of Mental Health, 1986).

means that an inmate who talks about killing himself (that is, who expresses what clinicians call suicidal ideation) may be attended to, whereas prisoners who are less obtrusively disturbed are neglected. The strategy could be defensible if its aim were to address inmate despondency, but the goal—suicide prevention—is one of controlling undesired behavior or avoiding legal repercussions rather than improving mental health.[44]

Suicide poses issues of consequence because it reflects societal ambivalence about mental illness and criminal behavior. Szasz points out that suicide attempts had been historically defined as violent crimes, but the advent of the insanity concept redefined the behavior as mental illness.[45] Similar redefinitions occur when people are committed to psychiatric settings, given that the prevailing hospital entrance requirements (danger to self or others) specify social harm, but treatment targets symptom reduction. To reduce a person's symptoms may reduce his or her dangerousness, but if this occurs it is a corollary of more significant achievements, such as restoring the person's contact with reality and ability to care for self. Mental health concerns, such as whether this person can feed and clothe himself or herself, follow a daily routine, lead an independent existence, and relate to other people, may have little to do with dangerousness, which defines treatment candidates at entrance or discharge.

The situation is one in which disturbed and criminal persons are defined as one or the other at different junctures in time, or in contact with different agencies, or to subserve different aims. The result is "humpty-dumptyish" in the sense that there is no integrated approach to the person as a whole. The situation also impedes the reconstruction of lives that cannot be understood unless the contribution of pathology to the genesis of misbehavior is recognized.

---

[44]H. Toch, 1975. A sad fact that makes the practice ironic is that despondent inmates who are isolated through suicide prevention in jails often experience exacerbated difficulties, including completed suicides.

[45]T. Szasz, "Insanity and Irresponsibility: Psychiatric Diversion in the Criminal Justice System," in H. Toch, ed., *Psychology of Crime and Criminal Justice* (New York: Holt, Rinehart & Winston, 1979), pp. 139–141.

# Describing the Careers of Disturbed Violent Offenders

We have suggested that there are difficulties in thinking about disturbed violent offenders as subjects of research. Some of these difficulties are conceptual and others are strategic. Conceptual difficulties can compound strategic difficulties, and this makes it necessary for a researcher to operate atheoretically at first, holding conceptual problems in abeyance. One must arrive at and adhere to operational definitions that lead to an internally consistent picture, though broader questions relating to the nature of crime (or violence) and mental illness remain temporarily unresolved.

One set of definitions one must arrive at has to do with the population that one will study. The subjects must be violent and disturbed, but few people are judged violent and disturbed at the same time. This means that the researcher must select one variable that is contemporary and that describes the person's current status while making do with a second variable that mainly describes his or her history. One must view persons who are currently definable as disturbed or criminal, with records of disturbed and/or criminal behavior. Different selection strategies yield different subpopulations with different attributes.

The two variables (violent crime and mental health) yield interrelationships, but one variable (violent crime) is primarily dependent in that it can be affected by the other variable (mental health) but is unlikely to affect it. Given the one-way nature of this relationship, offender status makes a more plausible criterion or outcome measure, and mental health status makes a less plausible one. A retrospective inquiry can plausibly start with a population of violent offenders whose mental health (as well as criminal) histories are available for review. The strategy has become increasingly feasible nowadays because mental health systems keep computerized records of the services they deliver to their clients.

Regardless of which selection strategy one uses, one must recognize that definitions of mental illness or criminality— official designations of offender and patient status—describe the responses of agencies as well as the behavior of the persons responded to by the agencies. One can at times correct for less-than-optimal definitions (for instance, one can independently assess the violence level of behavior by using descriptions of offenses), but one cannot escape the fact that a criminal conviction or a diagnosis is a judgment, not a behavior description.

Links between crime and mental illness present a compounded problem because they represent assumed relationships between assumed categories of behavior. Coexistence of observed behavior can be more safely asserted. One can describe temporal patterns, starting with the premise that behavior classifications that coincide in time or rapidly follow each other provide clues to interrelatedness, and that more extended sequences provide more enduring cues having to do with behavioral consistencies (if any) over time. The study of consistencies over time must also be a core concern of consequential motivation-related research because personality, as conventionally defined, means no more and no less than consistency of behavior.[46]

The inferences one can draw from one's research in this area depend on the range of behavior, particularly of "mental health problems," one can subsume. Restricted definitions are always neater but tend to describe extremes or (at worst) exotica. Moreover, neatness dissipates in longitudinal portraits given the checkered careers of the subjects one studies, and psychological careers are no less checkered than offense careers, which means that persons who at times are psychotic manifest less serious disabilities with greater frequency at other times. A more substantial argument against a restricted-range model is that it obfuscates the multiproblem nature of disabilities, which is already obfuscated by preclassifications of clients and the segmentation of services.

The liabilities of extended-range sampling (such as lack of precision) can be neutralized by sorting, grouping, or disaggregating populations in consequential ways. This benefit co-

---

[46]G. W. Allport, *Pattern and Growth in Personality* (New York: Holt, Rinehart & Winston, 1961).

incides with more pragmatic considerations because we must sort disturbed violent offenders into groups for other reasons, such as the fact that our variables of interest (mental illness and violence) can intersect in many and diverse ways. We must also sort people into homogenous groups if the key questions we want to speculate about are motivational (for instance, how does mental illness affect offense behavior?), because to answer such questions one must get as close to the individual as possible while preserving the capacity to generalize to similarly motivated persons.

*Consequential disaggregation* means that one must strive to select distinguishing attributes that have relatively substantial explanatory power, given the limitations of one's data set. Purely descriptive variables (such as the physical attributes of an offense) are probably dispensable because they carry only situational or criminalistic significance. And other recorded data (such as legal offense descriptions) must be beefed up to more closely approximate qualitative differences among people and their behavior.

Disaggregation yields subgroups or typologies, in this case, types of offenders who differ in the combination of problems (violence and mental illness) that they manifest. It probably is not critical whether one starts with subgroupings along one or the other of these problem areas because either sorting procedure (variations of violence across mental health groupings, or types of mental health problems across offense groupings) would permit one to review representative clusters of contrasting offenders.

One reason we have placed a certain emphasis on the past history of offenders is that we feel that research exploring links between categories of behavior makes the most sense if it can trace these links over time. In part this is so because sequences can illuminate changes from one behavior category to another. In particular, we see no way other than through a review of lives over time to describe the paradoxical sequences of destructiveness and nonresilience that may be represented among offenders who are at times violent and at times disturbed.

There is an additional virtue in combining typological and longitudinal views. When we portray grouped persons longitudinally, we ask not only what sorts of problems people have and how people's problems evolve but also how people with different problems experience the evolution of their problems and how people whose problems evolve differently differ from each other.

Though such ways of posing differentiating questions are similar, they are also different. The first strategy involves pre-classifying problems and tracking their course over time. In educational research, students can be divided into good students and poor students on the basis of averaged academic performance; next, typical histories can be charted. Poor students may be found to have short scholastic careers that begin inauspiciously and degenerate. Should this be so, one draws causal inferences, such as, Chances are, failure breeds failure.

Pure scientists delight in such inferences, but policymakers may need more discriminating data. The educator may have to ask questions (e.g., Which students offer hope or justify taking risks?) that call for closer scrutiny of career patterns. The same holds for reformers or interventionists, who need clues (such as spurts in desirable or undesirable behavior under specifiable conditions) to the impact of remedial interventions.

Such concerns increase the attractiveness of "career-based typologies" that use behavior trends as the basis for sorting people. This grouping strategy invites one to examine, for example, the downhill or uphill careers of students viewed separately, or the careers of chronic versus nonchronic offenders. The strategy does have "applied" advantages—for instance, it helps assess risk level where chronicity is predictive of difficulties. The approach also offers a way of posing questions about cause and effect sequences. By the same token, some questions become more difficult to ask when we concentrate on sequential (when) events and underemphasize content (what) concerns. It becomes harder, for example, to become aware of latent or qualitative shifts; chronics, for example, keep looking chronic, though they have problems that change complexion over time.

The nondifferentiation of problem content is a particularly serious issue when we know that "the problem" is a composite set of difficulties that vary independently. We know of our disturbed violent offenders, for example, that they have at least two problems (mental illness and a propensity to aggress) whose manifestations can be traced separately. This knowledge almost forces us to inject problem-related criteria of disaggregation (What are the person's precise difficulties?) into our career typology (How does the person manage over time?) to produce a composite portrait (How do the person's varying problems change over time?).

When we engage in this sort of compounded exercise we obtain a more differentiated but also more cluttered picture of career patterns. In mitigation of this lack of neatness we can offer only the prospect of viridicality, a sense of variegated permutations of "real life" careers. We can also claim a somewhat innovative perspective that describes a range of serious and complex offenders in a way that is different from the averaged portraits customarily found in the criminological literature.

# I

# A Study of Disturbed Violent Offenders

# 2

# Research Strategy

Newspaper headlines proclaiming "epidemics" of violence and of mental health problems or announcing the existence of yet another "crazed" murderer can give the impression that a large percentage of the population is violent or mentally ill. Although the salience given to such stories reflects the high level of concern society attaches to these problems, it belies the fact that from a researcher's point of view serious violent crime and serious mental disorder are relatively infrequent events. National data collected by the Federal Bureau of Investigation indicate that in 1993 between seven and eight violent crimes were reported to the police for every 1,000 persons in the general population.[1] Epidemiological estimates of mental disorder are harder to come by on the national level, but the evidence suggests that about 5% of the population have experienced serious mental illness such as schizophrenia, major depression, and manic episodes at some point in their lives.[2] In developing our approach to studying mentally disordered violent offenders we had to deal with this statistical reality.

---

[1]K. Maguire & A. L. Pastore, eds., *Sourcebook of Criminal Justice Statistics, 1993*, U.S. Department of Justice, Bureau of Justice Statistics (Washington, DC: U.S. Government Printing Office, 1994).

[2]L. N. Robins, J. E. Helzer, M. Weissman, H. Orvaschel, E. Gruenburg, J. D. Burke, & D. A. Regier, "Lifetime Prevalence of Specific Psychiatric Disorders in Three Sites," *Archives of General Psychiatry*, 1984, *41*, 949–958.

Because our interests were in persons who qualify as both mentally ill and violent, we could anticipate that the difficulties inherent in studying uncommon events would be exacerbated. The challenge we faced in designing our research was that of ensuring a sample of mentally disordered violent offenders sufficiently large for multivariate statistical analyses while working within real-world limitations, such as the usual constraints on resources and time. Given these considerations, we could rule out a number of design strategies. For example, we could eliminate a design in which we randomly sampled from an arrest population, given that a study of 1,382 police–citizen encounters uncovered only three incidents in which violent crimes were committed by persons who showed evidence of mental disorder.[3] We could increase the yield of this type of selection process by focusing on a more restricted population, such as a group of mentally disordered individuals or a group of violent offenders, but the evidence suggests that the improvement would be marginal. A recent follow-up study of 3,858 mental patients found that only 50 of them were arrested for a violent crime within 19 months of discharge to the community.[4]

What was needed, then, was a reliable and efficient procedure for identifying a substantial number of mentally disordered violent offenders. One such approach starts with a group of convicted violent offenders, then narrows it to those who have had recourse to mental health services. This procedure gave us a pool of recently violent individuals who at some point in the past may have been mentally ill. We could then refine our categorization of offenders as mentally disordered by collecting information on the nature and extent of services they had required.

## Selection of the Sample

We began our sample selection with an entry cohort of inmates sentenced to a term of incarceration in the New York prison

---

[3]This figure does not include traffic-related incidents. See L. A. Teplin, "Criminalizing Mental Disorder: The Comparative Arrest Rate of the Mentally Ill," *American Psychologist*, 1984a, *39*, 799.

[4]Steadman et al., 1978.

system after having been convicted of a violent offense. During the time period that defines the cohort we reviewed—January 1985 through December 1985—12,764 offenders were admitted to the prison system.[5] Of this group of offenders, 8,379 were sentenced for a statutorily defined violent offense, a criterion that covers a wide range, including some types of burglaries.[6]

Our next step was to match the names and birthdates of the violent offenders in the cohort against computerized client records maintained by the New York State Office of Mental Health.[7] The records are a historical listing of persons who received outpatient or inpatient treatment at any state-operated psychiatric facility, thereby providing an efficient screening device for identifying persons with a history of admission to psychiatric service. The comparison yielded a total of 1,833 matches, which means that 22% of the entering prisoners had experienced some contact with the state mental health system. Having identified the former patients and secured their client identification numbers, we then accessed computerized service delivery files and obtained a treatment history of each individual. The treatment information, which includes date, type of facility, and type of service, would later be used to infer the nature and severity of mental health problems.

On examining the service delivery records, we found that most (66%) of the offenders had been forensic (court-referred) clients, for whom there was little or no treatment information. This picture contrasted sharply with that of the civil psychiatric

---

[5]The prison intake cohort includes only new admissions. It does not include offenders returned to prison for violating parole.

[6]We used the statutory definition of violent offense, which includes a few crimes that traditionally might not be considered violent. In New York state, degrees of burglary are distinguished by whether there was threat or physical harm to a victim. (N.Y. Penal Law §§140.20–140.35 [McKinney 1988]). Legally defined violence extends to some property offenders because they may have threatened or harmed a victim. In addition, we note that the statutory definition of violence is the criterion that determines which criminals qualify for penalty enhancements under specialized violent offender laws, and the extension of these penalties to include some property crimes again reflects a concern for the violence potential of these offenses.

[7]Cross-referencing of computerized corrections records and mental health records was done on the basis of last name, first two letters of first name, and date of birth.

patients we identified, who for the most part had extensive treatment records. We also found that a significant number of offenders had been admitted to psychiatric facilities for alcohol and drug abuse problems. This finding was particularly interesting to us, because the relationship of substance abuse disorders to violence could plausibly differ from that of other emotional disorders.

At this point in our sampling procedures we had identified a group of "mentally disordered" violent offenders with the following characteristics: (a) most of the offenders were forensic patients for whom we could not otherwise confirm a history of serious emotional disorders; (b) some offenders had received psychiatric treatment primarily for alcohol and drug abuse problems, and because substance abuse treatment programs also are run by paraprofessionals in quasitherapeutic settings, inmates who were exclusively clients of these programs were not identified; and (c) the group did not include offenders who had received services only in private psychiatric facilities. In view of these considerations, we turned to another source of data—the correctional files—in order to refine our classification procedures.[8]

The New York State Department of Correctional Services maintains a file on each inmate at its central administrative office. The files contain a variety of records, many of which

---

[8]Psychiatric patients who have serious drug or alcohol abuse problems are one example of the multiproblem mental health client. A recent newspaper article documents the fact that the mental health system has difficulty treating persons with combined psychiatric and substance abuse problems. The article notes that between one-fifth and one-half of the mentally ill are substance abusers, and a state commission estimated that there are 100,000 such dually disabled persons in New York. Even though an effective treatment strategy has yet to be developed, mentally ill substance abusers consume a disproportionate share of mental health resources. In the article, the father of a schizophrenic alcoholic is quoted as complaining, "The alcoholism programs can deal with alcoholism. The mental health programs can deal with mental illness. But my son has both and they don't know how to deal with that." At least one reason for this situation is that treatment approaches of alcoholism programs, which are often confrontational, and of psychiatric programs, which often use drugs supplemented by emotional and social support, can be incompatible ("Mental Health System Fails Alcoholics, Drug Abusers," Albany *Times Union*, March 13, 1988, pp. A–1, A–4).

relate to the inmate's prison experiences. Of particular interest to us were documents generated during the intake and classification process that detail the offender's past mental health involvements and his or her criminal history. These records offered us another source of information on the offender's psychiatric history along with a complete chronology of adult criminal justice experiences.[9] However, because the information contained in these documents had to be retrieved manually, it was impractical for us to collect data on the entire offender cohort. We therefore invoked a sampling strategy, selecting all offenders with civil psychiatric records, a total of 625 inmates, for inclusion in the sample.[10] We also randomly sampled from the group of forensic patients we had identified (sampling ratio 1:7; $n = 145$) and from inmates with no record of treatment by the state Office of Mental Health (sampling ratio 1:12, $n = 540$). As we reviewed the correctional files, we abstracted information on mental health contacts and on participation in community substance abuse programs, later merging these data with the Office of Mental Health records and eliminating redundant entries in terms of date of contact and name of treatment institution. In addition, while searching the files, we coded the chronology of each offender's criminal history (dates and offenses) and the details of the violent incident for which the inmate was sentenced.

By invoking the correctional files as a source of information, we clarified the nature of treatment involvement for some forensic patients, and we uncovered some mental health clients who had not been identified by the computerized record search. In Table 2.1 we display the composite treatment histories (correctional files and mental health files) by the initial classifications (forensic, civil, no service) derived from mental health files. We were able to confirm the treatment status of nearly all (99%) civil patients, which includes a substantial proportion

---

[9]Many prison files contained information on juvenile offenses. We coded this information whenever available, recognizing that it may be missing for some offenders because of laws that order juvenile records sealed as confidential.

[10]We also included the handful of patients with extensive forensic treatment records in this group.

**Table 2.1**

*Results of Search for Service Delivery Information by Initial Classification of Mental Health Experience of Offender*

| Service delivery based on correctional and mental health files | Initial classification of mental health experience | | |
| --- | --- | --- | --- |
| | No history ($n$ = 540) | Forensic patient ($n$ = 145) | Civil patient ($n$ = 625) |
| Psychiatric evaluation only | 7% | 13% | 1% |
| Substance abuse treatment program | 8 | 8 | 5 |
| Psychiatric treatment program | 15 | 22 | 73 |
| Psychiatric and substance abuse treatment programs | 2 | 2 | 21 |
| No service delivery information | 68 | 56 | 0 |

(21%) who were treated for combined addiction–mental health problems. In contrast, we were less successful with the forensic clients, failing to locate any service delivery information on more than half (56%) the group. We inferred from this absence of information that treatment experiences were minimal and that these clients probably did not suffer from serious disorders. We were, however, able to discern that some forensic patients participated in treatment programs (22%) or had undergone psychiatric evaluation (13%) only. The figures on the group initially described as having no service history are interesting because they bear on the advantages of accessing multiple sources of information. For more than two-thirds of this group (68%) there was no evidence of mental health contact in the correctional files. However, we did find that 7% had been subject to psychiatric evaluation, 8% were clients of substance abuse programs, 15% had been psychiatric patients, and 2% were treated for combined psychiatric and substance abuse problems. Thus, these data indicate that although our computerized matching procedure was an efficient screening device, the accuracy of identifying mental health clients was substantially increased by tapping more than one information source.

As a final step we used the composite service delivery information to reclassify the sample into three mental health groups: substance abuse ($n = 83$), psychiatric ($n = 540$), and combined psychiatric and substance abuse ($n = 141$). Offenders with no history of mental health treatment, including those who were only subject to psychiatric evaluation, as well as the forensic clients for whom we were unable to verify service delivery, became the comparison group ($n = 543$).[11]

Before describing our analytic strategies, we must turn to issues that pertain to the generalizability of the sample. Specifically, we must consider how the results of this study can inform us about relationships between violence and emotional disorders and about other populations of mentally ill violent individuals.

Our sample derived from a group of violent offenders recently convicted and sentenced to prison. The criminal justice system is often likened to a sieve or filter in that at each successive juncture only some offenders continue in the process. We know that, among the factors that determine which offenders move forward, the most critical are offense seriousness and criminal history. Because ours was a prison intake sample, the violent individuals we studied have probably engaged in more serious violence and accumulated more extensive criminal records than other offenders who are not yet incarcerated.

Mentally disordered offenders were also identified on the basis of participation in outpatient and inpatient therapeutic programs. We know that not all persons with mental illness receive treatment, but among those who do we can be reasonably sure that most are experiencing emotional difficulties. The process by which persons with emotional disorders seek assistance is influenced by the availability of formal and informal treatment options, which, in turn, depends on the level of social and economic resources. Inmates largely come from

---

[11]In the final classification, substance abusers are defined as individuals who participated in either alcohol or drug treatment programs operating under psychiatric or nonpsychiatric auspices; psychiatric patients are defined as individuals who received outpatient or inpatient mental health treatment, exclusive of outpatient psychiatric evaluations.

socially disadvantaged groups, and the disturbed individuals in our sample were probably unable to afford private care-givers, which means their emotional difficulties were more likely to be a matter of public record. We also know that the caseloads of public mental health institutions contain many of the seriously disordered individuals in society.

Our criteria for defining substance abusers again referred to participation in treatment programs, and we knew from reading inmate files that our definition did not include a fair number of offenders who habitually used drugs or who abused alcohol. We assumed that we had identified those with the most serious addiction problems, but we could not be certain of this. However, many of our findings regarding these offenders (reported in chapters 3 and 5) were consistent with what is known about the relationship between substance abuse and crime.

The selectivity of our sampling procedures yielded several advantages. By concentrating on the extremes of the crime spectrum we deal with serious violence, which is a major social problem, as well as with chronic offenders, a group that is of clear policy interest and that is likely to show substantial career patterns. In addition, by focusing on treated disturbed individuals, relationships between violence and emotional disorder should be easier to identify because we have information on the nature of the illness and the dates of service delivery. We therefore are in a better position to raise treatment issues, including those pertaining to use of therapeutic alternatives to punitive responses.

# Data Analysis

Our data analysis procedures can be divided into two major sections: (a) comparisons of offenders and violent incidents, and (b) development of a career typology describing histories of violent offense behavior and mental health involvement.

In making comparisons between offenders, we focused on differences in criminal histories and mental health histories. We were especially interested in the frequency, nature, and timing of offense and mental-health-related involvements be-cause this information became critical to us when we tried to develop a typology that was largely based on history. Differences in social and demographic variables such as age, race, and marital status were also examined in the analysis.

Our comparison of violent incidents was based on the offense that led to the offender's current term of imprisonment. The information covered legal attributes such as statutory category and sentence length, as well as type of violent attack (for example, threat, physical assault), weapon use, location of incident, and the relationship of victim to offender. In collecting victim information we limited our coverage to two victims, giving priority to those who experienced the greatest injury. (This strategy did not prove too much of a limitation since only 15% of cases involved three or more victims.)

Because statutory schemes are developed as punishment-relevant classifications, they do not always describe the uses to which violence is put. Thus, legalistic descriptions may gloss over important commonalities between violent incidents. An offender who attacks his or her spouse in a jealous rage might be convicted of either murder or assault depending on the postattack condition of the victim, which in turn can be influenced by such factors as celerity of medical attention. Legalistic schemes may draw our attention to a distinction in one area (for example, the victim's physical condition) at the expense of another (for example, the offender's motivation). In similar fashion, burglary, usually a nonviolent offense, can involve either threatened or actual violence against a confronted victim. We therefore developed a supplementary classification of violent incidents to describe the type and level of violence. The coding was based on offense descriptions provided by the prison system in the "description of pattern of criminal behavior" document, which was generated as part of the inmate classification process.

In describing types of violence we tried to keep our categorizations as close to the act as possible. We divided violent acts into unmotivated, retaliatory, felony-related, sex—adult, sex—child, weapon-related, arson, against police, burglary, auto, and institutional violence. Although we sometimes used legal designations of offenses (burglary, arson), at other times we restated statutory categories in broader terms (sex offenses, weapon offenses) or made victim-related distinctions that were not always reflected in the designations of conviction offenses (victims as adults, children, police). When useful, we also incorporated motivational (unmotivated, retaliatory) or situational (felony-related, auto—as weapon, institution—as setting) elements to help describe violent behavior. The distribution of conviction offenses by type of violence is shown in Table 2.2. In the classification scheme that we constructed, some violence types (burglary, weapon offenses, and arson) are highly concordant with a specific offense, whereas other violence types (unmotivated, retaliatory, police victim, by auto or in institutions) contain a great deal of heterogeneity.

Because the violence type categories encompass substantial variation in levels of violence, we added a four-category ordinal scale to summarize the degree of harm inflicted on the victim. The categories used were no (personal) violence, less serious (threat or minor damage), serious (physical damage and non-consensual sex), and extreme (death, serious multiple injury, or sex with violence). This format allowed us to include non-violent encounters that are statutorily defined as violent, as well as less predatory offenses that involve only a potential for violence or that result in minor physical harm. In combination, the coding formats provided a richer classification of incidents, describing both type and degree of violence in ways that are not captured by statutory classifications.

## Eccentric Offense Behavior

We are obviously concerned with relationships between mental illness and violence and, in particular, with the ways that serious emotional problems can shape the expression of violence. In studying violent incidents, it struck us that some offenders, particularly offenders with a history of mental health involvement, did not come across as stereotypical criminals in that their offenses showed peculiar, odd, or eccentric features. These attributes were neither reflected in legal classifications nor fully captured by our supplementary coding formats. We therefore developed a third code of unusual or eccentric offense attributes to capture peculiarities of violent behavior. There are many such attributes, but the general categories we used are ineffectual behavior (e.g., turned self in to police,

# Table 2.2

*Percent Distribution of Conviction Offense by Type of Violence*

| | | | | Type of violence | | | | | | |
|---|---|---|---|---|---|---|---|---|---|---|
| Conviction offense | Retaliatory (n = 182) | Unmotivated (n = 50) | Felony-related (n = 559) | Sex—adult victim (n = 76) | Sex—child victim (n = 88) | Weapon (n = 68) | Arson (n = 29) | Police victim (n = 28) | Burglary (n = 199) | Auto/institution (n = 29) |
| Murder | 37% | 25% | 4% | 1% | 1% | 2% | 0% | 0% | 0% | 0% |
| Kidnapping | 1 | 0 | .7 | 3 | 0 | 0 | 0 | 0 | 0 | 0 |
| Arson | 0 | 0 | 0 | 0 | 0 | 0 | 97 | 0 | 0 | 0 |
| Robbery | 6 | 10 | 87 | 7 | 2 | 3 | 0 | 29 | 5 | 25 |
| Assault | 48 | 57 | 3 | 3 | 0 | 0 | 0 | 50 | .5 | 25 |
| Reckless endangerment | 4 | 2 | .2 | 0 | 0 | 0 | 0 | 4 | .5 | 0 |
| Rape | 0 | 0 | .2 | 64 | 43 | 0 | 0 | 4 | 0 | 0 |
| Sodomy | 0 | 0 | 0 | 13 | 38 | 0 | 0 | 0 | 0 | 0 |
| Sex abuse | 0 | 0 | 0 | 8 | 16 | 0 | 3 | 0 | 0 | 0 |
| Weapon | 3 | 4 | .7 | 1 | 0 | 91 | 0 | 7 | 1 | 4 |
| Burglary | 2 | 2 | 4 | 0 | 0 | 5 | 0 | 7 | 93 | 18 |

*Note:* Columns may not add to 100% because of rounding. The auto/institution heading serves as a residual category reflecting situations in which an automobile was used as the instrument of violence or in which the violence took place within an institution.

failed to leave the scene of the crime when given the opportunity, left behind personal identification or other highly incriminating materials, made several attempts at the crime before succeeding); frenzied mental state (e.g., violent overkill
including multiple stabbing or shooting, potentially fatal beating or assault, torture or mutilation); symptomatic behavior
(e.g., psychotic symptoms such as hallucinations or delusions,
paranoia, dazed, bewildered, confused, disoriented mental state,
poor personal hygiene, depressed, withdrawn, crying, self-
injury); no apparent motivation; and no memory of the event.[12]

## Career Framework

We have noted that any study of emotional disorders and
violence must accommodate the fact that mental health problems and offense behaviors, and relationships between the
two, change over time. A concept that helps to organize this
developmental complexity is that of an offense–mental health
"career." The dictionary tells us that, apart from a sequence
of vocational progression, a career can connote "a course of
continued progress as in the life of a person." Within the social
sciences, a career framework has been used to study a variety
of progressions, including the socialization of medical students, the development of drug addiction, and the community
adjustment of mental patients. In these contexts, a career describes sequences of experiences that are common to groups
of individuals.

The goal in our research was to illuminate sequences of

---

[12]We collected data on several types of eccentric offense behavior that are
not reported. One category, behavior disproportionate to stimulus, was
deleted because it appeared in over 50% of the cases and did not discriminate
between offender groups. In contrast, other eccentricity categories (matricide, fratricide, or infanticide; excessive destruction of physical property)
proved to be extremely infrequent. Still other eccentric behavior (arson,
sexual violence, child victim) is better described by the type of violence codes
we developed. The category unmotivated offense appears in both the type
of violence and eccentric offense behavior classifications. The type of violence
code describes the primary nature of the violence and thus applies only to
violent incidents. The eccentricity code includes nonviolent and potentially
violent encounters.

offender behavior in which the advent of criminal acts and of symptoms that are serious enough to justify diagnosis and treatment can be located in time. Such patterns of behavior over time permit us to show when a person is unambiguously disturbed, when he or she is engaging in crime, and when he or she is both. Given a large enough sample, temporal patterning permits the grouping of offenders into types that are characterized by different mixtures and sequences of offenses and symptomatology. Over a lifetime, such types describe composite careers of criminality and mental illness; over limited periods they describe composite career segments.

Career types are different chains of career segments that imply different relationships between personal problems and offense behavior. For example, offenses that are always committed when an offender has discontinued outpatient care and medication carry different implications from those that occur when the offender is receiving mental health services or when the offender has not yet been diagnosed. A career in which early emotional problems are followed by a long, rootless existence (unemployment, homelessness, etc.) that eventually leads to criminality is different from a career of chronic delinquency and of incarceration followed by a psychotic breakdown.

Composite careers of criminality and mental disorder, reconstructed from chronologically based records, can help to illuminate patterns of escalation and deescalation or continuity and discontinuity of problem behaviors. One such example of a composite career, taken from the *New York Times*, describes the history of a man shot dead by police after running naked through St. Patrick's Cathedral in New York City and killing an elderly usher with a prayer stand.[13]

---

[13]"A Killer in St. Patrick's: Hospital to Jail to Death," *New York Times*, September 23, 1988, pp. A1, B4.

The account reads as follows:

June 23, 1983 First admitted to Bellevue Hospital Center. Was brought in for smashing windows of a Broadway movie theatre. Was under arrest in prison unit. Discharged July 1.

July 2 First incarcerated at Riker's island, charged with third-degree assault. Released Aug. 8.

Aug. 19 Bellevue. Was brought in after being found swimming in Hudson river. Discharged Sept. 7.

Sept. 10 Rikers. Charged with third-degree criminal trespassing. Released Oct. 11.

Feb. 9, 1984 Rikers. Charged with first-degree robbery. Released April 6.

April 16 Bellevue. Discharged April 23.

April 25 Bellevue. Discharged May 10.

Dec. 19 Bellevue. Examined in prison unit and released to police custody.

Dec. 20 Rikers. Charged with criminal possession of stolen property. Released Jan. 5, 1985.

Jan. 19, 1985 Rikers. Charged with petty larceny. Released Sept. 17.

Dec. 10 Bellevue. Discharged Jan. 6, 1986.

Feb. 27, 1986 Manhattan House of Detention. Charged with second-degree criminal trespassing. Released March 6.

Aug. 11, 1986 Rikers. Charged with fourth-degree criminal mischief. Released Sept. 19.

Sept. 25, 1986 Rikers. Charged with fourth-degree criminal mischief. Released Oct. 10.

March 26, 1987 Rikers. Charged with criminal mischief. Released April 10.

April 1 Bellevue. Treated in emergency room and given an appointment.

April 27 Bellevue. Seen for appointment.

April 28 Rikers. Charged with criminal mischief. Released May 8.

Sept. 23, 1988 Shot dead by police.

The career concept lends itself to the development of a career typology depicting common patterns of experience over time. As a descriptive tool, a career typology can be particularly useful because it organizes large amounts of data into meaningful and relevant subcategories. By including both offender and offense attributes in the same typology we can develop a composite picture of persons, histories, and behavior, and such combinations can provide clues to offense motivation as well as to other psychological processes associated with offending.

Various strategies can be used to develop a typological scheme. When relatively few items compose the dimensions of the typology, all possible or logical combinations can easily be examined. However, when the number of items involved is large, this strategy becomes unwieldy, and a technique is needed to isolate significant combinations of variables.

A statistical procedure that is particularly well-suited to the development of a discriminating classification scheme is cluster analysis. Cluster analysis refers to a family of statistical procedures used to identify groups or classes of objects with common attributes, the results of which can be viewed as a natural confluence taxonomy. The procedures can be applied to a variety of objects—people, institutions, cultures, plants, animals—and are especially useful with complicated data. For example, psychologists have used cluster techniques to identify patterns of personality characteristics among mentally ill and other individuals.[14] The analytic strategy is that of partitioning a diverse set of objects into homogeneous subsets based on regularly occurring associations among variables. Because one way one learns to organize experience is by sorting things on the basis of like and unlike features, cluster techniques have intuitive appeal. Another attractive feature of cluster analysis is that by sorting a large heterogeneous group into smaller, more homogeneous subgroups, the technique can help one uncover otherwise hard-to-discern order and regularity in complex phenomena.

Applications of cluster procedures are considered atheoretical in the sense that hypotheses or theoretical propositions do not guide the statistical clustering process. However, there are several methodological issues that arise in the use of cluster analysis, and we briefly outline these areas, documenting the strategies we used to address them. The issues are (a) choosing variables for inclusion in the analysis, (b) selecting a clustering

---

[14]Louis M. McQuitty, *Pattern-Analytic Clustering: Theory, Method, Research, and Configural Findings* (New York: University Press of America, 1987).

technique, (c) measuring similarity, and (d) deciding on the number of clusters in the final solution.

The selection of variables to be included in a cluster analysis is important because there are limitless ways of describing objects and, by definition, omitted variables cannot be part of the taxonomy. One's judgment can be used to narrow the universe of descriptive items by eliminating those that seem conceptually irrelevant to the task at hand. Yet, after this step is taken many options still exist, and choices can make a difference in producing a more or less meaningful classification scheme. Because we were concerned with offense–mental health careers, we had to include historical information on mental health and criminal justice experiences in our analysis. We also had to enter a description of the conviction offense which, given the procedures used to identify the sample, represents the capstone of the offender's violence career. The conviction offense was recorded in terms of type and level of violence, which we coded as described above. On the negative side we decided to exclude most demographic variables from the analysis because we felt that an initial focus on static background characteristics would prove distracting, particularly in the context of most other items that were chosen to illuminate sequences of pathology and violence.[15] We did, however, list demographic variables as "covariates" in our description of final cluster solutions.

The second issue with which we were confronted was that of selecting a clustering technique. A number of types of clustering techniques have been developed, and within a given type there are a variety of specific methods.[16] We decided to use a hierarchical technique that is appropriate for the types

---

[15]We included age in the analysis because time, as it relates to opportunity (or in our case risk), is implicit in the notion of career, which describes developmental sequences.

[16]B. Everitt, *Cluster Analysis* (New York: Wiley, 1974), pp. 7–22. Among the more frequently used clustering techniques are hierarchical, optimization-partitioning, density or mode-seeking, and clumping. Hierarchical clustering methods include single linkage or nearest neighbor, complete linkage or furthest neighbor, centroid, median, average linkage between or within groups, and Ward's method.

of data we collected and is among the more commonly used clustering procedures. Hierarchical techniques operate in an agglomerative manner, which means that at each step two groups are joined together, becoming a single unit that is eligible for subsequent mergers. In a figurative sense, the technique fashions a tree by starting with many individual branches and ending with a single trunk.[17] The specific clustering method we used is average linkage between groups, which tends to produce more homogeneous clusters than the single linkage method.[18]

The third issue involves the choice of a proximity measure to indicate the degree of similarity or dissimilarity between objects. A problem researchers often face is that variables of different measurement levels are combined in an analysis, which means that selection of any single proximity measure involves compromise. In our situation, most of the variables in the analysis were nominal so that it was convenient to transform the data to binary (yes, no) format. We therefore generated dichotomous variables to represent the presence or absence of each of the nominal categories in the data set. In some cases, it was necessary to reduce the level of measurement (as in the case of age) to accommodate this scheme.[19] After trying several proximity measures, we decided to use the Jaccard measure, which is one of several used with binary data.[20]

---

[17]M. Anderberg, *Cluster Analysis for Applications* (New York: Harcourt Brace Jovanovich, 1973), p. 131.

[18]Average linkage is similar to single linkage, which is among the most popular clustering methods. However, average linkage is less influenced by extreme values and therefore less subject than single linkage to "chaining," which refers to the tendency for new clusters to be composed of a single case.

[19]Age was divided into three categories: low (21 years and younger), medium (22 to 30 years), and high (31 years and older). Arrest history was similarly divided into the following categories: low (three or fewer arrests), medium (four to eight arrests) and high (nine or more arrests). Low IQ referred to test scores of 80 or less. The category of offenders with a history of psychotic diagnosis included those who, at some time prior to entering the prison system, had received a clinical diagnosis (e.g., schizophrenia) involving psychotic symptoms (e.g., delusions, hallucinations). Offenders on probation or parole at the time of the offense were described as under supervision.

[20]In a $2 \times 2$ table with frequencies a, b, c, d in respective cells (1,1) (1,0)

The final issue is that of deciding on the number of clusters in the final solution. Hierarchical techniques generate from one to as many clusters as there are data points, and it is up to the researcher to decide where in the process to draw the line. Mechanical strategies have been developed to address this issue, but these methods are concerned with finding the "correct" number of clusters, a notion that is often of questionable relevance to hierarchical techniques. The conceptual "meaning" or "coherence" of items that defines the clusters was to us the important consideration, and we used this criterion in assessing various solutions. The point at which the disaggregation process no longer made useful or meaningful distinctions (or conversely, when the agglomeration process obscured useful distinctions) was the juncture that we identified as the final cluster solution.

---

(0,1) (0,0) the Jaccard measure is computed by $a/a+b+c$. Anderberg (1973) describes this measure as "the conditional probability that a randomly chosen data unit will score 1 on both variables, given that data units with 0-0 matches are discarded first. The 0-0 matches are treated as totally irrelevant" (p. 89).

# 3

# Results of Statistical Analyses

In this chapter we examine the social, criminal, and mental health background of inmates in our sample. This review serves several purposes. First, it is a descriptive device, providing contextual material that allows for comparisons with other offender populations. The review also provides a frame of reference for subsequent analyses in that some findings may highlight areas for investigation, and others may facilitate explanations of results. In addition, by scrutinizing the criminal history of mental patients we broach the question that motivated our study, which is, What are the relationships between emotional disorder and violence? And, finally, by mapping the nature and timing of criminal and mental health involvements, we create a foundation for the career typology that we describe in subsequent chapters.

Our first task was to provide detailed comparisons of violent incidents by emotionally disordered and other offenders; this material may strike some readers as excessively particularistic, but its representation is directly relevant to our main concerns, which center on the distinctive features of violence among offenders with emotional problems. Our approach to the analysis will move from legal classifications and conventional offense attributes such as victim–offender relationship as descriptive items, to comparisons based on the violence typology and the eccentricity codes we described in chapter 2.

## Social Characteristics and Criminal History

In Table 3.1 we display the social characteristics and criminal histories of offenders in the samples. We found that in all three mental health groups white, nonhispanic inmates were overrepresented, with the highest percentage found among offenders with combined substance abuse and mental health problems (57%). We also noted that inmates with a history of psychiatric problems showed the lowest level of preincarceration employment and were least likely to be married. Finally, we saw that inmates in the mental health groups tended to be older than other inmates, with the greatest difference found among the two groups of substance abusers. These findings are consistent with other research that has suggested that mentally disordered offenders tend to have less solid roots in the community than other offenders.[1]

We observed that violent offenders in our samples had accumulated substantial criminal records, with an average of 5.7 arrests for the comparison group. Offenders with mental health records had more extensive criminal backgrounds than other offenders, and this tendency included a greater number of violent offenses. The difference was greatest among substance abusers, who on the average had almost twice as many arrests as offenders in the comparison group. For this reason, it is unsurprising that inmates with substance abuse problems were more apt to have done time in prison. First contact with the criminal justice system occurred on the average at about 18 years of age for all inmate groups, so differences in criminal histories cannot be attributed to earlier onset of offender careers. Another possible explanation for the differences in arrest histories is that they are an artifact of age disparities, given that older offenders have had more time to accumulate contacts

---

[1]When Steadman and his associates compared demographic profiles between hospital patients who are arrested and other patients, differences suggested that the patient-arrestees resembled offender populations (i.e., young, minority group members with prior criminal records) (Steadman et al., 1978). On the other side of the coin we found that offenders with mental health backgrounds demographically resemble client populations of psychiatric hospitals (i.e., older, white individuals).

**Table 3.1**

*Social Characteristics and Criminal History by Mental Health Experience of Offender*

| | Mental health experience | | | |
|---|---|---|---|---|
| | No history (*n* = 544) | Substance abuse history (*n* = 83) | Psychiatric history (*n* = 540) | Substance abuse and psychiatric history (*n* = 141) |
| **Social characteristics** | | | | |
| Ethnicity | | | | |
| White | 15%** | 44%** | 39%** | 57%** |
| Black | 58 | 34 | 46 | 30 |
| Hispanic | 27 | 22 | 15 | 13 |
| Gender | | | | |
| Male | 98% | 96% | 96% | 96% |
| Female | 2 | 4 | 4 | 4 |
| Marital status | | | | |
| Single | 64%** | 65%** | 77%** | 71%** |
| Married | 36 | 35 | 23 | 29 |
| Highest education level | | | | |
| Grade school | 22% | 20% | 22% | 19% |
| Some high school | 64 | 61 | 56 | 59 |
| High school graduate | 16 | 19 | 21 | 23 |
| Age (years at prison entry) | $\bar{x}$ = 26.0$^a$ sd = 7.7 | $\bar{x}$ = 30.4$^a$ sd = 6.6 | $\bar{x}$ = 28.6$^a$ sd = 9.4 | $\bar{x}$ = 30.0$^a$ sd = 7.6 |
| Employed (at conviction) | 78%** | 82%** | 69%** | 85%** |
| **Criminal history** | | | | |
| Age at first offense (years)$^b$ | $\bar{x}$ = 18.4 sd = 6.1 | $\bar{x}$ = 17.6 sd = 2.8 | $\bar{x}$ = 18.4 sd = 8.0 | $\bar{x}$ = 17.8 sd = 4.4 |
| Number of prior offenses | $\bar{x}$ = 5.7$^a$ sd = 5.7 | $\bar{x}$ = 10.0$^a$ sd = 7.1 | $\bar{x}$ = 7.9$^a$ sd = 7.5 | $\bar{x}$ = 10.3$^a$ sd = 7.5 |
| Number of prior violent offenses | $\bar{x}$ = 1.4 sd = 1.7 | $\bar{x}$ = 1.9 sd = 2.4 | $\bar{x}$ = 1.8 sd = 2.2 | $\bar{x}$ = 2.0 sd = 2.2 |
| Prior prison experience | 27%** | 43%** | 31%** | 48%** |

**Chi-square, $p < .01$.
$^a$T-test, $p < .01$.
$^b$The conviction offense is used as the first offense for offenders with no criminal history.

with the criminal justice system. Yet when we grouped offenders into relatively homogeneous age strata, we found comparable differences in arrest histories by mental health background, showing that offenders with emotional problems had

**Table 3.2**

*Mean Number of Prior Arrests*

| | Mental health experience | | | |
|---|---|---|---|---|
| Age at conviction offense | No history | Substance abuse history | Psychiatric history | Substance abuse and psychiatric history |
| 20 years and younger | 3.4 | 4.1 | 5.0 | 4.6 |
| 21 to 25 years | 5.3 | 7.1 | 7.0 | 7.9 |
| 26 to 30 years | 6.6 | 9.1 | 9.5 | 11.1 |
| 31 to 35 years | 8.0 | 10.0 | 10.0 | 10.4 |
| 36 to 40 years | 8.9 | 17.1 | 8.6 | 10.9 |
| 41 years and older | 8.5 | 15.4 | 9.5 | 20.5 |

greater levels of criminal involvement regardless of chronological age.

Mean arrest rates across age categories and offender groups appear in Table 3.2. The data indicate that offenders with mental health backgrounds have more extensive criminal histories than other offenders across age groups. The difference is greatest for offenders with substance abuse problems, especially in the older age groups, where we found very substantial criminal records.

# Patterns of Prior Offenses

The number of prior violent crimes committed by an individual is strongly associated with the number of nonviolent crimes (Pearson correlation = .62). This finding confirms that criminals lead checkered offense careers, and raises the possibility that more extensive violence histories among offenders with mental health problems may simply reflect a more general increased propensity to crime. One strategy for addressing this issue is to examine the percent distribution of prior offenses by type, which provides an index of crime propensity that in effect is standardized for number of offenses. These data are shown in Table 3.3. Our discussion focuses on ratios across groups of offenders for types of crime, because these comparisons accommodate the diversity of criminal behavior by taking into account the fact that some crimes are infrequent for all offender groups.

The comparison group of offenders was about one and a half times more likely to have been arrested for robbery than other offenders. In contrast, those in the three mental health groups were twice as likely to have been arrested for public order offenses. Both groups of substance abusers revealed an inclination for burglary and drug offenses and stood out from the comparison group by being about three times more likely to have been arrested for driving while intoxicated (DWI). Offenders with relatively pure substance abuse problems were also about 15 times more likely to have been arrested for prostitution. Finally, we found that the psychiatric group was about one and a half times more likely than the comparison group to have been arrested for assault, including sexual assaults such as rape and sodomy, as well as for criminal mischief.

In order to investigate whether serious offenders with mental health backgrounds have a tendency to specialize in violence we examined the proportion of violent to total crimes among offenders with 10 or more prior arrests. The analysis revealed that the distribution of this proportion was virtually identical across offender groups. Descriptive statistics on the distributions appear in Table 3.4.

In summary, the data indicate that offenders with mental health histories, particularly substance abuse problems, have much more extensive criminal records than other offenders. Among the more significant findings is the fact that offenders with psychiatric histories show a greater propensity for assaultive offenses, including serious sexual assaults. Substance abusers are more frequently involved with possessing or selling drugs and DWI. They also show a greater inclination for burglary and prostitution offenses, activities that presumably help finance addictions. At the same time, all groups of offenders with mental health involvements show a disproportionate tendency for nuisance offenses, such as those considered breaches of public order.

The greater propensity that offenders with mental health

## Table 3.3

*Distribution of Types of Prior Offenses by Mental Health Experience of Offender*

| Type of prior offenses | Mental health experience | | | |
|---|---|---|---|---|
| | No history ($n = 3,067$) | Substance abuse history ($n = 810$) | Psychiatric history ($n = 4,179$) | Substance abuse and psychiatric history ($n = 1,429$) |
| Murder | .5% | .4% | .3% | .4% |
| Kidnapping | .1 | .2 | .2 | .3 |
| Arson | .5 | .6 | .4 | .5 |
| Rape, sodomy, sex abuse | 1.5 | 1.6 | 2.7 | 1.6 |
| Robbery | 14.0 | 9.4 | 8.9 | 9.1 |
| Assault | 6.7 | 5.6 | 9.5 | 6.9 |
| Reckless endangerment | 1.2 | 1.7 | 1.8 | 1.8 |
| Burglary | 14.3 | 17.7 | 14.4 | 16.9 |
| Grand larceny | 11.6 | 10.6 | 9.4 | 8.5 |
| Possess stolen property | 5.6 | 4.9 | 4.3 | 4.2 |
| Petit larceny | 8.3 | 8.4 | 9.2 | 10.6 |
| Forgery, fraud | 2.9 | 3.1 | 4.6 | 4.3 |
| Prostitution | .2 | 3.1 | .9 | .3 |
| Drug | 6.6 | 8.1 | 4.2 | 6.4 |
| Marijuana | 4.5 | 3.3 | 1.9 | 2.7 |
| Firearm | 4.0 | 3.1 | 2.9 | 2.4 |
| Public order | 3.2 | 5.1 | 6.1 | 5.3 |
| Criminal mischief | 2.1 | 2.7 | 3.8 | 2.4 |
| Criminal trespass | 3.9 | 2.3 | 3.9 | 3.3 |
| Harassment | 1.2 | 1.1 | 2.0 | 1.8 |
| Escape | .4 | .7 | .6 | 1.0 |
| Resisting arrest | 1.5 | 1.4 | 1.1 | 1.4 |
| Gambling | .7 | .5 | .8 | .1 |
| DWI | .7 | 2.5 | 1.3 | 2.2 |
| Other auto | 1.1 | 1.2 | 1.5 | 1.9 |
| Juvenile delinquency | 1.8 | .5 | 1.5 | 2.7 |
| Person in need of supervision | 1.0 | .1 | 2.1 | .7 |

*Note*: These data describe the number and proportion of prior criminal offenses for each offender group.

**Table 3.4**

*Proportion of Violent to Total Crimes for Offenders With 10 or More Arrests by Mental Health Experience*

| Mental health experience | Mean | Standard deviation | Median |
|---|---|---|---|
| No history | .22 | .15 | .19 |
| Substance abuse history | .20 | .16 | .16 |
| Psychiatric history | .23 | .18 | .19 |
| Combined substance abuse and psychiatric history | .20 | .16 | .17 |

histories have for both violent and nuisance offenses is somewhat paradoxical. The town drunk who panhandles and sleeps on park benches, or the mental patient who wanders the street determined to engage pedestrians in strangely symbolic conversations are not images that come to mind when we think of disturbed violent offenders. This observation led us to ask whether the tendencies for violence and nuisance offenses coexist in the same individual or characterize nonoverlapping subgroups of offenders. We pursued the issue by looking at the association between numbers of violent and public order offenses. The analysis revealed substantial Pearson correlations among substance abusers (.24) and among offenders with composite psychiatric–substance abuse problems (.37), and considerably lower correlations among offenders with a psychiatric history (.15) or with no record of mental health involvement (.13). Thus, substance abusers, particularly substance abusers with psychiatric histories, show a tendency to combine the two extremes, violence and nuisance offenses, in their criminal careers.

Our findings pointed to a connection between substance abuse problems and the kinds of crimes offenders commit, and we suspected that these relationships were obscured by the mix of alcoholics and drug addicts in the substance abuse groups. We therefore looked at criminal histories by type of addiction and found that alcoholics had a greater propensity to engage in arson, assault, reckless endangerment, public order offenses, and DWI (see Table 3.5). In contrast, drug

**Table 3.5**

*Distribution of Types of Prior Offenses by Type of Substance Abuse Problem*

| | Substance abuse history | | |
|---|---|---|---|
| | Alcohol ($n = 698$) | Drug ($n = 1,229$) | Both ($n = 312$) |
| Murder | .4% | .4% | .3% |
| Kidnapping | .4 | .2 | 0 |
| Arson | 1.1 | .2 | .6 |
| Rape, sodomy, sex abuse | 1.7 | 1.5 | 1.9 |
| Robbery | 9.6 | 9.1 | 8.7 |
| Assault | 8.3 | 6.0 | 3.8 |
| Reckless endangerment | 2.9 | 1.0 | 2.6 |
| Burglary | 13.6 | 18.6 | 19.9 |
| Grand larceny | 9.3 | 9.6 | 8.0 |
| Possess stolen property | 3.3 | 5.0 | 4.8 |
| Petty larceny | 8.9 | 10.4 | 9.6 |
| Forgery or fraud | 5.0 | 3.7 | 1.9 |
| Prostitution | .3 | 1.2 | 3.2 |
| Drug offenses | 2.4 | 9.8 | 6.4 |
| Marijuana offenses | .9 | 4.1 | 3.2 |
| Firearm offenses | 2.1 | 2.8 | 2.9 |
| Public order | 9.6 | 2.8 | 4.8 |
| Criminal mischief | 3.4 | 1.5 | 4.5 |
| Criminal trespass | 2.7 | 3.1 | 2.9 |
| Harassment | 3.2 | .9 | .6 |
| Escape | .6 | 1.3 | .3 |
| Resisting arrest | 1.9 | 1.0 | 1.9 |
| Gambling | 0 | .3 | .3 |
| DWI | 4.9 | 1.1 | 1.3 |
| Other auto offenses | 1.6 | 1.5 | 2.6 |
| Juvenile delinquency | 1.6 | 2.0 | 1.9 |
| Person in need of supervision | .3 | .5 | 1.0 |

addicts were disproportionately involved in burglary and drug offenses, including marijuana offenses. These findings confirm the argument that drug addicts can be financially motivated to commit property offenses in support of their addiction, and that criminal laws designed to curb the use of drugs turn addicts into repeat offenders when arrest is used in lieu of treatment options.

Contrasting criminal proclivities, such as engaging in social nuisance and violent offenses, were shown to have a greater tendency to appear in tandem among substance abusers. This finding requires us to bring a new perspective to the fact that offenders with alcohol problems disproportionately engage in a variety of antisocial behavior ranging in degree of seriousness from public order offenses to arson. It not only appears that portraits of alcoholics as disorderly drunks and as bellicose inebriates both contain an element of truth, but, more significant, we found that these representations often describe co-existing dispositions in the same intoxicated person. Also, we noted that the violence pattern (arson, assault, reckless endangerment) among alcoholics points to a phenomenon that supports another familiar argument postulating a link between severe drinking, emotional disinhibition, and impaired social judgment (see Table 3.5).

## Offender Career Patterns

We now examine mental health and criminal justice careers based on the chronology of treatment involvements and arrests for violence.[2] In order to simplify the analysis, we have characterized past events as remote (more than 3 years) or recent (3 years or less). We also have identified instances of mental

---

[2]Information regarding the timing of service delivery was not always available for mental health contacts recorded in correctional files. The fact that the degree of completeness of treatment chronologies varied a great deal presented us with a problem. If we limited our analyses to individuals for whom we had complete information on all contacts, a substantial number of cases would be excluded as missing data. On the other hand, if we analyzed only events with complete information, descriptions of many individual mental health careers would be incomplete. We resolved the dilemma by assigning mental health contacts to the remote history category when the year of contact was unknown. We chose this strategy because, among events with complete information, a disproportionate number occurred more than 3 years prior to the conviction offense. Although this procedure introduced a bias that led us to overestimate the frequency of remote mental health involvements, the error is probably less than if we listed events with missing dates in one of the other time categories. We also assigned June 30 as the date if only the year of contact was available, and we used the 15th of the month if only the day was missing. Finally, we included psychiatric evaluations at time of conviction in the career chronology, although these evaluations were not used in the initial classification of the mental health samples.

health treatment in connection with the violent conviction offense that defines the sample. This scheme has allowed us to
trace the timing and chronicity of criminal violence and indications of mental disorder.

Patterns of mental health contacts over time are displayed
in Table 3.6. We note that more than half (56.3%) the substance
abusers had a treatment history confined to the remote past,
whereas other disordered offenders showed signs of having
more current problems. If we tally offenders who have had
mental health treatment within 3 years of the violent conviction
offense, (i.e., combine all patterns except remote past only)
we find that three-fifths (60.7%) of the psychiatric group and
seven-tenths (70.3%) of the combined psychiatric–substance
abuse group demonstrated near-term evidence of emotional
difficulties. In addition, we note that offenders with substance
abuse and psychiatric disorders were most apt to have earned
a client status that spans both remote and recent past (42.6%).

**Table 3.6**

*Career Patterns of Treatment History by Mental Health Experience of
Offender*

| | Mental health experience | | |
| | Substance abuse (n = 80) | Psychiatric (n = 537) | Substance abuse and psychiatric (n = 191) |
| Chronology of treatment | | | |
|---|---|---|---|
| Simple patterns: | | | |
| Remote history only | 56.3% | 39.3% | 29.8% |
| Recent history only | 18.8 | 8.8 | 5.0 |
| At conviction | 3.8 | 8.8 | 3.5 |
| Subtotal | 78.9% | 56.9% | 38.3% |
| Combination patterns: | | | |
| Remote and recent | 12.5% | 12.7% | 42.6% |
| Remote and at conviction | 6.3 | 13.2 | 8.5 |
| Recent and at conviction | 1.3 | 5.6 | 4.3 |
| Remote, recent, and at conviction | 1.3 | 11.7 | 6.4 |
| Subtotal | 21.4% | 43.2% | 61.8% |
| Total | 100.3% | 100.1% | 100.1% |

*Note*: Remote history refers to events taking place more than 3 years prior to the
conviction offense, and recent history refers to events within 3 years of the conviction
offense. Columns total more than 100% because of rounding.

If we tally offenders in the psychiatric history group who received services at conviction, we find that the proportion is substantial (39.3%). However, treatment histories limited to this point in time are in the minority (8.8% of the group), because most offenders who received services at conviction had a record of previous mental health involvement. A similar though less substantial pattern holds for psychiatric patients with substance abuse problems.

If we define chronic histories as those with treatment involvements spanning the three time periods, we find that substance abusers show the least chronicity and psychiatric patients the most. In particular, we see that about one in nine (11.7%) of the purely psychiatric patients can be described as a chronic mental health client.

In Table 3.7 we display chronological patterns of violence. In this table, we confirm that the comparison group has the highest proportion of offenders with no violence history (38.6%), whereas the combined substance abuse and psychiatric group has the lowest proportion (22.7%). Whereas both substance abuse groups tend to have violence histories limited to the remote past (44.6% and 51.1%), all mental health groups show

**Table 3.7**

*Career Patterns of Violence History by Mental Health Experience of Offender*

| | Mental health experience | | | |
|---|---|---|---|---|
| Violence history | No history ($n = 544$) | Substance abuse history ($n = 83$) | Psychiatric history ($n = 540$) | Substance abuse and psychiatric history ($n = 141$) |
|---|---|---|---|---|
| No prior violence | 38.6% | 27.7% | 34.1% | 22.7% |
| Remote violence | 30.9 | 44.6 | 32.4 | 51.1 |
| Recent violence | 16.7 | 9.6 | 14.6 | 9.2 |
| Recent and remote violence | 13.8 | 18.1 | 18.9 | 17.0 |

*Note.* Remote history refers to events taking place more than 3 years prior to the conviction offense, and recent history refers to events within 3 years of the conviction offense.

greater chronicity of violence than the comparison group, with the psychiatric group being the most chronic (18.9%). Although the differences in the proportion of chronic violent offenders are not dramatic, for nearly one in five offenders with a mental health history the offense for which he or she was incarcerated represents at minimum the third arrest for a violent crime.

Next we examined the relationship between temporal patterns of mental health contacts and violence, and the results of this analysis are shown in Table 3.8. A remote violence history appears most characteristic of substance abusers, regardless of treatment chronology, and chronic substance abusers contain the largest proportion of chronically violent offenders (29.4%).

Both groups of psychiatric patients, those with relatively pure emotional problems and those with additional substance abuse problems, display similar relationships between chro-

**Table 3.8**

*Relationship Between Treatment Career Patterns and Violence Career Patterns by Type of Mental Health History*

| | | Violence history | | | |
|---|---|---|---|---|---|
| | Treatment history | No violence | Remote violence | Recent violence | Remote and recent violence |
| Offenders with a substance abuse history | Remote (n = 45) | 26.7% | 44.4% | 11.1% | 17.8% |
| | Recent (n = 18) | 33.3 | 50.0 | 11.1 | 5.6 |
| | Remote and recent (n = 15) | 23.5 | 41.2 | 5.9 | 29.4 |
| Offenders with a psychiatric history | Remote (n = 211) | 28.4 | 42.2 | 10.9 | 18.5 |
| | Recent (n = 94) | 52.1 | 13.8 | 19.1 | 14.9 |
| | Remote and recent (n = 232) | 31.9 | 31.0 | 16.4 | 20.7 |
| Offenders with a substance abuse and psychiatric history | Remote (n = 42) | 23.8 | 57.1 | 7.1 | 11.9 |
| | Recent (n = 12) | 50.0 | 25.0 | 8.3 | 16.7 |
| | Remote and recent (n = 87) | 18.4 | 51.7 | 10.3 | 19.5 |

*Note.* In this table, recent treatment history includes services delivered after the conviction offense.

nologies of treatment and violence. Offenders with a remote treatment history most often have a violence history limited to the same early time frame (42.2% and 57.1%), but half or more of those who only recently became mental health clients have no violence history (52.1% and 50%). Chronic psychiatric patients show nearly equal proportions of offenders with no violence history (31.9%) or a remote history of violence (31%), whereas those with additional substance abuse problems more often than not have a remote violence history (51.7%). Finally, both groups of chronic psychiatric patients contain a substantial proportion of chronically violent offenders (20.7% and 19.5%). In fact, among offenders with an extensive treatment history one in five also had an extensive history of violence.

Overall, we found that many offenders who had been psychiatric patients had long-standing treatment histories. More significantly, we saw that violent offenders who raised mental health issues at conviction usually had a prior record of emotional difficulty. In contrast, treatment chronologies of substance abusers tended to be more circumscribed, less often spanning the remote and the recent past. Substance abusers, who also tended to be the oldest offenders in our samples, also had violence careers that were limited to the remote past, whereas other offenders more often had a history of recent violence. Careers of violence showed somewhat greater chronicity among offenders with records of mental health problems, and this finding is consistent with our previous analyses.

The relationship between mental health and violence careers is reported in Table 3.8, in which we see a consistent and significant pattern among both groups of former psychiatric patients. Offenders with a history of psychiatric treatment originating in the remote past usually had a violence history confined to the same time frame. Similarly, convicted violent offenders who had only recently developed emotional difficulties tended to have no prior record of violence and were often first-time violent offenders. Psychiatric patients with chronic treatment histories were most likely to have chronic violence histories. Thus, as we tracked the course of mental health treatments over time, periods of serious emotional disorder consistently coincided with an increased propensity to violence. The pattern is significant because it suggests a connection between emotional problems and violence among seriously disturbed offenders.

# Offense Descriptions

In Table 3.9 we describe the offenses for which inmates in the samples were incarcerated. The data indicate that offenders with psychiatric histories more often stand convicted of murder, assault, rape, and sodomy, implying that the degree of physical injury inflicted on victims is highest for this group. On the other hand, offenders in both substance abuse groups are more apt to stand convicted of burglary, which suggests that these groups did the least physical damage to victims.

When we compared judicial sentences across groups of offenders, striking differences emerged for offenders with a history of psychiatric treatment. In particular, we found that offenders with psychiatric histories who were convicted of murder,

**Table 3.9**

*Conviction Offense by Mental Health Experience of Offender*

| | Mental health experience | | | |
|---|---|---|---|---|
| | No history ($n = 544$) | Substance abuse history ($n = 83$) | Psychiatric history ($n = 540$) | Substance abuse and psychiatric history ($n = 141$) |
| Conviction offense | | | | |
| Murder | 8.8% | 6.0% | 10.4% | 5.7% |
| Kidnapping | 0.2 | 0.0 | 0.9 | 0.7 |
| Arson | 1.1 | 2.4 | 3.0 | 2.8 |
| Robbery | 46.6 | 44.6 | 32.4 | 44.7 |
| Assault | 9.4 | 7.2 | 16.1 | 12.1 |
| Reckless endangerment | 0.4 | 1.2 | 1.1 | 1.4 |
| Burglary | 15.8 | 24.1 | 16.1 | 21.3 |
| Rape | 5.2 | 4.8 | 9.3 | 3.5 |
| Sodomy | 2.0 | 2.4 | 5.7 | 0.0 |
| Sex abuse | 1.1 | 2.4 | 2.4 | 0.0 |
| Weapon | 9.4 | 4.8 | 2.6 | 7.8 |

arson, sodomy and weapons offenses received much longer maximum sentences than offenders with no mental health involvement (182 mo. versus 163 mo., 73 mo. versus 50 mo., 103 mo. versus 88 mo., 67 mo. versus 50 mo.). In terms of more run-of-the-mill violent offenses, such as robbery, burglary, and assault, offenders with psychiatric histories received sentences that were comparable to those of ordinary offenders. It is interesting to note that similar patterns of more severe punishment did not emerge for offenders with substance abuse histories or for offenders with combined psychiatric and substance abuse histories.

In addition, we examined the proportion of offenders who were under community supervision at the time of their offense, convicted by trial, and sentenced to life imprisonment. The analysis did not reveal any significant differences across groups of inmates.

In summary, we find that inmates with psychiatric histories are more often convicted of serious violent crimes and substance abusers are more frequently convicted of burglary. Differences in conviction offenses thus parallel differences observed in arrest histories, and this confluence of findings is reassuring because it suggests that there are reliable differences in criminal propensity between groups of offenders. The fact that similar differences emerge across both arrest histories and conviction offenses also points to a continuity in offense behavior over time. Finally, although we have not examined the many factors that enter into sentencing decisions, the data support the argument that mentally disordered offenders receive more severe penalties than other offenders who are convicted of similar offenses, especially when sentenced for very serious violent crimes.

## Patterns of Offense Behavior

At this point we describe aspects of violent crimes (for example, location, weapon use, victim–offender relationship) that are often reported in criminological research. In doing so, we locate violent offenses by disturbed offenders within a broad context of situational attributes. As we reviewed these data, we noticed that a modal, or typical, pattern, around which there is modest variation, existed for each crime type. We therefore begin to report the findings with a composite description of "typical" offenses by the comparison group and then note any deviations from this pattern by offenders in the mental health groups. In Table 3.10 we present information on selected characteristics of violent crimes by the offender's mental health experience. It is important to keep in mind that this information describes violent offenses for which offenders were sent to prison.

Murderers commit most of their offenses on the street or at the victim's residence, using a gun, and are often accompanied by a co-offender. The victim is typically a male friend or acquaintance. In contrast, murderers with psychiatric histories are more likely to act alone at their own residences, using a blunt instrument as a weapon, killing a relative or spouse.

Murders and assaults share a similar pattern of offense characteristics. Among the comparison group, assaults tend to occur on the street against a male friend or acquaintance. The incidents frequently involve a gun, and the victim usually requires hospital treatment. Offenders with psychiatric histories are more apt to act alone in off-the-street locations, assaulting female strangers. They rarely use a weapon, but when they do, the preferred instrument is a knife, and the attack is less likely to precipitate hospitalization. Inmates with combined psychiatric and substance abuse histories disproportionately attack their relatives or spouse and, when a weapon is used, it is most often a knife.

Robbers constitute the largest offender group, and the typical scenario finds the offender on the street acting in concert with others and with a weapon, usually a gun. The victim is nearly always a stranger and suffers physical assault. Several contrasts with this picture are found among the substance abusers. Both groups (specialized and compounded) of substance abusers tend to commit their robberies without assistance against commercial establishments. The victim is usually threatened with a weapon, and the offender makes off with a substantial amount of money (over $250).

Sex offenders almost always act alone, committing the offense at their own or the victim's domicile with a relatively

## Table 3.10

*Selected Characteristics of Violent Incidents by Type of Offense and Mental Health Experience of Offender*

| | Mental health experience | | | |
|---|---|---|---|---|
| | No history | Substance abuse | Psychiatric history | Substance abuse and psychiatric history |
| **Murder** | ($n$ = 48) | ($n$ = 5) | ($n$ = 56) | ($n$ = 8) |
| 2 or more offenders | 37.5%* | 20.0%* | 16.1%* | 50.0%* |
| Location | | | | |
|   Residence | 34.0% | 40.0% | 48.2% | 50.0% |
|   Business | 19.1 | 20.0 | 14.3 | 0.0 |
|   Street | 42.6 | 40.0 | 33.9 | 37.5 |
|   Other | 4.3 | 0.0 | 3.6 | 12.5 |
| Weapon | | | | |
|   None | 0.0% | 20.0% | 5.4% | 0.0% |
|   Knife | 33.3 | 40.0 | 39.3 | 50.0 |
|   Gun | 56.3 | 40.0 | 30.4 | 37.5 |
|   Blunt instrument | 2.1 | 0.0 | 14.3 | 0.0 |
|   Other | 8.4 | 0.0 | 10.7 | 12.5 |
| Victim's relationship to offender | | | | |
|   Spouse, paramour | 12.5% | 20.0% | 17.9% | 12.5% |
|   Other relative | 0.0 | 0.0 | 3.6 | 0.0 |
|   Friend, acquaintance | 52.2 | 40.0 | 50.0 | 62.5 |
|   Stranger | 34.8 | 40.0 | 28.6 | 25.0 |
| Male victim | 75.0% | 60.0% | 76.8% | 75.0% |
| **Assault** | ($n$ = 51) | ($n$ = 6) | ($n$ = 87) | ($n$ = 17) |
| Two or more offenders | 23.5% | 0.0% | 14.9% | 0.0% |
| Location | | | | |
|   Offender's residence | 15.7% | 16.7% | 17.4% | 37.5% |
|   Victim's residence | 15.7 | 16.7 | 14.0 | 12.5 |
|   Business | 11.8 | 0.0 | 12.8 | 18.8 |
|   Street | 47.1 | 50.0 | 38.4 | 25.0 |
|   Other | 9.8 | 16.7 | 17.4 | 6.3 |
| Weapon | | | | |
|   None | 7.8% | 33.3% | 14.9% | 11.8% |
|   Knife | 31.4* | 50.0* | 51.7* | 64.7* |
|   Gun | 49.0** | 16.7** | 18.4** | 11.8** |
|   Other | 11.8 | 0.0 | 14.9 | 11.8 |

## Table 3.10 (*Continued*)

| | Mental health experience | | | |
|---|---|---|---|---|
| | No history | Substance abuse | Psychiatric history | Substance abuse and psychiatric history |
| Victim's relationship to offender | | | | |
| Spouse, paramour | 14.0% | 16.7% | 19.5% | 29.4% |
| Other relative | 2.0 | 0.0 | 1.1 | 11.8 |
| Friend, acquaintance | 54.0 | 33.3 | 35.4 | 41.2 |
| Police | 5.9 | 16.7 | 9.8 | 5.9 |
| Stranger | 28.0 | 33.3 | 40.2 | 17.6 |
| Victim hospitalized | 70.6% | 50.0% | 48.8% | 47.1% |
| Female victim | 27.5% | 50.0% | 42.5% | 41.2% |
| | | | | |
| Robbery | (*n* = 253) | (*n* = 37) | (*n* = 175) | (*n* = 63) |
| Two or more offenders | 70.8%** | 54.1%** | 47.4%** | 34.9%** |
| Over $250 | 23.4 | 35.5 | 26.8 | 37.5 |
| Location | | | | |
| Victim's residence | 13.5% | 10.8% | 16.7% | 17.5% |
| Business | 20.7** | 40.5** | 26.4** | 49.2** |
| Public transportation | 14.7 | 5.4 | 14.4 | 11.1 |
| Street | 47.4** | 43.2** | 38.5** | 17.5** |
| Other | 3.6 | 0.0 | 4.0 | 4.8 |
| Weapon | | | | |
| None | 29.8% | 16.2% | 31.8% | 19.7% |
| Knife | 23.0 | 37.8 | 27.2 | 29.5 |
| Gun | 43.7 | 43.2 | 35.3 | 47.5 |
| Other | 3.6 | 2.7 | 5.7 | 3.2 |
| Stranger victim | 84.5% | 97.3% | 83.4% | 81.0% |
| Most serious attack | | | | |
| Threatened | 35.3%** | 64.9%** | 35.6%** | 61.9%** |
| Hit, hand or object | 53.8** | 29.7** | 54.6** | 33.3** |
| Shot or stabbed | 10.4 | 5.4 | 8.6 | 4.8 |
| Raped | 0.4 | 0.0 | 1.1 | 0.0 |
| | | | | |
| Sex offense | (*n* = 48) | (*n* = 8) | (*n* = 94) | (*n*= 5) |
| Two or more offenders | 8.9% | 0.0% | 7.4% | 20.0% |
| Location | | | | |
| Offender's residence | 40.0% | 37.5% | 42.2% | 20.0% |
| Victim's residence | 26.7 | 25.0 | 27.8 | 0.0 |
| Street | 17.8 | 37.5 | 15.6 | 40.0 |
| Other | 15.6 | 0.0 | 14.4 | 40.0 |
| Weapon used | 28.9% | 12.5% | 24.7% | 40.0% |
| Male victim | 11.1% | 25.0% | 22.3% | 0.0% |
| Victim under 16 years | 55.6% | 50.0% | 58.5% | 20.0% |

**Table 3.10 (*Continued*)**

| | No history | Substance abuse | Psychiatric history | Substance abuse and psychiatric history |
|---|---|---|---|---|
| | | Mental health experience | | |
| Victim's relationship to offender | | | | |
| Spouse, paramour | 4.5% | 0.0% | 4.3% | 20.0% |
| Daughter, son | 13.6 | 37.5 | 14.3 | 0.0 |
| Other relative | 0.0 | 0.0 | 5.5 | 0.0 |
| Friend, acquaintance | 45.4 | 37.5 | 39.6 | 40.0 |
| Stranger | 36.4 | 25.0 | 38.5 | 40.0 |
| Weapon | ($n = 51$) | ($n = 4$) | ($n = 14$) | ($n = 11$) |
| Two or more offenders | 25.5% | 25.0% | 21.4% | 36.4% |
| Location | | | | |
| Residence | 23.5% | 25.0% | 21.4% | 0.0% |
| Business | 5.9 | 25.0 | 21.4 | 27.3 |
| Public transportation | 5.9 | 0.0 | 7.1 | 9.1 |
| Street | 64.7 | 50.0 | 50.0 | 63.6 |
| Victim physically attacked | 7.8% | 25.0% | 21.4% | 9.1% |
| Burglary | ($n = 86$) | ($n = 20$) | ($n = 82$) | ($n = 30$) |
| Two or more offenders | 48.8% | 30.0% | 35.6% | 23.3% |
| Over $250 | 45.3% | 41.2% | 50.7% | 47.4% |
| Location | | | | |
| Residence | 88.4% | 85.0% | 92.0% | 96.7% |
| Business | 9.3 | 10.0 | 4.6 | 3.3 |
| Other | 2.3 | 5.0 | 3.4 | 0.0 |

*$p < .05$; **$p < .01$; Chi-square, specified category versus all others.
*Note*: The chi-square test statistic is strongly influenced by the number of cases, which for some offender and offense combinations is very small. Percentages refer to the proportion of incidents with a given characteristic. Some columns may total greater than 100% because multiple victims with different characteristics are involved. The number of cases may vary as a result of missing data. Descriptive items are reported selectively because all items are not relevant to each offense type. Infrequently appearing categories are sometimes combined. The offender's residence is counted as the offense location in situations in which offender and victim live together.

young (under 16 years of age) female victim who is either a friend or stranger. Weapons are infrequently used. The mental health groups show the same pattern, with the exception of the psychiatric group, which is somewhat more likely to search out a male victim.

Burglars, acting in concert, usually target the private dwelling of a stranger. The crime often produces substantial material gain (over $250), and victims are rarely physically assaulted. A similar pattern emerges for mental health groups, except that these offenders show a greater propensity to act alone.

Weapons offenses often involve a lone offender who is discovered carrying a weapon on the street. Only in rare instances is there a victim who is attacked. A similar pattern is found among the mental health groups. However, incidents by offenders with psychiatric histories appear to carry a greater potential for violence, as indicated by a greater tendency to be found carrying weapons in commercial establishments and attacking a victim.

In summary, the composite picture that describes many, but certainly not all, murders and assaults among the comparison group is as follows: The violence is a product of street encounters among groups of male acquaintances in which a dispute arises and someone is shot. Major departures from this scenario for offenders with mental health histories, particularly psychiatric care, are: (a) the offender is more inclined to act alone, (b) incidents are less likely to take place on the streets, (c) the offender less often uses a gun, (d) murders more frequently involve nonstranger victims, specifically a spouse or relative, and (e) strangers and females run greater chances of being victims of assault.

Before discussing our findings we need to acknowledge that several explanations can be applied to the same set of facts. This is so because differences in criminal behavior may reflect variations in social activities or life styles of offenders, or may capture different motivational or situational aspects of violent encounters. In chapter 7 we examine violent incidents from a different perspective, one that will provide additional information on these issues. Nevertheless, we now venture a few interpretations of the data we have just presented.

The most consistent difference we find, one that applies to almost all types of crime, is that offenders with mental health backgrounds are more disposed to act alone. This fact suggests that group-influenced motivations are less apt to produce violence among mentally disordered offenders, which may reflect the familiar observation that mental patients tend to have relatively marginal life styles that include a greater degree of social isolation. The fact that mental patients use guns less often than other violent offenders suggests that disturbed offenders are less prone to share the view that possessing a gun is a necessary means of protection or a visible symbol of toughness. More generally, however, access to firearms depends on associations with persons who have access to illegal goods and markets, and in this regard mental patients may be at a disadvantage.

Relatives and spouses are disproportionately victims of murder, implicating domestic problems as situations that can provoke extremely violent reactions from mentally disordered offenders.[3] We also find that violence by mental patients occurs less frequently on the streets, reinforcing the conclusion that different types of social situations or encounters act as a catalyst to violence. One possibility is that intimate family encounters are a source of stress for emotionally disordered persons and may, over time, lead to an escalation of accumulated grievances (including legitimate, exaggerated, or imagined grievances). Yet, intimates will also be exposed to greater risk of victimization because disturbed offenders lead more reclusive lives.

In contrast, assault victims are more often strangers, which suggests that unprovoked attacks or short-term escalations of ordinary social encounters may also be prevalent among mentally disordered offenders. It is harder to explain why females are more frequently chosen as victims, but it may be that some disturbed offenders lack inhibitions including chivalrous norms which hold that women are out of bounds as sparring partners. Moreover, if some mentally disordered offenders selectively relate to weaker victims, a presumed lack of physical strength among females may make them attractive targets.

Among violent or potentially violent acts that incorporate a profit motive (that is, robbery), substance abusers stand out as heavily involved and ambitious actors. These offenders

---

[3]Although the proportion of offenders who murder a relative is small (5%), we find that matricide, fratricide, and patricide occur only among offenders with psychiatric histories.

(a) appear more comfortable working alone, (b) usually target lucrative commercial establishments, and (c) are likely to carry a gun, which hypothetically allows for effective control of the situation, thereby reducing the chances of physical violence.

# Patterns of Violence

We now examine differences in violence across groups of offenders based on the typology we developed in chapter 2. The data indicate that felony-related violence is the most common type of violence for which offenders are imprisoned (see Table 3.11). However, proportions of felony-related violence vary across groups, ranging from half of the comparison group to one third of the psychiatric group. The second most common offense type is burglary, which most people would consider a property crime. As before, we again found that burglars were disproportionately represented among substance abusers. Specifically, more than one fifth of the substance abusers (both groups) were burglars, which is about one and a half times the proportion of burglars in other offender groups. The next most common type of violence is retaliatory violence, and the proportion of inmates in this category does not differ significantly across groups.

The remaining violence types are relatively uncommon but show significant variations across groups. Both groups of inmates with a history of psychiatric problems engaged more frequently in unmotivated violence, which included situations in which the offender could not offer plausible explanations for his or her act. Although only 6.5% of the incidents committed by the psychiatric patients could be described as unmotivated violence, the proportion is five times greater than that of the comparison group. The difference is important because unmotivated attacks are by definition enigmatic, unpredictable, and undeserved and therefore are viewed as extremely threatening. Many unmotivated attacks are dramatically newsworthy and are often portrayed as characteristic of disturbed offenders. Thus, the results of our analysis are significant on two counts. First, we find that disturbed offenders hold a near monopoly on unmotivated violence. Yet we also

**Table 3.11**

*Type and Level of Violence and Eccentric Offense Behavior by Mental Health Experience of Offender*

| | Signifi-cance[a] level | No history ($n$ = 544) | Substance abuse history ($n$ = 83) | Psychiatric history ($n$ = 540) | Substance abuse and psychiatric history ($n$ = 141) |
|---|---|---|---|---|---|
| | | Mental health experience | | | |
| Type of violence | | | | | |
| Retaliatory | .40 | 12.5% | 10.8% | 15.7% | 14.4% |
| Unmotivated | .00 | 1.2 | 0.0 | 6.5 | 5.8 |
| Felony-related | .00 | 50.8 | 45.8 | 33.7 | 43.9 |
| Sex—adult | | | 7.2 | 8.5 | 2.9 |
| victim | .00 | 3.7 | | | |
| Sex—child | | | | | |
| victim | .00 | 4.5 | 3.6 | 10.7 | 0.7 |
| Weapon | .00 | 8.7 | 3.6 | 2.0 | 5.0 |
| Arson | .17 | 1.2 | 2.4 | 3.1 | 2.9 |
| Police victim | .31 | 1.7 | 3.6 | 2.8 | 0.7 |
| Burglary | .02 | 13.1 | 21.7 | 14.4 | 22.3 |
| Auto/institu-tion | .82 | 2.3 | 1.2 | 2.4 | 1.4 |
| Level of violence | | | | | |
| No violence | .11 | 18.9% | 20.5% | 15.9% | 24.5% |
| Less serious | .00 | 33.6 | 43.4 | 21.1 | 35.3 |
| Serious | .03 | 30.3 | 22.9 | 31.5 | 20.1 |
| Extreme | .00 | 17.2 | 13.3 | 31.5 | 20.1 |
| Eccentric offense behavior | | | | | |
| Ineffectual | .00 | 3.5% | 8.4% | 10.9% | 10.6% |
| Frenzied | .00 | 1.8 | 2.4 | 9.8 | 8.5 |
| Symptomatic | .00 | 1.8 | 0.0 | 7.8 | 4.3 |
| No motive | .00 | 1.1 | 1.2 | 8.0 | 4.3 |
| No memory | .00 | 1.3 | 10.8 | 6.1 | 13.5 |

[a]Chi-square, specified category versus all others.

find that such incidents are relatively infrequent and can hardly be described as characteristic of the type of violence committed by disturbed offenders.

The two disturbed offender groups were also more likely to commit sexual violence against both adults and children. The proportion of sex offenders was substantial in that it amounted to nearly one fifth of the psychiatric group. Inmates with substance abuse problems were more frequently sentenced for sexual violence, but only with adult victims. The differences are significant because it is often assumed that sex offenders have peculiar motivations and, in particular, that the behavior of child molesters is pathological.

Finally, we saw that the comparison group was more often convicted of weapon offenses, and that the distribution of crimes involving arson, violence against police, violence in an institution, and assault with an automobile did not vary across offender groups, although there was an indication of a difference for arson.

Possibly our most important finding is that seriousness of violence ratings show substantial variation across mental health background. In nearly one third of the offenses by persons with psychiatric histories the level of violence was extreme. The proportion is the highest observed, being almost twice that of the comparison group. If we combine ratings of serious and extreme violence, almost two thirds (63%) of incidents committed by offenders with psychiatric histories fall into this category, indicating that emotionally disturbed offenders are disproportionately involved with the most violent and most injurious crimes handled by the criminal justice system.

Other analyses we conducted show that recency of psychiatric problems is associated with extremity of violence. Among offenders who received psychiatric services at time of conviction, more than three quarters (77%) engaged in serious or extreme violence. We inferred from the data that many contemporaneously disordered offenders were seriously violent, but this conclusion should be tempered by the observation that perceived need for treatment can be influenced by degree of violence. However, although we acknowledge the possibility that persons are judged in need of treatment because they are violent, our analysis of career patterns showed that most offenders who became patients at conviction had mental health records predating the offense, which weakens the argument that violence is a contaminating diagnostic criterion. We also noted that the proportion of serious or extreme violence for offenders with a recent psychiatric history was 66% and for those with a remote history, 61%. These findings faintly suggest that among offender populations recency of emotional problems increases the likelihood of serious violence.

In contrast, we saw that inmates with substance abuse problems mostly engaged in offenses that involved little or no violence, and this finding might have been anticipated from previous analyses which showed that these offenders frequently engaged in burglary. It is also significant that violence levels among substance abusers with psychiatric problems were not greater than those among other substance abusers and were lower than those among other psychiatric patients.

On the other hand, the role of alcohol and drugs stood out in violence by offenders with substance abuse problems. Sixty percent of those with alcohol or drug problems and 64% of those with both psychiatric and substance abuse problems were described as under the influence of intoxicating agents at the time of their offense. These proportions compare with 38% of the psychiatric group and 27% of the comparison group who were intoxicated under similar circumstances.

The findings on violence by substance abusers are interesting because they both confirm and dispel popular images of criminalized drug addicts. On the one hand, substance abuse is associated with increased propensities for acquisitive crimes such as burglary, and presumably these offenses are attractive because they can help underwrite the costs of addiction. We also saw that many substance abusers committed crimes while under the influence of drugs or alcohol, which suggests that intoxicating agents can play a facilitative criminogenic role by lowering inhibitions. In contrast, the relatively nonserious violence levels of substance abusers' crimes do not support a view of addicts as wildly violent offenders, and the data do not support observations made by some psychiatrists that mentally ill substance abusers are especially violent.[4] As we read

---

[4]In a recent newspaper article, a psychiatrist, in discussing a delusional patient who was shot while attacking a police officer, stated, "He has severe mental illness, he has substance abuse, and that tends to precipitate the breakdown or make the breakdown more violent" (New York Times, September 23, 1988, p. B4). Of course, our data do not provide a rigorous test of this hypothesis, since not all offenders in the combined substance abuse— psychiatric group were necessarily disordered and using chemical agents about the time of the offense.

cases files, we were struck by the number of situations in which substance abusers were impaired by alcohol or drugs to such a point that they failed to behave as rational offenders or were unable to successfully carry out an offense. We include ineffective, counterproductive acts under the heading of eccentric offense behavior, and we now return to Table 3.11 to examine patterns of eccentricities among offenders in the samples.

# Patterns of Eccentricity

Eccentric violence was rare among members of the comparison group, with ineffectual behavior, the most frequently appearing item, characterizing only 3.5% of conviction offenses. Proportions of all incidents showing other types of eccentricity fell under 2%. In comparison, substance abuse offenders displayed more ineffectual or counterproductive behavior (8.4%), and often claimed to have no memory of the criminal event (10.8%). The most consistent pattern we found was that offenders with psychiatric histories were overrepresented in all categories of peculiar offense behavior. The pattern is a dramatic one, given that many violent incidents by psychiatric patients demonstrated ineffectual or counterproductive behavior, such as leaving behind incriminating evidence (10.9%), violent overkill or other behavior reflecting a frenzied mental state (9.8%), and conduct one generally thinks of as symptomatic of mental disorder (7.8%). In 8% of violent incidents there was no plausible motivation for the offense, whereas in 6.1% the offender could not recall his or her crime. Offenders with combined substance abuse and psychiatric problems showed the greatest difficulty recollecting details of their offenses (13.5% of incidents). This group was also overrepresented in other categories of eccentricity, but less so for motiveless and symptomatic violence when compared with the psychiatric group.

When we look at the relative incidence of eccentric features across mental health backgrounds, we see that the differences are substantial. Compared with offenders with no treatment history, violence by former psychiatric patients is roughly three times more likely to involve frenzied behavior, four times more likely to display symptomatic behavior, five times more likely to involve no memory of the offense, and seven times more likely to show no apparent motivation. In our opinion, the consistently disproportionate display of eccentric offense behaviors among former psychiatric patients, and in particular of symptomatic nuances, argues for recognition of "symptomatic violence," meaning situations in which clinically relevant motivations can be implicated in the violence picture of disturbed offenders. In this regard, we find that a history of emotional problems can influence violent behavior in dramatically different ways. Emotional disorders can reduce a person's competence as a violent offender, and they can also increase the damage that is done in acts of blind rage.

We therefore conclude that a view of mental illness and criminality as unrelated independent attributes is not appropriate for some patient-offenders. The argument for a more integrated perspective is strongest in cases in which symptoms and violence coincide, and we take a closer look at offenses of this kind in chapter 8. We also conclude that two contrasting images—that of the ineffectual criminal and that of the frenzied violent offender—emerge from descriptions of offenses by disturbed individuals. Such combinations of person-related attributes and offense-related attributes deserve further scrutiny, which is a principal goal of our cluster analysis.

# II

# Typological Clusters and Case Studies

# 4

# Offenders With Histories of Mental Health Problems

We now turn to the cluster analysis, which yielded types highlighting sharp contrasts on consequential variables. In this and the following two chapters we identify various types of offenders who differ in terms of types of offense, level of violence, and criminal and violence history. Substance abusers are often differentiated by diverse histories of drug or alcohol abuse. Within offense categories (burglary, robbery, extreme personal violence) types differ on historical variables—such as presence or absence of violence records—and demographics (e.g., age). Such distinctions are gratifying in view of the number of variables we clustered, which could combine in impressively messy ways given their substantial heterogeneity.

We have noted that our core sample is composed of violent offenders who were former clients of mental health services, excluding substance abuse services. Cluster analysis subdivided this sample of psychiatric patients into 10 diverse types (Table 4.1). We labelled these types as the impulsive burglar, impulsive robber, long-term explosive robber, young explosive robber, mature mugger, acute disturbed exploder, chronic disturbed exploder, disturbed sex offender, composite career offender, and compensatory offender. The types ranged widely in terms of the seriousness of the violence the offender had perpetrated and differed in the extent to which professional interventions were deemed necessary after the offender was

# Table 4.1

Results of Cluster Analysis for Offenders With Psychiatric Histories

| | Impulsive Burglar (n = 56) | Impulsive Robber (n = 39) | Long-term Explosive Robber (n = 53) | Young Explosive Robber (n = 40) | Mature Mugger (n = 22) | Acute Disturbed Exploder (n = 51) | Chronic Disturbed Exploder (n = 90) | Disturbed Sex Offender (n = 65) | Composite Career Offender (n = 60) | Compensatory Offender (n = 19) |
|---|---|---|---|---|---|---|---|---|---|---|
| **Offense type** | | | | | | | | | | |
| Unmotivated | 0% | 0% | 0% | 0% | 0% | 26% | 19% | 5% | 0% | 0% |
| Retaliatory | 0 | 5 | 2 | 8 | 0 | 51 | 39 | 8 | 5 | 11 |
| Felony-related | 0 | 74 | 85 | 75 | 100 | 12 | 7 | 9 | 17 | 58 |
| Sex—adult victim | 0 | 10 | 2 | 5 | 0 | 2 | 19 | 14 | 8 | 11 |
| Sex—child victim | 0 | 3 | 6 | 8 | 0 | 2 | 4 | 43 | 20 | 11 |
| Weapon | 2 | 0 | 0 | 0 | 0 | 0 | 0 | 5 | 12 | 0 |
| Arson | 2 | 5 | 2 | 3 | 0 | 0 | 0 | 12 | 3 | 11 |
| Police victim | 0 | 0 | 4 | 3 | 0 | 6 | 3 | 3 | 5 | 0 |
| Burglary | 96 | 0 | 0 | 0 | 0 | 0 | 0 | 0 | 28 | 0 |
| Auto/institution | 0 | 3 | 0 | 0 | 0 | 2 | 9 | 2 | 0 | 0 |
| **Violence level** | | | | | | | | | | |
| No violence | 98% | 0% | 0% | 0% | 0% | 0% | 0% | 5% | 35% | 0% |
| Less serious | 0 | 62 | 50 | 53 | 100 | 0 | 0 | 0 | 10 | 11 |
| Serious | 2 | 21 | 47 | 43 | 0 | 0 | 0 | 89 | 52 | 90 |
| Extreme | 0 | 18 | 4 | 5 | 0 | 100 | 100 | 6 | 3 | 0 |
| Alcohol/drug influence | 55% | 44% | 34% | 33% | 32% | 22% | 46% | 31% | 32% | 47% |
| **Eccentricity** | | | | | | | | | | |
| Ineffectual behavior | 7% | 5% | 8% | 8% | 5% | 29% | 11% | 11% | 12% | 21% |
| Frenzied mental state | 0 | 3 | 2 | 3 | 0 | 35 | 30 | 2 | 0 | 5 |
| Symptomatic behavior | 0 | 5 | 4 | 0 | 0 | 29 | 8 | 14 | 3 | 11 |
| No apparent motive | 2 | 3 | 2 | 0 | 0 | 29 | 18 | 9 | 0 | 0 |
| No memory | 5% | 5% | 3% | 0% | 5% | 10% | 10% | 6% | 5% | 11% |
| Psychotic diagnosis | 5 | 5 | 23 | 5 | 23 | 53 | 28 | 25 | 37 | 53 |
| Low IQ | 9 | 5 | 20 | 25 | 23 | 22 | 22 | 20 | 18 | 53 |

| | | | | | | | | | |
|---|---|---|---|---|---|---|---|---|---|
| **Violence history** | | | | | | | | | |
| None | 63% | 100% | 0% | 0% | 27% | 59% | 0% | 85% | 2% | 5% |
| Recent | 27 | 0 | 47 | 88 | 27 | 24 | 47 | 6 | 27 | 68 |
| Remote | 18 | 0 | 100 | 33 | 55 | 18 | 94 | 9 | 98 | 42 |
| **Arrest history** | | | | | | | | | |
| Low | 32% | 87% | 4% | 40% | 23% | 67% | 7% | 51% | 2% | 42% |
| Medium | 48 | 13 | 4 | 45 | 64 | 28 | 28 | 35 | 37 | 58 |
| High | 20 | 0 | 93 | 15 | 14 | 6 | 66 | 14 | 62 | 0 |
| **Psychiatric history** | | | | | | | | | |
| Instant | 27% | 28% | 19% | 10% | 23% | 78% | 31% | 65% | 37% | 84% |
| Recent | 41 | 28 | 40 | 28 | 46 | 53 | 41 | 32 | 37 | 79 |
| Remote | 70 | 67 | 85 | 83 | 73 | 55 | 89 | 63 | 93 | 79 |
| **Age** | | | | | | | | | |
| Low | 68% | 82% | 15% | 98% | 0% | 0% | 13% | 15% | 0% | 11% |
| Medium | 29 | 13 | 68 | 3 | 100 | 53 | 46 | 37 | 8 | 84 |
| High | 4 | 5 | 19 | 0 | 0 | 47 | 41 | 48 | 92 | 5 |
| Prison experience | 18% | 0% | 53% | 8% | 18% | 2% | 51% | 14% | 73% | 16% |
| Under supervision | 32 | 15 | 36 | 45 | 32 | 10 | 24 | 12 | 30 | 37 |
| **Covariates** | | | | | | | | | |
| Single | 77% | 95% | 77% | 90% | 76% | 80% | 63% | 77% | 59% | 94% |
| High school graduate | 25 | 13 | 26 | 0 | 14 | 33 | 21 | 25 | 34 | 33 |
| White | 60 | 31 | 42 | 23 | 29 | 35 | 31 | 60 | 45 | 26 |
| Employed | 71 | 54 | 73 | 58 | 68 | 71 | 67 | 71 | 86 | 67 |

arrested. As one might expect, the offenders had substantial histories of mental health contacts, and in most of the groups they also had histories of violence.

# Types of Offenders

## Impulsive Burglars

The first type we isolated stands out because it is one whose members are not violent offenders (54 of 56 are convicted burglars), though 4 of 10 had committed violence in the past. The offenders are mostly young, and a surprising number (over half) were intoxicated at the time of their offense.

We call members of this group impulsive burglars because (a) they are nonprofessionals who (b) demonstrate mixed motives for burglary offenses that are often ineffective and self-destructive and (c) reflect long-term difficulties.

A case in point is that of an 18-year-old man who was imprisoned for a spree of four burglaries, in which he stole mostly jewelry. The offender's problems began early with learning disabilities compounded by displays of anxiety and destructiveness. Antisocial acts in school included disruption of classes and theft of a teacher's purse. There was also a burglary (at age 13) involving an abandoned building. A year later there was another burglary in which the offender broke into a house and stole jewelry and a pair of socks; he was placed in a residential program from which he absconded. This sequence was followed by other burglaries, other residential placements, and more escapes.

After his last offenses the man was inducted into the Job Corps. There, staff reported that "he had numerous behavioral problems." The following examples of his behavior were recorded while in the Job Corps:

> Assaulted another student with a chair during an argument over a candy cane.

Carried two small cans of gasoline to the dorm with the idea of setting the dorm on fire.

Numerous fights with other male students over trivial matters.

Suspected of being involved in a break-in of a center residence and the center canteen.

This offender was ultimately jailed and soon required mental health services. The jail staff reported that

he was hospitalized twice in the Forensic Unit of the County Jail because of suicidal potential. First admission was after he attempted to hang himself in the bullpen with his shoelaces. He was discharged in an improved condition [and] was re-admitted because a noose was found in his cell and he threatened to kill himself in order not to go to state prison. On second admission he also exhibited psychotic symptoms, an underlying schizophrenic condition.

The offender ascribed his suicide attempts to difficulties he experienced in obtaining drugs. The same passive, infantlike stance characterized the man when he entered prison, where staff complained that he "seems to be lacking in . . . motivation."

A similarly nonprofessional flavor permeated a second case, that of a 23-year-old burglar. This man's difficulties began at age six and included "family problems." Among these were a sadistic, abusive father, who "used to beat him and handcuff him to his bed or a back porch railing," and a half-brother who sexually abused him.

One site the man burglarized was a program from which he had received services. He also broke into the home of a friend who had helped him with legal fees, clothing, and shelter. The man appeared unable to refrain from committing offenses when placed on probation and parole, requiring that he be institutionalized. A social worker observed that "he seems almost to want to be punished or at least caught, particularly in light of his constant, flagrant violations of probation and curfew." The offender himself said that he was "a person who can be talked into anything" and claimed he was "afraid some-day someone will talk him into killing someone." Such state-ments are doubly revealing because they were not designed to invite lenient dispositions despite their disarming honesty and self-effacement.

## Impulsive Robbers

Impulsive robbers are youthful robbers who have no histories of violent crimes and negligible criminal histories. Like im-pulsive burglars, such young offenders have childhood prob-lems, including mental health problems.

The pattern is illustrated by a 20-year-old man who was serving his first prison sentence for robbery after he broke into an occupied house whose owner he threatened and manhan-dled but did not seriously hurt. The offender had been a drug and alcohol abuser, and he was intoxicated at the time of the offense. He had also been a long-term patient, having been hospitalized for 8 years starting at age 11. He had most recently committed himself to a hospital after seeing his mother stabbed by her boyfriend and had to be rehospitalized as soon as he arrived in prison.

The offender had been a victim of child abuse and had been brain-injured in infancy. He was virtually illiterate and was borderline mentally retarded. He was also psychotic and claimed he heard voices that instructed him to hurt himself and other people.

The man was easily intimidated, which caused him many problems in prison. Other problems had to do with his im-pulsive aggressivity, which impelled him to assault other in-mates and destroy furniture. However, the man was deathly afraid of guards (he thought they would beat him for "not making his bed right") and invited exploitation by peers, to which he then clumsily reacted.

This offender's prison career consisted of transfers between the prison hospital (where his deportment improved under medication) and disciplinary segregation settings. As a result of this pattern his chances for program involvement became slim and his prospects of community adjustment negligible.

This offender is somewhat more disturbed than most impulsive robbers but typifies this group in his combination of youthfulness, rootlessness, and inadequacy, which augurs an inauspicious career.

## Long-Term Explosive Robbers

Long-term disturbed robbers are older robbers who have high arrest records and extensive histories of violence. They also have longstanding mental health problems and have led checkered—and singularly unsuccessful—careers. Many (30%) are intellectually deficient.

One robbery offender who typifies this serious and obdurate pattern is a 28-year-old man who had evolved a propensity for beating women during the process of stealing their pocketbooks. He explained that he had to assault his victims because they refused to part with their bags. He further indicated that he covets bags "because my mother has money in her pocketbook all the time." He also explained that he did not victimize men "because I don't want them to come after me."

The offender was a chronic schizophrenic who had been hospitalized frequently. He was mentally retarded and was described by prison staff as "simplistic, polite, and cooperative." Despite his extensive offense history (10 prior felony arrests) and his predatory crimes, the man had to be placed in protective, structured settings, where he did well under continuing medication.

Another 28-year-old robber had been arrested 19 times in 10 years. He had most recently robbed a supermarket at knifepoint and resisted arrest, injuring a police officer. In a prior offense he had entered a cookie store, demanding samples, and had assaulted a customer who turned her back on him and "didn't apologize."

The offender had been committed to several different hospitals and on one occasion had been found incompetent to stand trial. He had also attempted suicide. In prison the man was described as "bizarre, babbling, and [showing an] incoherent speech pattern." When he was not in hospital, the man "dwelled on the subject of masturbation inordinate amounts of time," refused to wash, and "presented a fire problem."

Such deficits are typical of the group and make such men odd exemplars of hardened recidivism.

## Young Explosive Robbers

Young disturbed robbers have violence histories but have not served time in prison, though they are often on probation when they are arrested. These robbers also tend to commit offenses that involve appreciable levels of violence, if one considers the extreme youthfulness (98% young) of the cluster.

One offender fitting this precocious category is a volatile 19-year-old man who served his first prison term for a robbery with a sawed-off shotgun. Like other young robbers, this man had been raised in a succession of institutions, starting with special schools in which he had to be placed after he failed kindergarten. He did not do better in such special schools, from which he was mostly suspended for temper tantrums in which he attacked teachers and fellow students.

Some settings would not accept the man because he was explosive, and others discharged him after they discovered they could not accommodate his explosions. The man was also a problem because he was badly retarded (his IQ was 63) and demonstrated emotional instability that yielded imperfectly to medication.

The man had been arrested twice for criminal assaults and had served time in a youth institution for robbing an elderly woman at knife point. After he was released from this placement, the man pistol-whipped an acquaintance and committed the shotgun robbery for which he was incarcerated. He arrived in prison announcing that he had enemies among fellow inmates, though he refused to tell staff who they were.

A second young offender stood convicted of a mugging in which the victim was knocked down before being robbed of his possessions. The offender had spent 8 years in psychiatric settings, first as a young child, with the notation that "[his] hospitalization has been made necessary as a result of hyperactivity, unmanageable behavior, assaultiveness, and aggressiveness toward smaller children." He was thereafter diagnosed as suffering from childhood schizophrenia and organic brain damage with impaired intellectual functioning; he did not do well on a trial release from the hospital, during which he assaulted members of his family.

The man's last conviction involved a car theft for which he was sentenced to 9 months in jail. In prison, the man was deemed victim-prone because he was mentally retarded, but he saw himself as tough and picked fights with other inmates.

The combined aggressivity and vulnerability of young explosive robbers create a problem for prisons, which is exacerbated by the fact that the offenders (not one of whom has graduated from high school) have remedial programming needs.

## The Mature Mugger

Mature muggers are a contrasting group of offenders of median age who commit robberies involving nonserious violence, typically the sorts of crimes committed by younger offenders.

One example is a 35-year-old man who had mugged a woman and was cornered by her neighbors. He explained that he "had more than his two-drink limit," had discovered he was "feeling very hungry," and "knew there was no food at home." He also testified that he "saw the victim, who was nicely dressed, and thought she would have some money and that 'it wouldn't hurt her if I took a couple of dollars.'" He explained that he had once attempted a similar offense under similar circumstances, and "some men saw what happened and chased me and beat me up."

The man had been hospitalized on 13 occasions, for periods from 1 week to 1 month, and diagnosed as suffering from paranoia and depression. He indicated that whenever he felt the onset of such an episode, he would walk to the hospital and commit himself. A probation officer suggested that "the defendant seems to need the hospital at times for a complete rest and the security and the extra care it gives him. He also likes their food."

Hospital staff wrote that the man was "generally nonviolent and extremely passive-dependent . . . respectful of authority figures and trusting of them and very cooperative in our program." They also testified that the man "recompensates quickly while in the hospital and usually responds well to medication and milieu therapy."

The offender was childlike. He had made no effort to earn a living; he had no plans to work. When questioned about his future, he could envisage only "starvation ahead."

A second mugger used an unloaded gun to threaten pedestrians, explaining that he "didn't know how to load it." The man's IQ ranged between 43 and 59, depending on who had tested him. He had been treated for brain damage in childhood. He had also been treated for "a tendency toward explosive, rather bizarre behavior" which consisted of setting his mother's bed on fire and threatening to shoot other relatives.

In prison the man was placed in a special program. Here he did well, and staff reported that other "inmates on the block appeared to like [him] and made special efforts to protect him." Later, staff wrote,

> He carries out simple tasks well. . . . He has developed a cooperative attitude and a willingness to please those in authority. He has made lesser progress in the area of personal hygiene and grooming skills and needs reminders to wash his clothes.

The man managed prison as a result of the relatively tender care he was afforded. Prison staff explained that "he gets around by following the person in front of him; new situations can't be handled." Staff concluded that "it is unlikely that he would be able to manage without assistance," which means that "he will always need a sheltered, supervised program and may prove unable to function in an unsupervised living situation."

## Acute Disturbed Exploders

The individuals we have designated disturbed exploders are invariably dangerous offenders and perpetrate extreme—and often bizarre—violence. The acute disturbed exploder group contains inmates who are often diagnosed psychotic, are viewed as disturbed at the time of arrest, and commit eccentric offenses. Two thirds of these inmates, however, have low arrest records, and half have no histories of violence, despite the fact that the group tends to be relatively old. Its violence is, there-fore, late-blooming.

Fairly typical of exploders is a 26-year-old schizophrenic con-victed of manslaughter. The man had no offense history, but as a youth became fearful and led a reclusive life. His relatives reported that he "even had tar put on the roof, thinking that if someone wanted to get him they would get stuck in the tar."

This history is significant because before he committed his last crime the man reexperienced the onset of his delusions:

> He started talking about drug dealers, big crime and the communists taking over. . . . A few days before the shoot-ing his mother stated that he asked her if she had heard a van pulling into the driveway at about 3 AM, claiming that some people in the van wanted him to come outside so that they could shoot him. . . . He used to hide . . . putting pillows on his bed so that people would think that he was there.

The man's delusions focused on gangs of drug dealers, and he decided to kill a person he suspected of such membership. He could not find his intended victim, however, and shot one of the man's associates. Thereafter he attempted suicide in jail, had to be hospitalized, and assaulted a nurse in the hospital. In prison he continued to be fearful and complained of psy-chosomatic problems. Staff reported that

> he became suspicious, thought the Mafia was after him, and that his father was going to kill him with a gun. He became inappropriate, tense, unable to sleep and had little appetite, as he felt someone was trying to poison his food.

At other times the man's delusions took a more ethereal form, such as in a letter to the victim he had killed expressing his remorse and revealing that he had become concerned about space invaders:

> In discussing his delusions he indicates that FBI agents and drug dealers are no longer the source of his difficulties, but

that through the assistance of another inmate he has been able to see that certain human beings are, in fact, space creatures who have been placed on the earth and have assumed human form for the purpose of harassing and controlling certain people, of which he is one.

Throughout his tenure in prison the man functioned as a mental health client, commuting fearfully between prison clinics and hospital settings.

Another offender, also in his midtwenties, had earned no criminal record to date though he was a drug addict who had led a nomadic life, centering on residence in flophouses. In one such transient establishment the man killed a neighbor by stuffing clothing down his throat after he became convinced that this neighbor was conspiring against him. He subsequently had to be hospitalized from the jail, refused to eat, and needed to be fed through a tube. He also attempted suicide by hanging.

Released on probation, the man attacked members of his family and was resentenced to prison. He arrived in prison confused and withdrawn, refused meals, and walked into walls, but recovered under medication. He had to be hospitalized repeatedly from the prison. Between hospitalizations the man "was not interested in any programs . . . but only liked to read magazines, newspapers, and then would sit back and sleep in his chair." This was a nonviolent behavior pattern, but violence-related concerns were raised about the future because the man blamed his mother for his imprisonment and had threatened to kill her.

## Chronic Disturbed Exploders

Chronic exploders are the largest cluster of disturbed offenders. They are also a distinctly violent group, both because their offenses are invariably extremely serious and because they have histories of violence. The offenders often have substantial arrest records and long-term mental health problems.

Some chronic exploders show consistency in their crimes. One offender was imprisoned for injuring four people in a knife attack. One of the man's victims was his former spouse whose face the offender had slashed in a previous incident. Before being sentenced for his second offense, the man declared that he intended to kill his ex-wife (and himself) and "insisted that [his probation officer] include such statements in his report."

The offender was first institutionalized at age 11, after he had been adjudicated a neglected child. At the time he was seen as a problem client. He maintained his reputation in the army, from which he received an undesirable discharge. He served prison time for forgery, then graduated to kidnapping. At this juncture he was judged disturbed and was twice declared incompetent to stand trial. After he was finally imprisoned he spent much time in the prison hospital, where he was diagnosed "schizoid." However, he viewed himself throughout as nondisturbed. He still insisted that he had no mental health problems as he reentered prison, though he asked a psychiatrist for medication.

A second exploder was involved in a sadistic episode in which an elderly victim was stomped, beaten, sexually abused, and robbed. The man had a history of prior arrests, yielding five convictions. One of his arrests involved sexual abuse, which the man described as consensual sex with an underage girl.

The man started life in foster child placement and was hospitalized at age eight after his foster parents concluded that they could not control him. He spent 5 years in a hospital, where staff wrote that "he has not been able to transcend his traumatic and extremely deprived childhood. . . . At this time, the prognosis for reintegration into the community is poor."

Thereafter, the man spent 20 years leading a transient existence interspersed with crimes ranging from burglary to robbery and assault.

## Disturbed Sex Offenders

This cluster contains sex offenders who mainly victimize children and are by definition responsible for serious violence. These offenders are also disturbed. They are often seen by mental health staff at the time of their offense, and one in four (28%) has been diagnosed as psychotic. They are older offenders, mostly Caucasian, and usually have no history of violence or of imprisonment.

One sex offender in our sample was a man in his late thirties who had victimized his daughter and infant son. He described these predations as "hug therapy" designed to prevent his children from having misconceptions about sexuality. He also claimed that he had been sexually abused as a child and described himself as a practitioner of Satanism.

The man had no prior contacts with the criminal justice system. However, he had been caught smuggling marijuana in the navy and had admitted to drug and alcohol abuse. The man declared that he was upset at being arrested. He went on a protracted hunger strike in the jail, and said that he was not doing so out of guilt but because he feared prison, where he knew child molesters were unpopular. He complained that "if he had been a 'murderer or airport bomber' he would be a prison hero but due to the nature of his actions he would not do well in prison."

The man arrived at prison reception depressed and in tears and was placed in a protective setting in which he did fairly well. He was not deemed disturbed, but staff wrote that "he has a strange outlook on life." They later upgraded their views after the man attempted suicide. He had become depressed because he had been turned down by the parole board and his wife had divorced him. The parole board had suggested that the man undergo therapy, and he followed their recommendation. He was judged to have made progress, because he no longer announced that he would kill himself after his release. He also resolved his religious conflict (between Christianity and Satanism) by professing that "he tends to lean toward God."

A second sex offender resembles the first. He was imprisoned for sodomizing his daughter, attempted suicide in confinement, and had to be hospitalized from the prison. The man was in his thirties and had long-standing problems. He had been sent to a boarding school as a child because he could not be managed at home. In this institution he "alleged that during his first week he was sodomized by another boy who repeatedly sodomized him over the next 5 years." After leaving the institution the man was hospitalized for "nervous breakdowns." He later married, but a social worker recorded that "his attempts at leading a semblance of a normal life were unsuccessful."

The man was arrested while on probation for another sex offense involving an underage victim. He then tried to hang himself in jail, where other inmates attempted to strangle him and scald him with boiling water. He also professed guilt and alleged that his offenses "will torture me for the rest of my life."

In prison, the man had to commute between protective and mental health settings, including the prison hospital. In the hospital he was again assaulted by a fellow inmate, who also attacked him in the prison. After two serious psychotic relapses, prison staff wrote: "It appears that [this inmate] for the time being at least will continue to experience difficulties maintaining himself within the correctional system, and may well require extended psychiatric intervention."

## Composite Career Offenders

The composite group contains older offenders with long-term mental health histories and long-standing records of violent involvements. The crimes these offenders commit are diverse, and most have been previously imprisoned.

The hallmark of the group (like that of long-term disturbed exploders) is that the offenders have long histories of mental health problems and records of offenses and are both career criminals and career patients. An illustrative composite career is that of an offender serving a life sentence for an armed robbery. The man was in his thirties, but he was a veteran offender who had been convicted of a burglary at age 10. His first adult offense (at 16) was one in which he assaulted and injured a police officer. He was subsequently convicted of rape, robberies, assaults, escapes, and weapons offenses.

After the man's arrest for robbery he was declared incompetent to stand trial and diagnosed as suffering from paranoid schizophrenia. He had also been declared incompetent and hospitalized 9 years earlier. Thereafter he had been sent to prison, where staff noted that he "is severely suicidal and can act out violently when he doesn't get his way." At the time the man listed his occupation as "hustling," which was accurate because he had never worked and was a multidrug user.

In prison the man had to be committed and tried to hang himself in the prison hospital. Psychiatrists there described him as psychotic. They reported that he "experiences auditory hallucinations, hears his mother's voice calling him different names, feels there are spies out to kill him, was autistic and withdrawn, appeared slovenly and dirty." Yet the man made a recovery, left prison, and reembarked on his criminal career.

The man reentered prison denying his criminal history and "claim[ing] he is the victim of racial prejudice." He also declared that he would not participate in programs because he had been unjustly incarcerated. He nonetheless adjusted to prison, did well in prison programs, was well regarded by staff, and appeared to have found a long-term home.

## Compensatory Offenders

This small cluster of very disturbed persons comprises chronically disadvantaged offenders, over half of whom (10 out of 19) have been diagnosed psychotic. These offenders tend to have clear-cut intellectual deficiencies, mostly commit serious violence (often robberies), and have histories of violence. They tend to be intoxicated and ineffectual at the time of their offense. They lead a rootless and isolated existence, as exemplified by the fact that 18 of 19 are unmarried, though few of them are young.

The crimes of this group reflect the multiple inadequacies of its members. A typical incident is described as follows: "The instant offense finds [the offender] under the influence of alcohol and drugs, cutting the purse strap of a seventy-one (71) year-old female, knocking her to the ground and stealing the purse." The offender was described at prison entry as "a high school graduate with no work history due to a psychiatric disability [who] has been diagnosed as a paranoid schizophrenic, which has been somewhat exacerbated by alcohol abuse."

The man was hospitalized when in his teens and maintained on medication. Prison staff diagnosed him as a schizophrenic in remission with a "passive–aggressive personality" and learning problems. They suggested counseling and remedial education.

A parallel offender assaulted a 70-year-old man, returned to the scene, and was caught. Before this offender was sentenced he was subjected to a competency examination because he was severely retarded. He was also a school dropout, had been hospitalized (diagnosed as manifesting "schizophrenia, latent type"), and had been an alcohol and drug addict. He had not been in prison before but had an offense history consisting of aborted muggings.

A third offender set fires that "appear to be an attention-getting device." He did so when he was intoxicated, which he was very often. After his last fire, he gave himself up to the police. The offender was retarded and had hallucinations, for which he had been treated in hospitals. He had also committed offenses other than arson (none major), which he again attributed to intoxication.

## Reconstituting Humpty Dumpty

These vignettes illustrate differences among clusters but also highlight the continuum of which the clusters form a part. This is so because violent offenders often have multiple problems and present similar dilemmas to service providers. Among the features that these individuals—regardless of type—seem to share are (a) the advent of symptoms or behavior problems at early ages leading to (b) early institutional placement followed by (c) *ad seriatim* institutionalization and (d) an unproductive, marginal, migratory existence that includes (e) brushes with the law. The offenders often (f) have combinations of deficits, such as emotional problems exacerbated by substance abuse, that (g) color some of their offenses, raising questions of competence, and (h) impair their ability to manage in prison and profit from prison programs; this (i) decreases their prospects of successful community adjustment, thus (j) increasing the chances of recidivism, including (k) violent recidivism.

Other links between the clusters are more specific. One such link has to do with the fact that age-specific clusters can be

career junctures that follow each other in time. Impulsive robbers can therefore become long-term robbers, and impulsive
burglars can turn into composite career offenders, given time.
Levels of violence and pathology can also change, separately
or in tandem. Acute exploders, for example, are typically late
bloomers, both as offenders and patients. Long-term robbers,
by contrast, often deescalate one or both elements of their
careers.

Chapter

# 5

# Offenders With Substance
# Abuse Histories

Chapter 4 surveyed violent offenders with histories of mental health problems, and this chapter extends the review.
We again examine offenders who have received services in the
community, but we now view persons for whom services included treatment for substance abuse problems. In the second
half of this chapter we turn to clients of exclusively specialized
services.

The difference between offenders who have received substance abuse services and the offenders we have already discussed is admittedly one of degree, because emotionally disturbed offenders often report abusing drugs or alcohol. The
substance abuse histories we review in this chapter, however,
are more salient. They also contain more detail, thus permitting
disaggregation by type of substance abuse. More important,
the data we have about alcohol or drug addiction over time
can be used as a disaggregating criterion, so that types can be
based on the offender's long-term and short-term history of
substance abuse.

## The Mental Health–Substance Abuse Sample

Our first (compound) sample contains recipients of both specialized and nonspecialized services. The sample, as noted in
our summary typology (Table 5.1), yielded five clusters. We
labeled the types as the dependent burglar, skid row robber,

## Table 5.1

*Results of Cluster Analysis for Offenders With Compounded Substance Abuse and Psychiatric Histories*

| | Dependent Burglar (n = 20) | Skid Row Robber (n = 9) | Skid Row Exploder (n = 35) | Compounded Career Offender (n = 37) | Multi-problem Robber (n = 28) |
|---|---|---|---|---|---|
| **Offense type** | | | | | |
| Unmotivated | 0% | 0% | 6% | 16% | 0% |
| Retaliatory | 0 | 0 | 37 | 14 | 4 |
| Felony-related | 0 | 100 | 11 | 54 | 71 |
| Sex—adult victim | 0 | 0 | 6 | 5 | 0 |
| Sex—child victim | 15 | 0 | 0 | 0 | 4 |
| Weapon | 0 | 0 | 9 | 3 | 0 |
| Arson | 0 | 0 | 9 | 3 | 0 |
| Police victim | 0 | 0 | 3 | 0 | 0 |
| Burglary | 85 | 0 | 17 | 3 | 21 |
| Auto/institution | 0 | 0 | 3 | 3 | 0 |
| **Violence level** | | | | | |
| No violence | 95% | 0% | 20% | 3% | 21% |
| Less serious | 5 | 89 | 9 | 43 | 57 |
| Serious | 0 | 11 | 31 | 40 | 18 |
| Extreme | 0 | 0 | 40 | 24 | 4 |
| Alcohol/drug influence | 65% | 89% | 80% | 54% | 46% |
| Eccentric behavior | 10 | 11 | 29 | 32 | 14 |
| Psychotic diagnosis | 5 | 11 | 6 | 27 | 7 |
| No memory | 10 | 22 | 23 | 8 | 14 |
| Low IQ | 20 | 0 | 17 | 8 | 14 |
| **Violence history** | | | | | |
| None | 25% | 0% | 9% | 5% | 75% |
| Recent | 20 | 11 | 43 | 30 | 14 |
| Remote | 70 | 100 | 71 | 89 | 14 |
| **Arrest history** | | | | | |
| Low | 5% | 0% | 17% | 0% | 61% |
| Medium | 15 | 11 | 43 | 27 | 39 |
| High | 80 | 89 | 40 | 73 | 0 |
| **Psychiatric history** | | | | | |
| Instant | 25% | 11% | 26% | 14% | 25% |
| Recent | 25 | 33 | 60 | 27 | 32 |
| Remote | 85 | 78 | 54 | 92 | 68 |
| **Drug history** | | | | | |
| None | 10% | 89% | 86% | 0% | 43% |
| Recent | 55 | 11 | 14 | 19 | 25 |
| Remote | 50 | 0 | 0 | 87 | 36 |
| **Alcohol history** | | | | | |
| None | 85% | 0% | 6% | 89% | 64% |
| Recent | 10 | 33 | 57 | 5 | 21 |
| Remote | 5 | 89 | 54 | 5 | 18 |

**Table 5.1 (*Continued*)**

|  | Dependent Burglar (*n* = 20) | Skid Row Robber (*n* = 9) | Skid Row Exploder (*n* = 35) | Compounded Career Offender (*n* = 37) | Multiproblem Robber (*n* = 28) |
|---|---|---|---|---|---|
| **Age** |  |  |  |  |  |
| Low | 0% | 0% | 14% | 3% | 39% |
| Medium | 65 | 0 | 49 | 46 | 36 |
| High | 35 | 100 | 37 | 51 | 25 |
| Prison experience | 50% | 89% | 37% | 73% | 4% |
| Under supervision | 50 | 22 | 31 | 32 | 25 |
| **Covariates** |  |  |  |  |  |
| Single | 60% | 44% | 86% | 62% | 86% |
| High school graduate | 10 | 22 | 21 | 27 | 25 |
| White | 75 | 67 | 54 | 49 | 61 |
| Employed | 90 | 89 | 88 | 81 | 85 |

skid row exploder, compounded career offender, and multiproblem robber.

## Dependent Burglars

Like all our inmate samples, the compound sample includes a group of burglars whose offenses are invariably nonviolent. But burglars with mental health and substance abuse problems are a distinctive group. For one, they tend to be older and Caucasian, and they have substantial arrest records. Most of the offenders also have long-term histories of violent involvements and of mental health contacts, they have been treated for drug addiction, and more than half (13 out of 20) are intoxicated when they commit their burglaries.

An offender who provides an illustrative case is a 28-year-old man who burglarized a neighbor. He committed this visible offense, according to a person who interviewed him, because "at the time he was high after taking three quaaludes and smoking PCP, [and] because of his intoxicated state he got an urge to get up and steal." The man claimed complete lack of premeditation. In further exoneration, he pointed out that his performance was clearly substandard, arguing that "if this was planned, I would have used gloves."

The man had never used gloves. His difficulties had begun in early childhood (when his recorded IQ was 67, though he later tested at 102), and he took up drugs at age 12. He ambivalently boasted that he averaged 10 marijuana cigarettes daily, that he had used angel dust for a decade and "had taken over one hundred LSD trips." These facts matter to us because the man engaged in circular reasoning, in which he attributed his problems to his addiction and his addiction to his problems. He reported that he failed parole because "I can't do it on my own . . . the pressures are unbelievable." He absconded from drug treatment, he said, because "weekly contacts are not enough," and he engaged in group offenses because of an "inability to separate himself from a negative peer group."

The offender had been a penny ante recidivist. He served an earlier prison sentence for an aborted burglary in which he was intoxicated. He later had problems in prison that included being caught in the act of injecting himself with drugs. Prison staff complained about the man's "supercilious attitude and perceived macho/gangster type image" but protected him from his peers, who filled him with anxiety. The dilemma faced by the staff was that the man proved to be a shamelessly dependent person who relied on outside support (which is unhealthy), but that one had to reinforce his pattern, like it or not, because he could not manage without support. The same dilemma was faced by the man's parents, who "on numerous occasions bailed him out of jail, paid his legal fees and allowed him to remain in their house," nevertheless earning his ingratitude.

A second burglar, who took little responsibility for his acts, had a similar dependency problem pattern. The man was a substantial recidivist who had committed a rape, which he loudly disclaimed. He also minimized his last offense—he was caught burglarizing—by maintaining that "he was really only a bystander." After this burglary offense the man attempted suicide in jail and was hospitalized (in installments) for close to a year.

The man's criminal career was continuous, beginning in grade school where he had stolen from purses, mailboxes, and desks, and had urinated in classrooms. He had also deployed more blatant attention-getting measures, such as having intercourse with an inflatable dummy used as a demonstration device in health classes.

The man was an addict who had ingested a variety of drugs (he had even inhaled gasoline fumes). He did not care to have anyone deal with his problem, however. According to the record, he "absconded from a drug program because the stress of facing issues relating to his drug use and emotional problems was too much." Mental health staff also classified the man as treatment-resistant and reported that he "had a problem keeping appointments."

The offender's entry into prison proved inauspicious because he took the view that he "couldn't do a maximum security sentence, as he would be killed." Most of the time he lived in prison protection cells, and he invested most of his effort arranging transfers between prisons. He set fire to his cell in one setting and assaulted a guard in another, while depending on guards to extricate him from environments he feared.

## Skid Row Robbers

The second cluster contains few (only nine) offenders, all middle-aged male alcoholics who commit robberies. The men have long offense histories, including violent offense histories, and tend to be drunk at the time they commit their offenses.

A typical group member "states that he has been drinking for 20 years and drinks a couple of six packs of beer per day and a fifth of Scotch." On the day of his last offense (an armed robbery of a cabdriver) the man had consumed five bottles of wine, and the arresting officer described him as "very, very flushed." The probation officer noted that

> it is possible that the defendant really was so drunk that he didn't know what he was doing, since the arresting officer concurs with the idea that the defendant was highly intoxicated. In that case, a lifestyle of intoxication on the part of the defendant may be a primary source of his continuing criminality.

The man's extensive offense history included an arrest for assault (dismissed), two convictions for driving under the in-

fluence of alcohol, several burglaries, and an insurance violation. The man's alcohol problems had been attended to at a
VA hospital (he was a Vietnam veteran), where he was de-
toxified "once every other year." The offender also was past
president of a local chapter of Alcoholics Anonymous.

A second offender robbed a gas station, then embarked on
a high-speed chase in which he threw several objects—including the proceeds of the robbery—from his car window.
He was drunk at the time and reported steady drinking for
some 7 years, averaging a quart of alcohol a day. The offender
was also a discharged veteran. Before becoming an alcoholic
he had been a drug addict and minor dealer, and many of his
(18) arrests were drug-related, though he had also been convicted of larceny, burglary, possession of weapons, and driving
while intoxicated.

The man had been diagnosed as a very serious alcoholic
who suffered from "bouts of blackouts, liver and pancreatic
damage." He had been treated for these conditions in a variety
of programs, but the ministrations proved less than successful
because the man insisted that he had no alcohol problem he
could not handle. The man was a success in prison, however,
where he functioned well as a skilled carpenter.

## Skid Row Exploders

A contrasting pattern to that of skid row robbers is that of
alcoholics whose violence is diversified and explosive. The
arrest record of these offenders is often low, but the offenders
tend to be seriously emotionally disturbed and tend to be
drunk when they commit their crimes.

An example of such an offender is a middle-aged woman
whose difficulty (as assessed by others) consisted of the fact
that "when intoxicated [she] becomes extremely hostile, abusive and profane." In a past incident this woman had become
embroiled in an argument after an all-night drinking session.
She was dissatisfied with the resolution of the dispute and
burned down her apartment building, killing a guest (a drinking companion) whose presence she had forgotten.

The last offense she committed was similar in that she was
intoxicated (she claimed she had "blacked out") and held a

grudge against her victim. The victim—a female neighbor—
reported that

> she [the victim] came home from work and noticed [the
> offender] was talking very strangely, as though in a trance.
> [The victim] stated [the offender] left, and she was in bed
> just going to sleep when there was a knock of the door.
> [The offender] entered with a knife in her hand and began
> yelling at her and calling her names. . . . [The offender]
> then proceeded to stab [the victim] six times.

The offender in turn blamed alcohol and testified that she
"only remembers standing in the hall with a knife in her hand
and [the victim] bleeding."

There had been incidents in the woman's life involving diverse brushes with the law. She had been arrested for arson,
assaults, and impulsive property offenses. She had also attempted suicide and had been institutionalized for alcohol abuse
and for chronic schizophrenia, for which she was medicated.
She participated in treatment willingly, though she assaulted
a nurse in the prison because "she did not want [her dose of
thorazine] diluted with water." She also had other disciplinary
problems in confinement, which had to do with "temper tantrums and arguments."

Because the offender was not intoxicated when she was in
the prison, her outbursts suggest that her readiness to take
offense and to respond with retaliatory rage transcended her
drinking episodes. Alcohol added obliviousness to her indifference to the consequences of her acts; intoxication also added
to her rage, and emotional problems played an aggravating
role because they distorted—and steeply escalated—grievances grounded in minuscule disputes.

## Compounded Career Offenders

Compounded career offenders are the most disturbed of the
offenders who have substance abuse and mental health problems. These offenders have long-term histories of contacts with
service providers; they also have serious criminal histories,

including histories of violence. In addition, the offenders suffer from long-term drug addiction.

The pattern is highlighted by a violent robber who had hurt his victim, choking her and pushing her into a wall. The man then went on a mystifying rampage in which he destroyed the victim's apartment, wildly scattering her possessions as the police arrived. He staged this scene after being released from prison, where he had served time for a similar offense. During this period he was also involved in a rape.

The man was in his midthirties, but his crime and mental health problems dated to an early age. He had first seen a psychiatrist at 15; 3 years later he had been hospitalized, diagnosed as a chronic schizophrenic, and certified as a drug addict. On his release he became involved in weapons offenses and was convicted of robbery.

Service providers described the man's double (or triple) problem. Juvenile workers recorded that he "impresses as a disturbed youth who relates in a hostile and withdrawn fashion." Hospital staff reported that he had to be "treated with psychotropics and was a management problem." Detention officials noted that "he had to be transported in a straitjacket from the jail to the hospital." Staff of a community drug program complained that the offender "states his interests are 'partying, basketball, getting high and fooling around.'"

The man arrived in prison "extremely surly" and "exhibited a hostile and negative attitude." Two years later, a "progress" report noted that

> his horrendous custodial adjustment continues this 6-month period with four reports that resulted in 225 days sentenced to keeplock. [He is] a confrontative individual who has little regard for rules and regulations and who has poor rapport with staff and is only marginally acceptable with peers.

This assessment parallels that of an earlier prison stay in which officials had complained that "the inmate's behavior constitutes a real and constant physical threat to both peers and staff in spite of 'tailor-made' programs." Though the man's eccentricity was fully recognized, the impression he made was that of a dangerous, embittered, angry, and irritable person with a gigantic chip on his shoulder rather than that of a person with mental health problems.

## Multiproblem Robbers

Our last group of offenders is contrasting in that they commit little serious violence, have strikingly low arrest records, and are apt to be seen as disturbed. The offenders, moreover, are likely to have salient problems involving alcohol or drugs.

A case in point is that of a man who was imprisoned for several robberies that he had attempted while on probation. In these crimes the man used a threatening extortion note that sometimes produced money but was often disregarded. The man had this note in his possession when he encountered the police.

The offender had been arrested in the past for minor offenses but had violated probation by discontinuing drug treatment. He had undergone drug rehabilitation repeatedly, but without success. He had also been hospitalized for depression, and had been diagnosed a paranoid schizophrenic. Such difficulties continued to manifest themselves when the man was in prison, where he had to be hospitalized. He was otherwise a despondent inmate and was described as "having some difficulty coping" with various stresses of confinement.

A second offender tried to rob a bank after ingesting a large amount of alcohol and taking drugs. He was not only unsuccessful but later pointed out that "he has no recall of the offense." He regretfully noted that his "substance abuse usage had snowballed [because] he was abusing alcohol, pills and cocaine."

The offender had held respectable civilian jobs but had destroyed his career by attempting white-collar offenses. He had been depressed—possibly by self-induced failure—and had attempted suicide. He had been involved in therapy, both in and out of hospitals, since adolescence. His drinking had begun at 12 and his drug addiction at 15. At the time of his arrest, the man combined use of vodka, barbiturates, and cocaine, all of which he used daily.

The offender demonstrated limited coping competence and approached prison as a structured treatment environment, hoping for drug rehabilitation as well as a belated college education.

# Postscript

The offenders we have discussed so far in this chapter differ markedly from the prison population in that the majority of the offenders are white.

The substance abuse sample described in the next section also differs from typical state prisoners, but to a lesser degree. The sample is heterogeneous, older than average (though less so than the disturbed inmates), overrepresents white inmates (to a somewhat lesser degree), and shows the influence of alcohol or drugs in the commission of crimes.

# Clients of Substance Abuse Services

Inmates in the specialized sample have received mental health services only for drug and alcohol problems. This offender sample contains two small clusters and two larger ones (Table 5.2). The small clusters comprise inmates who are engaged in nonserious violence and have no violence histories. The larger clusters contain more violence-involved inmates, who are usually intoxicated while committing their crimes. We labeled the types from this sample as the addicted burglar, addicted robber, alcohol exploder, and drug exploder.

## Addicted Burglars

The first cluster consists of burglars, some of whom were on probation at the time of their offenses. These offenders were drug addicts, and 3 of the 11 members of the group had problems of retardation. The offenders had arrest records, but mostly no violence histories.

The careers of these offenders are unremarkable, except for testimonials they offer to the obduracy of addiction and to the unregeneracy of otherwise unimpressive criminal careers. A case in point is that of a 30-year-old man who had broken into

# Table 5.2

*Results of Cluster Analysis for Offenders With Substance Abuse Histories*

| | Addicted Burglar ($n = 11$) | Addicted Robber ($n = 11$) | Alcohol Exploder ($n = 33$) | Drug Exploder ($n = 20$) |
|---|---|---|---|---|
| Offense type | | | | |
| Unmotivated | 0% | 0% | 0% | 0% |
| Retaliatory | 0 | 0 | 15 | 20 |
| Felony-related | 0 | 91 | 36 | 55 |
| Sex—adult victim | 0 | 0 | 12 | 5 |
| Sex—child victim | 0 | 0 | 6 | 5 |
| Weapon | 0 | 0 | 6 | 0 |
| Arson | 0 | 0 | 6 | 0 |
| Police victim | 0 | 0 | 6 | 5 |
| Burglary | 100 | 9 | 9 | 10 |
| Auto/institution | 0 | 0 | 3 | 0 |
| Violence level | | | | |
| No violence | 100% | 0% | 12% | 5% |
| Less serious | 0 | 91 | 27 | 55 |
| Serious | 0 | 0 | 39 | 25 |
| Extreme | 0 | 9 | 21 | 15 |
| Alcohol/drug influence | 27% | 55% | 70% | 27% |
| Eccentric behavior | 0 | 9 | 27 | 0 |
| No memory | 0 | 0 | 24 | 5 |
| Low IQ | 27 | 9 | 9 | 10 |
| Violence history | | | | |
| None | 73% | 64% | 21% | 0% |
| Recent | 9 | 18 | 30 | 40 |
| Remote | 27 | 18 | 70 | 85 |
| Arrest history | | | | |
| Low | 9% | 46% | 18% | 0% |
| Medium | 55 | 55 | 39 | 5 |
| High | 36 | 0 | 42 | 95 |
| Drug history | | | | |
| None | 27% | 0% | 70% | 5% |
| Recent | 27 | 27 | 18 | 15 |
| Remote | 55 | 82 | 12 | 90 |
| Alcohol history | | | | |
| None | 73% | 91% | 6% | 85% |
| Recent | 27 | 9 | 46 | 10 |
| Remote | 0 | 0 | 67 | 10 |
| Age | | | | |
| Low | 9% | 27% | 12% | 5% |
| Medium | 82 | 46 | 36 | 40 |
| High | 9 | 27 | 52 | 55 |
| Prison experience | 18% | 9% | 39% | 70% |
| Under supervision | 45 | 27 | 33 | 40 |
| Covariates | | | | |
| Single | 64% | 55% | 85% | 40% |
| High school graduate | 18 | 36 | 24 | 5 |
| White | 36 | 45 | 63 | 30 |
| Employed | 73 | 70 | 82 | 90 |

homes. The man was intoxicated at the time of his crimes and had testified against his crime partner, whom he then regarded (correctly) as a prospective enemy.

The man was a heroin addict but had also indulged in cocaine, valium, quaaludes, and marijuana. He had been a confirmed addict since age 16. His 16th birthday also marked the beginning of his crime record, which included six arrests for criminal possession of drugs, six burglary arrests, and a conviction for driving while intoxicated. During most of the man's life he had been treated (unsuccessfully) in outpatient drug programs, as well as in a veterans' hospital. The man cooperated eagerly in such treatment and expected more of the same. He told prison authorities, for example, that he wanted to undergo drug therapy and that he intended to become a drug counselor after he was paroled.

A second addicted offender was somewhat older and was convicted of offenses he had committed while on probation. In one incident the man entered a store that someone else had broken into and stole a television set. In a second offense he sold drugs to an undercover officer, and in a third incident he burglarized a neighbor who was an acquaintance.

This ill-starred offender had started life in a reformatory, to which he was committed at age 11 at his mother's request. Here he had spent his adolescence. He then managed to become a career addict who had a substantial habit ($100 a day) but absconded from rehabilitation programs because he saw no point in abstaining from drugs.

## Addicted Robbers

The second cluster consists of addicts who commit nonserious violence and who have no records of violence and very modest criminal histories. One offender in this cluster reported that he had "a $400 to $500 a day cocaine/heroin habit." To sustain this redoubtable habit, the man participated in an attempted robbery of a health club. He had also sold counterfeit money, which earned him a federal prison sentence. The man's arrest record was otherwise modest (a fine for driving while intoxicated and an incident involving unlawful possession of marijuana), and he had owned a business, which he lost.

The offender had participated in several drug treatment programs, and one such program medicated him for "atypical depression" after he lost his mother. The man adduced his mother's death as a contributing factor to his crime and also pointed out that "he needed money for Christmas" and had no way to earn it.

The man's capacity for deception—and for self-deception—in the short run stood him in good stead. For a time, he became a model inmate. His deportment earned him membership in a temporary release program in which he worked as a jackhammer operator for a construction company, but the privilege was promptly rescinded after he took unauthorized vacations and submitted false pay receipts.

A second, younger offender committed a street robbery while "high on marijuana and beer." The offender failed after doing well in prison. He was released on parole but repaid the confidence by mugging an 83-year-old pedestrian. Drug programs found the man similarly uncooperative, but on other occasions he requested treatment as a way out of difficulties.

The man had been a precocious delinquent. After placement in a juvenile facility, he graduated to a career as an addict and burglar. (Along the way he tried other ways of sustaining his drug habit, such as stealing from his family.) The man's last probation officer commented wryly on his prospects. He concluded that the man's "degree of maladjustment, particularly along the lines of changed social attitudes, is such as to warrant a reasonable belief and expectation that [he] cannot get along without further conflict with the law."

## Alcohol Exploders

Addicted offenders are unreliable persons, whereas exploders are volatile. The alcohol cluster contains violent offenders who tend to be drunk at the time they commit their offenses and often do not remember what they have done. Many of the offenders are middle-aged, two thirds are Caucasian, and all have histories of alcoholism.

Prison intake staff wrote about one such offender that "intellectual limitations combined with his alcohol abuse and social instability appear to account for his criminal involvement."

The man's career showed a penchant for driving while intoxicated and also included arrests in which the man was charged with carrying a gun. This propensity culminated in a bloody incident in which the man, while drunk, tried to kill a drinking companion with whom he had had an argument by shooting him in the head.

Another alcohol offender attacked a whole family over a traffic dispute, lacerating the father with a car antenna. The man was very drunk at the time and had a history replete with offenses involving intoxication. One such incident was described as follows:

> A statement by [the victim] indicates that she was entertaining some friends at her home when [the offender and two companions] came to her house and insisted they were going to have a party there and drink beer that they had brought. She told them no. They got mad and started slamming and kicking at her front door, causing it to break. They then started throwing her kids' toy wagon around the front yard yelling very loudly and throwing items at vehicles in her driveway. [The offender] then broke a window out by hitting it with his fist.

There was further evidence of explosiveness in that the offender had assaulted his daughter and had been subjected to child abuse charges based on the physical damage he had done to her.

The man was an undisputed alcoholic. A disgruntled probation officer complained that "[the offender's] life style has been a continuous saga of alcohol abuse and alcohol-related criminal activity. His alcoholism has interfered with every area of his life." The officer pointed out that the offender had "consistently refused to continue alcohol treatment." The man was once placed in a halfway house for alcoholics but was soon expelled "for using marijuana." He was later terminated from a hospital program for noncooperation and left a third program because he "does not feel that he has a drinking problem."

## Drug Exploders

A fourth cluster consists of drug addicts with histories of violence and criminal involvements. The offenders are inveterate recidivists, and they tend to be high on drugs at the time they commit their crimes.

A case in point involves an offender who was in his thirties and "recently specialized in armed robberies of cabdrivers." The man attacked his victims at knife point while under the influence of drugs. He was also reliably intoxicated during offenses in which he resisted arrest, and on one occasion "gunned a car toward a police officer, hitting him, causing injury to his back."

The man was a career criminal, with a dossier of arrests dating to his adolescence. He saw this criminal career as subservient to his drug career, which a prison psychiatrist described as follows:

> At the age of fourteen (14) he was initiated to the drug culture—he started with smoking marijuana and later experimented with other narcotic drugs, using LSD, cocaine and amphetamines and finally became an addict to heroin. He was spending $50 a day and the funds were provided by illicit activities like stealing, burglary and robbery. He said that under the influence of heroin he felt carefree and nothing bothered him.

The man had participated in several drug programs and claimed that some had occasioned respites in his habit. He also adjusted well in prison, where he held responsible jobs and participated in therapy. Despite such involvements the man invariably recidivated, graduating from less serious to more serious offenses.

Another drug offender had committed robberies in which he held a knife to his victims' throats. He had no compunction about victimizing acquaintances, and one of them noted that "he looked like he was on drugs, with his eyes glassy and red." Police who arrested the man confirmed this condition and discovered a hypodermic needle in his pocket.

The offender had been apprehended on 18 occasions since

his 17th birthday. Most of his arrests were for felonies, including some he had perpetrated shortly after leaving prison. The man had participated in methadone maintenance programs in the community. He had also been involved in drug therapy while in prison, without impact on his postgraduate career.

Vignettes such as these are typical of careers in which offenders who are seriously addicted to alcohol or drugs reach middle age with violence-cum-addiction patterns that are intertwined, chronic, and discouragingly recalcitrant.

# 6

# Offenders With No Mental Health-Related Histories

In this chapter we disaggregate our comparison sample, which contains offenders who have no record of having received mental health services, at least not in the data sources available to us. Cluster analysis subdivided the sample into eight types (Table 6.1). We labeled the types as the inexperienced burglar, experienced burglar, acute exploder, patterned exploder, pre-career robber, early career robber, late career robber, and generalist. Five of these types contain larger numbers of inmates; of these five types, four are composed of robbers. The sample contains two groups of relatively nonviolent offenders (mostly burglars) and three groups of offenders whose violence is serious.

## Types of Offenders

### Inexperienced Burglars

The least violence-related group in our sample is that of burglars who have low arrest histories (60%) and no past violent involvements (68%). The inexperience of these burglars surprised us because we expected nonviolent offenders to be imprisoned only as a last resort, on the strength of past felonious conduct. We inferred, therefore, that there must be special reasons why these offenders appear recidivistic, such as short-

**Table 6.1**

*Results of Cluster Analysis for Offenders With No Mental Health History*

| | Inexperienced Burglar (n = 60) | Experienced Burglar (n = 38) | Acute Exploder (n = 67) | Patterned Exploder (n = 30) | Pre-career Robber (n = 73) | Early Career Robber (n = 76) | Late Career Robber (n = 50) | Violence Generalist (n = 63) |
|---|---|---|---|---|---|---|---|---|
| **Offense type** | | | | | | | | |
| Unmotivated | 0% | 0% | 5% | 0% | 0% | 0% | 0% | 0% |
| Retaliatory | 0 | 0 | 36 | 87 | 0 | 3 | 0 | 13 |
| Felony-related | 0 | 0 | 15 | 0 | 99 | 83 | 96 | 51 |
| Sex—adult victim | 0 | 0 | 8 | 7 | 0 | 3 | 0 | 13 |
| Sex—child victim | 0 | 0 | 22 | 3 | 0 | 0 | 0 | 10 |
| Weapon | 37 | 37 | 0 | 0 | 1 | 7 | 2 | 0 |
| Arson | 0 | 0 | 6 | 0 | 0 | 0 | 0 | 3 |
| Police victim | 0 | 0 | 3 | 0 | 0 | 1 | 0 | 5 |
| Burglary | 63 | 63 | 0 | 0 | 0 | 3 | 2 | 0 |
| Auto/institution | 0 | 0 | 49 | 13 | 0 | 5 | 0 | 37 |
| **Violence level** | | | | | | | | |
| No violence | 90% | 95% | 0% | 0% | 0% | 4% | 0% | 0% |
| Less serious | 10 | 5 | 0 | 0 | 66 | 66 | 96 | 0 |
| Serious | 0 | 0 | 57 | 7 | 22 | 22 | 2 | 89 |
| Extreme | 0 | 0 | 43 | 93 | 12 | 8 | 2 | 11 |
| Alcohol/drug influence | 15% | 26% | 39% | 57% | 26% | 16% | 16% | 32% |
| Eccentric behavior | 0 | 3 | 21 | 27 | 6 | 4 | 0 | 5 |
| No memory | 2 | 0 | 2 | 7 | 0 | 3 | 0 | 0 |
| Low IQ | 17 | 16 | 30 | 10 | 15 | 21 | 10 | 25 |

| | | | | | | | | |
|---|---|---|---|---|---|---|---|---|
| Violence history | | | | | | | | |
| None | 68% | 0% | 99% | 13% | 99% | 0% | 0% | 5% |
| Recent | 20 | 13 | 2 | 43 | 0 | 75 | 40 | 35 |
| Remote | 13 | 97 | 0 | 67 | 1 | 45 | 98 | 84 |
| Arrest history | | | | | | | | |
| Low | 60% | 0% | 75% | 30% | 90% | 53% | 0% | 13% |
| Medium | 33 | 24 | 22 | 60 | 8 | 36 | 46 | 32 |
| High | 7 | 76 | 3 | 10 | 1 | 12 | 54 | 56 |
| Age | | | | | | | | |
| Low | 45% | 3% | 18% | 13% | 52% | 86% | 0% | 2% |
| Medium | 37 | 45 | 58 | 17 | 41 | 9 | 72 | 65 |
| High | 17 | 53 | 24 | 67 | 7 | 5 | 28 | 33 |
| Prison experience | 8% | 79% | 6% | 13% | 0% | 20% | 64% | 48% |
| Under supervision | 27 | 50 | 9 | 13 | 8 | 42 | 44 | 24 |
| Covariates | | | | | | | | |
| Single | 66% | 53% | 57% | 55% | 81% | 80% | 49% | 52% |
| High school gradu-ate | 20 | 16 | 18 | 24 | 19 | 12 | 6 | 10 |
| White | 34 | 8 | 22 | 21 | 16 | 5 | 10 | 19 |
| Employed | 81 | 79 | 81 | 93 | 79 | 62 | 88 | 77 |

term trends in their offenses or cumulative impressions that include a concern about chronic delinquency.

An example is that of a young offender who had earned one adult arrest (which was dismissed) but whose conviction covered three incidents in which he had broken into homes. More important, the man had a juvenile history proving to the court that low-order deterrence had never impressed him. On several occasions this youth had been arrested for burglaries while on probation, and a disgruntled probation officer observed, "The defendant, a school dropout with a history of excessive truancy and an unstable work record, has run away from home on at least ten separate occasions, and has a pattern of hanging out with negative companions." The probation officer concluded that the young man "appears to have a pattern of anti-social criminal behavior."

The other side of the coin is the offender's lack of aggressivity. This is illustrated by the fact that this man had signed himself into protective custody when he arrived in prison, which confirmed the impression at prison intake that he was not a hardened criminal.

A second burglar was older (22) but appeared equally nonsturdy. The man had a low IQ (77) and had been perfunctorily diagnosed as having "severe emotional problems." He had spent much of his life in reformatories and had grown up to "a rather transient existence, sleeping in cars, home-made tents, with friends and in emergency housing."

Unsavory companions involved the man in burglaries in an ancillary capacity. On his own, he had stolen cars, filed false fire alarms, and committed nuisance offenses. The man had also given the impression of being nondeterrable. Placed on probation, he was rearrested a week later; sent to jail (with probation revoked), he reoffended when paroled.

Imprisonment of such offenders responds to the perceived need for a backup option when all else has failed. It may also embody the hope that incipient careers can be short-circuited through shock effects when lesser discomforts have made an insufficient impression.

## Experienced Burglars

Our second group contains burglars who are older, more recidivistic, and violence-experienced. A typical member of the group is a 35-year-old man who had been caught breaking into a store. The man's prison sentence was disproportionate to his crime because he was on parole at the time of his burglary and because one of his prior offenses was a rape. His record lists 19 other arrests and 12 convictions. Though the latter were mostly for burglary, the police viewed the man as a menace to the community.

The man had been in the army, where he had spent time combating fellow soldiers. He received an undesirable discharge but proudly recalled that he had "fought an officer and threw him through a window." After his unpromising army career the man settled into a routine of committing crimes to support a drug habit. He continued to commit crimes thereafter, despite the fact that he had discontinued drug use.

In prison the man was placed in lower-security settings, attended college classes, and underwent vocational training. The man is in his thirties and may have matured in confinement, but prior to his imprisonment he had persevered in his chosen career as a burglar, despite some occasional lapses into more serious violence of the kind that characterizes his cluster.

The group also contains individuals convicted of weapons charges. One such offender was arrested when police stopped him for speeding and discovered he had a loaded gun; he was found to be a parole violator. After the man arrived in prison, staff recorded that he "claimed no one ever got hurt in his crimes," though he had been convicted of an attempted rape. The man also recalled an episode of "delivering female masseuses to a pornography place," for which he had been arrested. The offender had spent a good portion of his 40 years in prison. His crimes included armed robbery (his next-to-last offense), burglary, interstate transportation of stolen property, petit theft, assault with intent to commit rape, criminal conspiracy (prostitution), drugs, profanity, driving while intoxicated, and reckless driving.

A third member of the cluster was convicted of two burglaries. After the first burglary he was arrested with the proceeds, and the second almost cost him his life because the victim (a police officer who was a markswoman) shot him in the head. The man was in his thirties and had been a burglar since his teens. In his only violent offense (at 20) he was convicted of arson after setting an occupied building on fire because he held a grudge. The man was intoxicated at the time of this offense. He was also described as acting in a bizarre fashion (reporting hallucinations) and was examined to see whether he could stand trial. He was narrowly certified competent but diagnosed as suffering from an "untreated psychosis." Prison psychiatrists later found no active psychosis but classified the man as an "inadequate personality" with a "past history of heroin." No one suggested that the man be treated, however, and he therefore qualified to join our non-disturbed (comparison) group as a veteran offender.

## Acute Exploders

The third cluster is important to us because it comprises offenders who, though they have limited arrest records and no histories of past violence, commit very serious violence. These offenders are often intoxicated when they are violent or show other signs of eccentricity. Some members of the group (30%) are intellectually limited, and their predominant violence categories are retaliatory violence and sex offenses against children.

A somewhat typical example is a first-time felon who was convicted of arson. The man had burned down three buildings in a row. One of the buildings was occupied at the time, and the police discovered that the man had a grudge against a young woman tenant: "The officers learned that the girlfriend of [the offender] lived in one of the buildings and that the fire marshall was informed that [the offender] had threatened to kill her and she had an Order of Protection against him." This explosive individual was a 21-year-old man of borderline intelligence (his IQ was 76); he had no criminal record other than two minor drug-related arrests to warn of his impending violence.

A second member of the cluster is an illegal alien whose credentials were otherwise unblemished. The man's offense covered a series of explosions that started with minor altercations. He had argued with a passenger in a van and pursued the van and tried to stop it, displaying a counterfeit police shield. The real police appeared, however, at which point the man became helplessly enraged, and the following sequence ensued:

> [The offender] sped away, but shortly thereafter was observed deliberately driving into the side of an occupied stationary police vehicle, causing injury to two officers. The arresting officer observed [the offender] reach for a .22 caliber handgun. [The offender] was pulled out of the car through the window and arrested after a struggle. . . . [The offender] also attempted to run down the arresting officer following a court hearing.

Paradoxically, the man required protection in prison after other inmates threatened him, which suggests that his capacity for rage is evoked by specific frustrations and perceived affronts, whereas other threats and affronts inspire fear or flight.

## Patterned Exploders

The fourth cluster is relatively small, but the offenders who compose it are responsible for the most extreme acts of violence, chiefly crimes of revenge. More than half commit their violence while intoxicated; almost all have violence histories, though few (13%) have been imprisoned. The offenders are mostly middle-aged and respectably employed.

These offenders show consistencies, but not in the sense that they replay violent offenses. Rather, their records often describe lesser violence that in retrospect foreshadows more serious violence. By reviewing past incidents we can often infer violence-related predispositions, but such inferences must be cautiously held, given that postdiction is cheap when we already know the outcome of the story. What is safe to note is that patterned explosive offenders have violence histories that make their offenses less atypical than those of other explosive offenders.

A representative offender from this group is a 50-year-old man who knifed another man during a drunken argument. The man described his violence as "self-defense," though the police reported that "he stabbed [the victim] repeatedly in the back, under his arm, and in the stomach near the heart, thereby attempting to cause said complainant's death." Other indications of the man's violence-proneness are that his past arrests include assaults and a warrant for "violence and battery of a law enforcement officer."

The man was an immigrant who had moved around the country for 2 decades. He had not learned to speak English and was "functionally illiterate" in his native language. Combined with these educational deficits was the fact that the man's intelligence was substandard (his IQ was 76).

The man appeared to be invoking violence to resolve disputes in which his language skills proved deficient, but his more general pattern was described by prison classification analysts, who concluded that "his criminal pattern is one of assault and serious violence against persons, reportedly when under the influence of alcohol."

A second exploder had a more specialized pattern. He described his offense as "a crime of passion," though he had gone out of his way to ambush his mistress and a male friend and had shot them to death. He also tried to kill a police officer, who returned the fire and injured the man. The offender's past difficulties with the law had been few but included an arrest for assault and a sentence for attempted murder, which was revealingly attributed to "personal domestic problems."

A third patterned exploder was younger and on probation for assault. His incident was preceded by convivial drinking and a ball game, during which an argument broke out. In the course of the argument someone punched the offender, who responded by knifing the person who had punched him. His victim narrowly missed bleeding to death.

Police pointed out that the offender and his peer group "have a long-established pattern of settling arguments with violence." This pattern appeared to have started early, in that the offender (whose intelligence was "dull normal") had been suspended from school because of constant involvement in fights.

The probation officer's summary of the man's career was that "the defendant has a predisposition toward violence, which in this case nearly resulted in a tragedy." The statement is similar to characterizations one can advance about other members of this same cluster.

## Precareer Robbers

The sample contains three groups of offenders who were convicted largely of robberies. The first group differs from the other two groups in that its members have no histories of violence or of imprisonment and have nonserious records of arrests.

Despite their unblemished dossiers, precareer robbers are often seen by the system as problem persons whose prospects are grim, as illustrated by the following assessment: "A first felony offender, the defendant's actions herein would appear to demonstrate his capacity for aggressive and reckless behavior. Accordingly the prognosis for his future societal adjustment at this time necessarily is extremely guarded."

The man about whom this was written had participated in a mugging in which the victim, who refused to part with his money, was kicked onto the tracks of a subway. This offense was obviously serious, but the man's prior offenses (trespass, criminal mischief, delinquency) were unimpressive, and his mother argued that her son was disturbed rather than delinquent. The man's peers had taken him more seriously. They had seen him as a threat and had assaulted him with a knife, injuring him. The man had reacted by trying to hang himself, and personnel in jail had to move him to protect him.

Similar profiles describe other offenders. One man (age 19) was involved in *ad seriatim* muggings, in one of which the victim was injured. The man was seen as disadvantaged by some ("the product of a broken home who displays immaturity, poor self-control, lacking in skills") but as unregenerate by others ("has not responded to discipline, therapy or probation supervision in the past. . . . future prognosis in sentencing this individual is poor"). He was also described as violence-embued, such as in prison, where the record tells us that the man expressed "anger and aggression toward either staff or peers."

Novice robbers are individuals who appear to have arrived at a critical juncture of their careers: They have not been adjudicated as violent offenders in the past but impress some observers as having become violent offenders who are slated for a career of serious crime.

## Early Career Robbers

Members of the second robbery cluster are uniformly young but have entered on a robbery career and been arrested for violent offenses. One out of five has been imprisoned for a prior offense, and many (42%) are on probation or parole at the time of their arrest.

The lengthy offense histories of these robbers start early, and the descriptions of their offenses are redundant. One adult criminal record, for instance, starts with the account of a team mugging in which the offender's partner "grab[bed] the victim by the neck" while the offender (age 15), "displaying a broken beer bottle, pointed it at the victim's face and indicated that they wanted the victim's money." Months earlier, the record describes the same offender as "acting in concert with three others, allegedly removing $35, a gold chain, and gold watch from an individual."

The man entered prison for the second time for an offense in which "acting alone, he forcibly snatched two gold chains from a female victim. . . . The victim's neck and chest were scraped as a result of this offense." Prison staff asked the man about this crime, and he explained that he used angel dust every day and that this habit is expensive.

Like other members of the early career cluster, the man had spent much time in institutions and had been a recalcitrant client. The first juvenile setting to which he had been sent (after stealing from his mother) complained that "the resident exhibited a negative pattern . . . many conflicts with both staff and residents, abusive language, destructive behavior, and frequent indulgences in marijuana." A second setting reported that "he began stealing from other residents, fighting with residents and staff, truanting from school and involving himself in illegal activity. He finally absconded from this facility."

When the man arrived in prison he boasted to staff that he "had many disciplinary reports during his last [prison] sentence, including several fights resulting in keeplock." He also announced that "if he has any problem with other inmates he will not go to the 'police' but will handle it himself." The man later proved as good as his word and had to be transferred to an adult prison. Here he rejected treatment, insisting he had no drug problem.

The man's status as an established career offender was thus cemented. His chances were assessed by a probation officer after his last robbery:

> The defendant's actions in the instant offense reflect the defendant's desire to remain active in a criminally deviant subculture involved in both drugs and strong-arm robbery. . . . Furthermore, the defendant's prior legal history and his actions in the instant offense are almost identical in that his actions were crimes perpetrated on the city streets aimed at unassuming and innocent individuals. . . . While on parole supervision, the defendant managed to be arrested on two separate occasions. . . . The defendant's actions in the instant offense are relevant to his past criminal behavior, and despite the defendant's youth, reflect behavior consistent with that of a habitual offender.

## Late Career Robbers

Our third robbery cluster contains older robbers who have long-term violence experience and extensive criminal histories. Most of the group have prison records, and many (44%) are nominally under supervision when they reoffend. However, the violence the offenders commit late in life is often less serious than that of young robbers, including themselves when young.

The members of the group often have long-term difficulties. One offender's career was summarized at prison intake as "a long history from childhood of social maladjustment, fighting and violent criminal offenses that are following him to adulthood." The criminal career referred to had begun at age 10, when the offender participated in his first recorded robbery. Earlier, the man's mother had been subject to a neglect petition, to which she responded that her son was "the most maladjusted and disruptive child in the neighborhood."

The man absconded from the juvenile facility in which he was placed, incurred 13 arrests (for burglary, robbery, and larceny) before he qualified as an adult and graduated to a reformatory. Later the man specialized in stickups in which he threatened his victims with a gun. In his last offense he robbed a cabdriver, evicted him from his cab, and led police on a high-speed chase.

The man's third prison sentence was a long one. After an unpromising start the man—who when he had left school was reading at a second-grade level—graduated from junior college, applied to a drug program, and cemented his relationship with his son, suggesting that there had been a possible turnabout in his career.

Another late-maturing career is that of a man whose first offense was a serious assault on a female victim. The man later became involved in rapes, robberies, and combinations of rape and robbery. In one incident he and a fellow sadist placed a bag over a woman's head and raped and robbed her. On another occasion the man threatened, beat, raped, and robbed a neighbor, ostensibly because of money she owed him.

The man's last offense was a more conventional robbery, in which he carried a gun. His prison sentence was long because he was also convicted of having jumped bail, and he decided to enroll in a prison program designed to rehabilitate violence-prone persons. In addition he took a vocational course, in which he performed creditably.

The cluster heading under which these men fall describes offenders in the late stages of their career. This means that violence deescalation may occur, and career desistance is possible.

## Violence Generalists

Our last category consists of offenders who engage in variegated serious violence. They have dense arrest histories and long-term violence problems. Some (25%) are mentally deficient, and others (32%) are intoxicated when they commit crimes.

The group combines attributes of exploders and robbers. Its violent offenses are often felony-related but at the same time, or at other times, are irrational and impulse-ridden.

Some members of the group have substance abuse problems. A case in point is that of an offender who was an alcoholic and also a drug addict and mentally retarded. A psychiatrist in the prison speculated about the link between the man's problems. He commented, "[This offender] probably had difficulties coping with the environmental requirements and as a result, he was seeking refuge in alcohol and cocaine in order to overcome his insecurity and anxieties."

In turn, alcohol had created more problems for the offender. He developed a penchant for drunk driving, which included running over police in an effort to escape. He had also attempted a robbery in which he assaulted his victim. In a third incident, he shot at a school full of children and explained that "I had nothing better to do at the time." The police to whom he delivered this account concluded that "the defendant was under the influence of alcohol at arrest" and that he was dangerous.

Another alcohol-involved offender had a barroom argument and slashed a woman in the abdomen, causing very serious injuries. The man had a long criminal record, including convictions for assault, burglary, robbery, larceny, resisting arrest, and ringing false fire alarms. At prison entry, he was described as "a predicate felon, if not a persistent felon." He in turn informed prison staff that he wanted "individual counseling in order to better understand himself with the hope of not returning to prison."

Members of the generalist cluster are often candidates for services, such as substance abuse services, which they have not received. The omission makes the offenders "nondisturbed" (because mental health status hinges on services received) and draws attention to other attributes they share. Unfortunately, these attributes are chronicity of offending and a penchant for violence, which evoke images of predatory careers, though the offenders are fringe figures whose careers are really only haphazard collages of frequently impulse-ridden involvements.

## The Mental Health Continuum

A reader might well conclude that differences between offenders who have mental health histories and those who lack such histories are not striking. This impression would not rest on the suspicion that disturbed offenders are unfairly stigmatized but on doubts about whether "nondisturbed" offenders earn many bills of mental health. Our vignettes (which are admittedly sparse) hint at careers of deprivation, deficits and nonresilience, addiction and self-destructiveness, impulsivity and perversity, heteronomy and explosiveness. In this respect, the accounts are no different from the range of histories covered in thousands of presentence summaries the reader might peruse elsewhere.

Few offenders we have described seem to be models of mental wellness as most of us would understand the phrase. These "nondisturbed" offenders are not sturdy professionals competently engaged in illegal occupations. They are not persons who resolutely elect unfortunate sources of income or drastic solutions to their problems. Many of these offenders have long-term "careers," but they drift, seemingly helplessly, from one career juncture to the next. Even when the offenders' crimes are substantial, the perpetrators are often limited and driven, or exude incompetence and marginality.

That is not to say that the offenders we described can be classified as disturbed, but that they are not mentally healthy. This means that they are not likely to receive help as long as mental health services subserve (as they do) the "medical model," which targets attention to diagnosed maladies—a far cry from promoting health. Persons who fall in the definitional penumbra (nonhealthy–nondisturbed) fall between the cracks of "health professions" that have become "illness professions" in practice.

What makes the situation ironic for offenders is that proposals to incorporate a more salient concern with mental health— that is, with personal effectiveness or coping competence—in correctional settings invite objections on the grounds that most offenders are nondisturbed, which makes the medical model inapplicable. Treatment will therefore continue to be constrained until we entertain the unfashionable notions that a continuum exists from (mental) illness to health, and that movement along the continuum from mental illness toward mental health can be a goal of intervention.

# 7

# The Disturbed Violent Offense

The study of offenders who have emotional problems differs from the description of offenses that are affected by emotional problems. Like other behavior, a violent crime can be a symptom of a person's psychological difficulties, but we have noted that disturbed persons are often capable of committing offenses that are indistinguishable from those perpetrated by nondisturbed offenders. The other side of the coin is that many offenses of ostensibly sturdy offenders can reflect nonsturdy motives such as loss of control or impulsivity.

Both of these facts are compatible with some contemporary thinking which rejects the notions that (a) violence and irrationality are the monopoly of a group of people who are different from the rest of us, and that (b) illness–normalcy and crime–law-abidingness represent dichotomous behavior. The first point is emphasized by a report from a Violence Commission task force, which includes the observation that

> A popular view of psychoanalytic and psychiatric theories is that they explain why "crazy" people behave as they do. While specialists in these fields do work most often with disturbed people, they also have a general view of life in which antisocial behavior is always present, either in potential or actual form. At the same time, they seek to understand the special role that violent behavior may serve for people who are deeply sick—or at least sicker than others.[1]

---

[1] D. J. Mulvihill & M. M. Tumin, with L. A. Curtis, eds., *Crimes of Violence.*

The second point is underlined by Seymour Halleck, among others, who writes,

> Most modern psychiatrists look upon mental illness as a process. Mental health and mental illness are both viewed on the same continuum. The behavior of some individuals may at times become so ineffective, so self-punitive or so irrational that the psychiatrist deems it advisable to define them as ill."[2]

In another passage Halleck suggests that crimes and symptoms may be interchangeable variations on maladaptive behavior, which means that "the same individual may show symptoms of schizophrenia on one day and of obsessive preoccupation on the next. On the third day he might commit a crime, and on the fourth he might be entirely docile and comfortable."[3]

The point implied by such statements is that any segment of behavior can be examined independently of the judgments one makes about the behaving person, though once one has enough of a person's conduct to assess, one can describe behavioral trends involving change or consistency. Halleck also implies that the labeling of behavior as disturbed does not require exotic expertise in that "ultimately, most of our decisions to call people mentally ill are based upon judgments of reasonableness."[4] An offender who commits a professional robbery, for example, is mostly viewed as a "rational" offender, because "it is assumed that the criminal is seeking goals that everyone can understand and accept, goals such as financial profit or status."[5] If the same person attempts to commit robberies while he is drunk, our assessment may become more reserved, on the grounds that "a reasonable man would not undertake a difficult criminal task while intoxicated.

---

*A Staff Report to the National Commission on the Causes and Prevention of Violence* (Washington, DC: Government Printing Office, 1969), Vol. 12, p. 459.

[2]S. L. Halleck, *Psychiatry and the Dilemmas of Crime* (New York: Harper & Row, 1969), p. 40.

[3]Halleck, 1969, p. 40.

[4]Halleck, 1969, p. 47.

[5]Halleck, 1969, p. 48.

If he must depend upon crime to earn his living, he is behaving no more reasonably than a surgeon who would try to operate while inebriated."[6]

Such ratings of the "reasonableness" of specific crimes need not imply, of course, that the offenders are reasonable or unreasonable. But it should be obvious that offenses can be psychologically revealing acts to the extent that they permit us to infer goals and concerns of individual offenders, and provide clues about the level of their skills and deficits, including intellectual, emotional, and social deficits. If deficits are substantial, one expects that crimes will be contaminated by them, sometimes subtly and sometimes dramatically and blatantly. Should this occur, the sum of many "unreasonable" offenses approximates a composite disturbed perpetrator:

> When the criminal fails to pursue acceptable goals in a logical, consistent or effective manner, we must assume either the he is inept at solving ordinary problems, that he has met with environmental circumstances which he cannot master, or that he is driven by motivations which are not apparent and which deviate from those which society would consider reasonable. These are all qualities that could just as easily describe the mentally ill. We, therefore, must return to our earlier assertion that if the judgments by which we designate unreasonable behavior were consistently applied to the law violator, we would have to agree that many criminals behave in a manner that is not too dissimilar to that of the mentally ill.[7]

As it happens, our data permit us to explore the strategy of behavior ratings that Halleck suggests. We can do so because we have concise descriptions of most offenses for which members of our samples were convicted. We also have an eccentricity code (described in chapter 2) that approximates Halleck's conception of "unreasonableness" in crime. This code lets us explore the range and quality of offenses that raise questions

---

[6]Halleck, 1969, p. 49.
[7]Halleck, 1969, p. 49.

about the offender's mental state at the time of offending. The point is not to document the extent to which criminals are mentally disturbed, because statements about the prevalence of mental illness cannot be based on impressionistic judgments. The point, rather, is to venture hypotheses about the ways in which specialized dispositions of violent offenders (psychological problems) can affect some of the offenses they commit.

## Random Violence

The most uncontaminated relationship between violence and emotional disorders exists in incidents in which strangers are assaulted without provocation and seemingly at random. Such violence is most apt to be perpetrated by Disturbed Exploders and has repercussions that transcend its numerical importance. This is so because victims have no way of predicting or preventing their victimization when offenders offer no cue to their impending resolve and strike out of the blue. Random violence also makes disturbed persons in general objects of fear, because it is the sort of violence that is exclusive to (though unrepresentative of) pathologically tinged offenses.

The reason random violence can without exception be ascribed to serious mental disorders is that its inception is invariably associated with psychotic delusions or hallucinations. The offense may appear motiveless because the offender usually assigns private, symbolic attributes to victims who happen to be available at the time the offender's delusions or hallucinations reach climactic junctures. To the extent to which external stimuli play a role in provoking the offender's violent act, the role is always bizarre and improbable, one in which the victim becomes a repository of grievances that the offender derives elsewhere. An illustration of this sequence is provided by the following scenario:

> The offender—a man in his midthirties—paced a subway platform mouthing the words "push, push, push," scanning his surroundings in what was described as "a nervous manner." The offender then approached a young Asian woman

waiting for a train and pushed her under an incoming engine, which crushed and decapitated her. The offender was overheard saying, "Now we're even. I did it. Now they'll see at school." After being arrested, the man had a telephone conversation with his sister in which he explained, "This is not my fault. It is the Board of Education."

The antecedent sequence in this incident was that the offender had been a teacher and was placed on medical leave after experiencing the onset of a schizophrenic condition. He was hospitalized and treated as an outpatient but discontinued his therapy and medication against the advice of his physicians. He then returned to his job, but his performance proved substandard, and he received letters of admonition from his principal. The resulting anxiety contributed to a resurgence of the man's psychosis, which now centered on a delusional system that made him the target of a conspiracy. On the day of his offense the man had had lunch at a Chinese restaurant, and the waiter had asked him what he did for a living. This question led the man to conclude that the Chinese community was in league with his superiors, who were the source of his difficulties. He also concluded that the Chinese as a group were "interfering with his mind and poisoning him to make him homosexual."

A second offender who attempted (unsuccessfully) to throw a stranger under an incoming subway train had spent "90 percent of twenty years" in psychiatric settings. In this instance, psychological difficulties had a remote origin and dated to the man's military service decades earlier. The man's behavior included angry outbursts and actions that were irrational and impulsive. He could offer no reason for committing his offense, and after he was incarcerated the prison intake analyst observed that "in every way he is an institutionalized psychiatric patient who belongs in a hospital rather than a prison."

Personal experiences that precipitate random violence can generalize from one target to another in psychological chain reactions. A case in point is that of a female patient who had been living on the street. One month previously this patient had been raped, and she had acquired a screwdriver to "defend herself." She had also become obsessed with delusions revolving around birth and maternity concerns, which culminated in a random attack on an infant in a stroller. The child's mother fought off the incursion, but in the course of the melee the patient turned her attention to an elderly bystander, whom she stabbed with her screwdriver.

Another chronic outpatient became involved in the following sequence:

> The patient walked the streets in an agitated state, mumbling to himself. A pedestrian asked him whether anything was the matter, and in response he pulled a knife and stabbed the pedestrian in the face. By this time a crowd had gathered and the offender slashed two of the bystanders. The police arrived, and the man menaced one of the officers with a knife and was shot in the leg.

In another example,

> The offender walked up to a stranger on the street, grabbed him and cut his throat and chin. He subsequently explained that "his friend, with whom he had worked, had died of cancer. He felt that two other people would die. He was suspicious that he was being attacked."

In other incidents the offender's concerns have more focus, in that they attach to a particular individual who triggers a specific obsession. Examples include the following scenarios:

> The offender entered a laundromat armed with a knife and encountered a stranger. The stranger left the laundromat and was followed by the offender, who stabbed him in the back and threw bottles at him. The offender told the victim, "I'll kill you if I see you [again] on this street."

> \* \* \*

> The offender peeked through a window and saw a woman taking a shower. He entered the house, picked up a knife and knifed the victim in the arm, neck, and back, subse-

quently indicating he had "no idea why" he had committed the offense.

In some instances delusional concerns center on the offender's perceptions of the victim's behavior, and the violence becomes quasi-random rather than random. This means that the victim has at some point dealt with the offender, but that the connotations the offender assigns to the victim's acts are overblown, improbable, and bizarre, and thus unpredictable. An example is the following chain of events:

> Two days prior to his violent crime, the offender had gone to a welfare office to inquire about his check. The caseworker was not in the office and the offender left a message. On the day of the offense, the offender returned and wordlessly stabbed his caseworker with an icepick. He explained, "I had to get my rent paid. I was afraid I would be thrown out of my place. [If I had used my hands instead of the weapon] I would probably have to go back there over and over again to see about my check."

Another example involves a disturbed female parolee who knifed a woman in a washroom, explaining that "the victim bumped into me and didn't apologize."

Most random violence one encounters is an uncontaminated product of delusions and bizarre impulses, but some random violence (though not an appreciable proportion) includes some contribution of alcohol or drugs to the offender's explosive state of mind at the time of the offense. The following examples are cases in point:

> The offender ran up to a woman who was waiting for a bus, and hit her in the face with a tree limb, breaking her nose; the woman fell, and the offender continued to assault her. He then "vigorously" resisted arrest and police concluded that he "[was] high on angel dust."

*  *  *

> The offender who had been drinking heavily in a tavern, exited and pointed a crossbow at passersby. Two off-duty police officers interceded, and the offender stabbed them.

Not surprisingly, offenders who commit random violence often state themselves that motives for their behavior are unascertainable. The offenders' inability to "explain" their violence relates to their confusion and agitation at the time of their explosions—which cannot be recaptured in retrospect—but also has to do with the complexity of motives that underlie random violence. We have noted that more than other violence, random violence is a product of overdetermined delusional ruminations. This means that the motives for the violence are related to the dynamics of the offender's emotional difficulties, including their long-term developmental origins. Such relationships must at best be inferred, as in classic examples in which sex-related anxieties lead to panic that is ascribed (via delusions) to external danger. The instances in which offenders themselves can pinpoint such dynamics are rare. On some occasions this identification occurs, however, as in the following incident:

> The offender—who was a transvestite—drove his car through a red light. When he was flagged down by police, he sped away, and crashed into a wall. Approached by the police he exited his car, swinging a knife and shouting, "I'll kill you. Kill me!" The offender indicated that at the time he was "extremely upset over his masculinity," and had been suffering bouts of depression. He recalled that when his car crashed "he truly hoped the police would kill him."

## Arson and Emotional Disturbance

A second category of violence that is almost always associated with emotional problems is incendiary violence or criminal arson, which is most often perpetrated by Disturbed Sex Offenders, Compensatory Offenders, and Skid Row Exploders. The dynamics of arson offenses are variegated and are insufficiently understood, but some offenses shed light on prevalent motivational patterns. One such pattern combines impulsivity, impotent rage, and a sense of lingering resentment. The following examples are cases in point:

While walking by a house in an intoxicated state, the offender remembered an altercation with the owner of the house that had occurred several years previously. Inspired by this recollection, the offender smashed a bowling ball through the victim's car window, poured gasoline through the window, and set the automobile on fire.

\* \* \*

The offender—whose intelligence was extremely limited—had done work for his landlord in exchange for promised compensation. Instead of a reasonable wage, the landlord paid the offender a very small sum (4 dollars). The offender felt resentful, got drunk, and started a fire in his closet. He also set fire to his apartment on another occasion after fortifying himself with alcohol. On this date he had not received a promised food donation and had discovered that a neighbor to whom he felt attached "does not like him."

\* \* \*

The offender, who was drunk, set fire to an apartment building, doing minor damage to the building's garage. The offender reported that the owner had called her "names." She indicated that she had reported the affront to the police, who "refused to do anything."

\* \* \*

Another offender had set five fires, resulting in damage of $300,000. One fire destroyed the garage in the offender's father's house. The offender reported disagreements with his father. After these acrimonious arguments, he testified, he got drunk and set fires.

\* \* \*

The offender, while intoxicated, incinerated a bedroom to injure her sleeping husband, with whom she had had an argument.

In incidents such as these one factor we invariably encounter is the offender's feeling that he or she is overwhelmed or resourceless in conflicts with opponents who are powerful.

This suggests that the offender has a low level of self-esteem and a limited sense of self-efficacy. Another denominator that cuts across the incidents is that the offender drinks alcohol as a precondition to fire-setting to work up his or her resolve.

Though resentment and a sense of impotence are a frequent motive for arson, some more complex patterns are detailed by a few offenders. One ambiguous account, for example, emerges in the following incident:

> The offender—who suffered from retardation—had set two fires in a motel that did extensive damage. He was a former employee who had been recently discharged, but claimed, "I had nothing against the motel . . . without thinking I would just go and light a fire anywhere." The man explained that he set fires in response to hallucinations in which he saw the face of an individual who had killed his sister, and that he set the fires to "get even" and to reduce tension he felt; "then everything builds up and I do it over again."

As it happens, the offender's account was incomplete, in that his fire-setting proved to be a long-term pattern. The offender had set several fires preceding the incident (his sister's death) that he regards as catalytic. This fact is not surprising, however, in that predispositions to arson are often chronic, while specific stimuli (such as feeling rejected) enter as shorter-term, reinforcing motives.

It is also not surprising that arsonists attribute their offenses to immediate antecedents, because longer-term motives are hard (if not impossible) to characterize. This difficulty contributes to the fact that arsonists' self-descriptions often include claims to rational, goal-directed, or calculated behavior. The following incidents are illustrative:

> The offender broke into a construction office to "look around" and stole a pen from a desk. He decided to "cover up finger prints" to avoid capture by strewing flammable liquid over the office, burning it down and causing several million dollars' worth of damage.

* * *

The offender had been rejected by a female friend and set her house on fire. He claimed he has done so to "play hero" by rescuing his friend's children, thereby inspiring her to renew their liaison.

Some offenders react to the difficulty of trying to explain their irrational acts by attributing their offenses to intoxication ("when I drink I set fires") or highlighting the enjoyment they derive from watching fires after they are set. Both observations are relevant, but neither gives adequate weight to longer-term motivational states documented by the mental health status and histories of arsonists.

## Mental Health Problems and Retaliatory Violence

Retaliatory violence is committed by a wide range of people, including those who have no criminal histories, those who have extensive involvements with violence, and those with emotional problems, substance abuse difficulties, and cognitive disabilities.

There is no distinguishably different pattern of "crazy retaliation," but some retaliatory violence resembles quasi-random violence (for example, a man cuts a person's face repeatedly for throwing a snowball at him); other incidents can combine retaliatory motives with concerns that are in fact symptoms of mental illness (for example, a man kills his wife after having an argument with her and hearing voices that tell him to kill her). In other instances the motives for the violence are contaminated by eccentric overtones or implausible premises that run through explanations of offenses, as in the following examples:

The offender—who had been hospitalized on occasion for treatment of schizophrenia—engaged in arguments with her fiance two days before her wedding. During the course of these arguments, she stabbed her fiance to death, and later explained that she "was choked to death by light-complected members of the black race who had joined in a conspiracy to destroy her via [the boyfriend's] death." She also said that the police had substituted the murder weapon for a "dagger" brandished by the victim.

\* \* \*

A man killed his brother-in-law with a twelve-gauge shotgun, called his sister [the victim's wife] and asked her "to clean up the mess." He claimed the victim had sexually molested his two daughters and "taunted him about performing sexual acts with him." He complained that he had shared such concerns with relatives, but "no one would believe him."

Retaliatory offenses are responses to perceived affronts, but it is not uncommon for disturbed retaliators to add unusual twists to standard acts of retribution, which include inappropriate and highly unusual behavior during or after the offense:

The offender suspected that his wife was involved in extramarital liaisons. He stabbed the sleeping wife in the neck, then choked her with a telephone cord. The police found the offender "dazed" and described him as "incoherent."

\* \* \*

The victim was the offender's ex-girlfriend, whom he had harassed "in order to get her back." In the incident the offender took a shotgun and held the girl for 16 hours "trying to get up the courage to kill himself in front of her." He used the gun, shooting out windows, before giving himself up to the police.

\* \* \*

The offender was a homosexual, and was also retarded. The victim was the man's lover, who had provoked him by becoming attentive to another man. The offender stabbed his lover in the back, ate dinner and asked a neighbor to call the police, who found the victim dead.

The irrational extreme among acts of retaliation is behavior involving disinhibited (angry, explosive) overkill, including massive, disproportionate rage in response to seemingly minor provocations. Explosions of unrestrained rage are not confined to any special group of offenders. Among some alcoholics, however—most notably, Skid Row Exploders—carefree, indiscriminate expressions of anger suggest a contribution of alcohol to the genesis of retaliatory resolves. Examples of disinhibiting alcohol involvement include the following acts of revenge:

> The offender had been "drinking excessively." A police officer found him blocking the exit to a bus terminal and asked him to move. The offender responded, "You're done, motherfucker," and attempted to shoot the officer with his service revolver.

*   *   *

> The offender was a supervisor in a rooming house. While intoxicated, he encountered a nonresident using a bathroom without permission. He armed himself with a baseball bat, waited for the victim to exit, and beat him to death.

*   *   *

> The offender assaulted a fellow patron in a bar, kicked and beat two female police officers who tried to restrain him, and assaulted a male officer, kicking him in the groin. After the man was nominally subdued and taken to a hospital, he assaulted doctors and nurses by spitting at them.

*   *   *

> The offender was a chronic schizophrenic who had been described as a man who "becomes paranoid and wanders aimlessly about." He had been drinking with the victim in the latter's apartment. The victim asked him to leave, and the offender stabbed the man in the heart.

Drug disinhibition (notably that induced by PCP and cocaine) is also sometimes associated with acts of retaliatory overkill, and there are instances in which the effects of drug and alcohol disinhibition seem to occur in combination:

> After an argument, the offender killed the victim, striking him with blunt instruments and then strangling him to death. The offender "states he was drinking and smoking angel dust, and does not remember the incident."

* * *

> The offender had a fight with an elderly drinking companion over a bottle of wine. During the fight, he stabbed, punched, and choked the victim in such a frenzy that others could not stop him. He claimed to have been drunk and "high on PCP."

The most dramatic disinhibition occurs among offenders whose violence has a tantrumlike flavor. In such violence the offender appears to run helplessly out of control and can do a great deal of harm, as in the following incident:

> The offender injured an acquaintance after an argument. He also injured police officers who tried to arrest him, lifting them and "banging them against a wall." A repeat performance occurred in the prison, during which four officers tried to subdue the offender and were seriously injured. Prison staff noted that "it seems that [the offender's] size and occasional episodes of dull-witted behavior may make him look like an easy target for others to pick on to prove themselves, although, due to his mental state, he is also capable of misinterpreting others' intentions and reacting explosively without real provocation."

The offender in this example reliably inflicted damage because he was large and threw repeat tantrums. The man's size dramatized his susceptibility to perceived affronts, but the combination of chronicity and promiscuous explosiveness occurs elsewhere among offenders with mental health histories. The following are some cases in point that involve recurrent and redundant retaliatory explosions:

The offender's difficulties included early referrals for "uncontrollable temper tantrums," including breaking a teacher's fingers and "destroying property at school." In the most recent incident he shot at a man he had previously stabbed, against whom he harbored a "grudge." He had also thrown a knife at a sister (puncturing her leg), threatened to kill his brother and grandmother, and "sexually attacked" a female acquaintance.

\* \* \*

The offender had spent 6 years in a psychiatric hospital. He was imprisoned for explosions in which he (a) stabbed a former girlfriend's new boyfriend; (b) blinded the girlfriend by stabbing her in the face, and (c) beat up the girl's father, threatening to burn down his house. In prison the man remained assaultive, "admits having no control over his explosive nature and does not care what he does to others."

\* \* \*

In jail, the offender, who was awaiting trial for an assault, attacked a corrections officer because his shampoo was missing, threw hot water in the face of an inmate with whom he had argued, and injured two officers who tried to restrain him.

The offenders involved in these incidents had histories of diagnosed difficulties, but explosive violence also occurs among men and women who have no such histories, most notably among Patterned Exploders. A propensity to disinhibition—the tendency to allow oneself to explode under stress—draws attention to the contributing role of reality-obfuscating factors we have referred to, which may be intoxicants (alcohol and drugs) or psychological deficits. The latter are obviously important and include emotional lability and cognitive dysfunctions that impair appraisals of threat or assessments of response options.

## Vehicular Violence

Among unusual forms of violence that reflect the influence of disinhibition are some extreme violent assaults in which cars are used as weapons. Serious vehicular violence can involve destructive impulsivity, panic, and indifference to consequences (including one's own survival). Though such violence often features alcohol as an impairing influence, it also provides a role for other disinhibitors, such as those associated with emotional problems.[8]

Vehicular violence by disturbed offenders includes serious incidents such as the following:

> The offender had tried to break into his inlaws' home. When police arrived, the offender backed a stolen car into three officers, then attempted to escape on foot. One officer sustained a hip and a head injury when the car was backed into him. Another officer was dragged 100 feet down the street. The offender explained that he had arrived to talk to his wife, who he thought had died in a plane crash. He was also there to see a friend from Venus, who had returned to help with his problems, and felt the police had interrupted his colloquy with his extraterrestrial friend.

*  *  *

> The offender had a history of assaulting police officers and prison guards. Preceding his offense he had been ordered to stop his car. He sped away but later returned, tapped the office on the shoulder, and asked him whether he had a problem. He locked himself in his car, and when ordered to exit drove the car into the officer, into a parked car, and into a police vehicle that responded to the scene.

*  *  *

> The offender was a disturbed juvenile escapee. He stole a pocketbook and was intercepted by a witness as he stole a van. He drove over the witness and dragged him down the street, killing him. He explained that "I got crazy the way things were going."

---

[8]The same point can be made about fatal accidents in which the victim and perpetrator are the same person. For an excellent discussion of the dynamics of traffic fatalities, see J. R. Finch & J. D. Smith, *Psychiatric and Legal Aspects of Automobile Fatalities* (Springfield, IL: Charles C Thomas, 1970).

These incidents show admixtures of confusion, anger, and fear. The same ingredients characterize more conventional incidents, but (a) the break with reality may be less drastic in conventional vehicular violence than it is among some disturbed offenders, and (b) the role of alcohol may make the contribution of any psychological problems that the offenders may have less salient:

> The offender was a former mental patient who lived in a trailer park. He was intoxicated and announced that he was going shopping, but a neighbor prevented him from driving off. The offender then agreed to go to bed, but later changed his mind, threatening his neighbor (offering to burn down his trailer) if he did not relinquish his ignition keys. He drove out with tires spinning, killed a pedestrian, and announced that he was leaving town to avoid "going to jail for life this time."

*   *   *

> The offender accused a man of stealing from his girlfriend, drove over the man repeatedly, then aimed his car at the girlfriend, who he alleged had been "paying too much attention" to the victim.

One motive that may at some level form part of disinhibiting sequences involving the use of automobiles is indifference to survival, but the role of this factor (which at minimum consists of a cavalier disregard of danger to oneself) becomes less salient when others are killed or injured than in more conventional DWI offenses, in which no victimization is intended (see footnote 8).

## Sexual Violence

Persons with mental health or substance abuse histories are overrepresented among offenders who commit sexual assaults against adults or (more so) against children. This statistical fact confirms that deep-seated dispositions figure among routine motives for rape and sodomy and that the dynamics of sexual violence are often complex. In view of this observation, it is not surprising that sexual violence is frequently recidivistic as well as impervious to deterrence through imprisonment, though relatively few disturbed sex offenders have experienced prison. Adding to the seriousness of this picture is the fact that victims of sexual violence are frequently depersonalized and callously dealt with by offenders whose obsessiveness and incapacity for empathy is extreme. Victims in such offenses are responded to as objects of need-satisfaction, and in the most serious incidents are treated with quasi-sadistic disregard for their physical survival:

> An offender abducted a 12-year-old girl, raped and sodomized her, and left her zippered in a suitcase.

> \* \* \*

> An offender abducted a woman at a party, raped and beat her and left her under subzero conditions in which she narrowly survived.

> \* \* \*

> The offender raped a mother and beat and kicked her four-year-old daughter.

> \* \* \*

> The offender raped a deaf-mute girl, who had to be hospitalized as a result of serious injuries.

> \* \* \*

> The offender sodomized a 7-year-old boy at knife point, urinated in his mouth, and left him covered with abrasions.

> \* \* \*

> The offender attacked a patient suffering from cerebral palsy, abandoned him in freezing weather, and stole his wheelchair. His comment to the victim (who almost died) was, "Good-bye, sucker."

Offenses such as forcible rapes of infants and assaults on

persons of advanced age are predations in which victims can be preselected for their helplessness as well as for their implausibility as sexual targets. Additional pathological nuances sometimes manifest themselves in the details of unfolding incidents, such as in the following examples:

> The offender entered the victims' apartment, knifed the husband and tried to rape the wife. When police arrived he threw a bottle at them, and told them they could not arrest him without a warrant. The man's blood alcohol was .16; he had convulsions and was taken to a hospital.

> \* \* \*

> The offender forced his way into an occupied apartment, complained that it was a pigsty, and made the occupant wash dishes. He then kissed her while watching himself in a mirror and explained to her that everyone gets raped, including himself in jail. He then raped the victim and told her that he would drown her in her bathtub.

> \* \* \*

> The offender abducted a pedestrian and tried to rape her. He explained that he was intoxicated, and had heard voices instructing him to have intercourse with a woman.

Students of abnormal behavior assume that some sexual assaults—particularly of children and other powerless victims—are compensatory efforts by persons who feel (and often are) inadequate.[9] In this view, men who are afraid to approach adult partners can gain sexual satisfaction and forceful dominance against helpless, and therefore nonthreatening, targets. The generality of this explanation is in some dispute, but illustrative documentation of inadequacy includes incidents such as the following:

> The victim was intoxicated, was sleeping soundly in the subway, and remained asleep while the offense took place.

---

[9]A. N. Groth, *Men Who Rape* (New York: Plenum, 1979).

The offender (a mental patient) subjected the victim to oral sex while another man (not associated with the offender) tried to rape her.

\* \* \*

The offender exposed himself to an elderly woman, took off some of her clothes, and fled. The next day the victim saw the offender in front of her home, where he hung out, and he was arrested.

\* \* \*

The offender was a mentally defective outpatient who partially disrobed a female pedestrian, but was subdued by other pedestrians before he could attempt to rape her.

# Mismanaged Offenses

Offenders who appear limited or disturbed at the time of their offenses, such as many Acute Disturbed Exploders and Compensatory Offenders, can have their efficacy as crime perpetrators reduced.[10] Though the proportion of disturbed persons who fail as career criminals is surprisingly small (which suggests that crime in general is not an occupation calling for sophisticated skills), some persons are clearly too impaired to function effectively in carrying out specific offenses.[11] Among

---

[10]Charles S. Silberman pointed out that bungled offenses are a testimonial to the spontaneity and lack of planning with which many offenders approach their vocation. He suggested further that such offenses are partly responsible for the fact that clearance rates (which for some offense categories are low) do not describe the probability of being arrested (which for repeat offenders is high). See *Criminal Violence, Criminal Justice* (New York: Random House, 1980).

[11]In a recent column, Dan Lynch (1994) wrote that "when you're talking about the phenomenal increase in crime in this country over the past 15 years, you're really . . . talking about people who can't read, who can't count past their fingers and toes, who can't begin to think and who have only the vaguest idea of what planet they live in. Go into any criminal courtroom in any community in the nation, and you'll see . . . an endless stream of people so immensely stupid, so utterly mystified by life and all its routine demands that you'll begin to wonder how their tiny brains generate enough energy to make their legs move."

In relation to such inadequate offenders, Lynch (1994) notes as a dilemma that "only somebody with the capacity to grasp justice as a penalty can be punished. A person too stupid to get the point can only be hurt." (See "Crime and Stupidity," Albany *Times Union*, April 10, 1994.)

instances of failure caused by impairment are robberies in which offenders try to follow standard robbery procedures but become unconvincing because of their obvious instability or eccentricity:

The offender gave a supermarket cashier a note that said, "I don't mind dying; you'll go with me if you don't give me a stack of twenties and fifties." The cashier could not open her register because of nervousness. The offender took his note and left the store. He was promptly overtaken and arrested.

\* \* \*

The offender approached a subway booth he had robbed, apologized to the attendant, and told her he was going to mug someone. He did and was arrested.

\* \* \*

The offender robbed a gas station. He was recognized because he had been in the station before and had filled out employment applications listing his name and address. He was described by the victim as "very nervous" at the time of the offense.

\* \* \*

The offender entered a gas station wielding a knife and announced, "This is a stickup." The owner and two sons responded, "You've got to be kidding." As they subdued the offender, he yelled, "I am an officer; call the police. I'm a detective." The police arrived and arrested him.

\* \* \*

The offender entered a bank claiming to have a bomb and demanding money. The teller laughed at the offender and he fled. A short time later he jumped over the counter, took money, and was arrested. He claimed to have no recollection of the incident, because he was under the influence of alcohol and drugs.

*   *   *

The offender tried to rob different banks using deposit slips of other banks and was informed that he was "in the wrong bank." He eventually did rob a bank and left a deposit slip with his name on it.

In incidents such as these, the offender's failure as a criminal can arise from (a) ambivalence or lack of self-confidence, (b) inappropriate behavior that reduces the credibility of his threats, or (c) self-destructive behavior that increases the probability of capture. Similar traits can reduce the efficacy of residential burglaries, as in the following example:

The offender had spent his paycheck on a drinking binge. He entered an apartment but fled when the occupant woke up. He entered a second apartment and again woke up the occupant, who stepped on him as he tried to hide. He tried to flee but was grabbed by the occupant of the first apartment, who found him "in a daze."

*   *   *

The offender talked to an answering machine of a former employer indicating that he was going to burglarize the man. He did and was arrested.

*   *   *

The offender burglarized a home and lingered to take a shower. He burglarized a second house and lay on a lounge chair on the porch, where a neighbor observed him and called the police.

*   *   *

The offender's IQ was 55. He burglarized an apartment, left behind his shoes and his wallet, and later explained that he was intoxicated.

*   *   *

The offender broke into an unoccupied apartment and stole property, but abandoned his hat and jacket. He also left feces on the floor.

In incidents such as these, the perpetrator shows that he or she lacks the capacity to complete an offense without risking apprehension. In other instances, offenses are undertaken on the spur of the moment (for example, the offender drinks and runs out of money, crosses the street to rob a bank, and returns to resume drinking), and they thus qualify as clumsy expressions of half-baked impulsivity rather than as manifestations of resolve, planning, or "criminal intent."

## Violence Overkill in Burglaries and Robberies

Very different from self-destructive inadequacy is the use of gratuitous violence in committing property-related violent offenses. Offenders with mental health histories are less prone than offenders without such histories to commit violent property offenses, but they are more likely to use excessive violence when they do commit such offenses. This fact is hardly surprising because violence overkill is not a "rational" way to conduct criminal business, in that it is unnecessary to achieve the ostensible goal (monetary gain) of the offense.

Extreme violence among disturbed offenders can express long-term traits (such as a disposition to be gratuitously assaultive or to casually take life) or shorter-term situational motives (such as blind excitation or rage). Compounded irrationality can increase the sadistic flavor of violence, such as in the following incidents:

> The offender robbed a gas station, then took the attendant into the woods and stabbed him with a machete, broke his arms and legs, and slashed his neck and chest, leaving him for dead. In a previous offense he had locked a cabdriver into the trunk of his cab and abandoned the cab, which was not found until 4 days later. The offender was a mental patient and a member of a satanic cult who "from adolescence has been a bizarre, violent, warped sadomasochist," who declared that he "is not afraid to die nor eliminate anyone who antagonizes him."

\* \* \*

The offender participated in the robbery of a fast food establishment. After the robbery, he went into the store and shot the manager in the head. He told a cabdriver he had kidnapped, "I had to shoot that motherfucker. . . . Twenty-five years don't mean nothin' to me. No one wants me anyway. I'll shoot you too."

\* \* \*

The offender robbed four stores. In the first, he shot the owner three times in the head. He shot his other victims in the chest, killing one of them. He was a chronic outpatient who had no criminal record and claimed no recall of the offenses.

\* \* \*

The offender entered the home of a paralyzed veteran, dragging him from room to room and beating him. He kept beating his victim because he was "infuriated" that the man had no money.

\* \* \*

The offender entered a house, stole property, then shot and killed the family pets—a retriever and a ferret. He testified that "he remembers little of that day as he had been drinking heavily and had taken PCP."

\* \* \*

The offender beat an elderly woman with a cane and kicked her in the face while mugging her. He was a disturbed transvestite with a history of robbing older, defenseless women.

\* \* \*

The offender threw his victim against a wall and demanded money, and the victim handed over his wallet. The offender removed money and then demanded the victim's shoes and jacket. Thereafter, he tried to strangle the victim, threw him down a flight of stairs and kicked him in the head. He explained that he was "high on angel dust."

Some offenders mention drugs as contributing to their readiness to use gratuitous violence, but patients with drug histories are underrepresented in the more extreme felony violence incidents. This suggests that drug-caused excitation is mostly not the only causal factor at work. To the extent to which drugs and emotional problems combine to spark violence overkill, mood enhancers (such as angel dust) may simply reinforce preexistent violent dispositions.

Extreme felony violence is not a psychotic symptom, in the sense that it is not behavior that responds to command hallucinations or delusions. If a common motivational denominator exists, it is an effort to demonstrate power through one's ability to maim or kill. Victims trigger the violence by being helpless, which makes them easy, inviting proving grounds for the potency the offender senses that he lacks. One cue is that cruelty often coexists with self-destructive behavior, including suicide attempts, and periodic despondency. This paradox derives from the offenders' view of the world as a dog-eat-dog place in which one is alternatively a victim and a victimizer. The offender is also typically tense, highstrung, and irritable, and full of bitterness and pent up rage. This emotional state, combined with his or her outlook on life, creates his destructive disposition.

# III

# Policy Issues

# 8

# The Extremely Disturbed but Minimally Violent Offender: The Problem of Sentencing

A s is discussed in chapter 9, some offender subgroups are made up of chronically disturbed and very violent persons who are obvious candidates for imprisonment because they pose serious threats to society. Such individuals tax prison resources and are at best warehoused in the prison, but they must be incapacitated for long periods to protect the community from extreme and unpredictably explosive conduct.

Other offenders are also disturbed but they pose lesser risk; more to the point, such offenders lack any "criminal intent" in the conventional sense of the term[1] and suffer from a variety of handicaps that create the adjustment problems under which much of their offense-related behavior can be subsumed. The need for incapacitation is not a pressing goal for such persons, the probability of deterrence is usually negligible (because offenses are at best impulsive), and the concept of equitable

---

[1]Criminal intent (*mens rea*) literally means evil or guilty state of mind and refers to the "mental element" of any offense. Seymour Halleck, a forensic psychiatrist, notes that "in the modern era, our courts have rarely been concerned with the mental state of an offender as an exculpatory factor unless the state can be characterized as a disability sufficiently severe as to meet the legal standards defining insanity. The *mens rea* or mental element accompanying a crime has become narrowly defined, so that simple awareness of conduct, the circumstances under which it occurs, and its probable consequences are usually sufficient to assure intent or guilty mind" (Halleck, 1986, p. 54).

punishment seems inapplicable, given that the harm that is done tends to be a corollary of clumsiness and confusion.

The type of disturbed offender who is not a public menace stands out unhappily as a prison inmate and tends to impress correctional staff as a victim of inappropriate, insensitive, or inhumane sentencing.

In a recent legislative hearing Commissioner Thomas Coughlin, the official in charge of New York prisons, expressed reservations about the disturbed and retarded offenders who are routinely sentenced to prison despite their obvious handicaps.[2] The commissioner advocated increased attention to this problem at the juncture of sentencing.

Coughlin said, in part:

> Pre-trial identification of these individuals should be intensified. A number of mentally retarded inmates with abysmal coping skills have been tried, pled or convicted and sentenced to DOCS [the prison system's] custody. In some instances, these individuals were in noncorrectional custodial care when the crime of conviction was committed. . . .
>
> As an agency, DOCS is not equipped to deal with these individuals. Although the most severe cases are few in number, they account for a disproportionate amount of staff intervention. Their presence in correctional facilities is highly disruptive to both staff and other inmates.
>
> Although [these offenders] have been adjudicated as being legally responsible for their actions, they function at an intellectual and social level well below that of the general inmate population.
>
> I would recommend that the lack of pre-trial services for developmentally disabled individuals be addressed by this committee. The current lack of such services is probably a

---

[2]Throughout this chapter we refer to disturbed offenders. Attention to our illustrations will remind us, however, that many of the inmates we discuss have multiple problems, combining (in varying degrees) serious retardation, learning deficits, and manifestations of mental illness.

contributing factor to the inappropriate incarceration of these individuals.[3]

# The Problem of Routine Adjudication

Our review of prison files confirmed that questions about the appropriateness of a prison sentence for the offender can often be easily raised. Such questions particularly arise in situations in which (a) the offender is clearly not a menace to the public, (b) his or her offense is irrationally motivated or reflects the influence of serious disabilities, (c) the offender remains disturbed in the period following arrest and preceding trial, and (d) he or she continues to be disturbed at intake into the prison.

Examples of cases that meet these four criteria are not hard to locate, though the number of inmates involved is impossible to determine with precision, given that delicate judgments must be exercised and that information on which to base such judgments is often sparse. However, it is the nature of the problem, rather than its magnitude, that must be the first of our concerns.

What is the nature of the problem? It is that some inmates are primarily disturbed and secondarily offenders but have been disposed of as if they were primarily offenders and secondarily (if at all) disturbed. Such actions are not reprehensible

---

[3]Excerpts from the "Testimony of Commissioner Thomas A. Coughlin Before the Assembly Standing Committees on Correction and Mental Health, Mental Retardation and Developmental Disabilities, December 9, 1987," *Public Hearing on Persons With Developmental Disabilities and the Criminal Justice System*. Coughlin advocates expansion of supportive services in the prison but recognizes that "in the short term, pressure [must] be put at the front end of the system, the courts, the prosecutors and the defense bar. Chronic schizophrenics with IQs of 67 should not be allowed to plead guilty and be sent to prison" (Coughlin, personal communication, December 29, 1987). The timeliness of Coughlin's testimony is illustrated by the fact that on the same date on which his remarks were publicized, a newspaper story appeared in which a county judge was quoted as objecting to procedures in the courts that allow "incapacitated persons to avoid criminal proceedings, [creating] a class of persons immune from the criminal justice system and given carte blanch [*sic*] to commit crime" (J. Cather, "Judge Cites Loopholes for Mentally Disturbed," Albany *Knickerbocker News*, December 10, 1987.)

because they deprive mentally ill persons of treatment, given that mental health services are available in many prisons. The problem is rather that fragile individuals must now receive services in a setting that poses tough challenges to the limited coping capacities of nonresilient personalities.[4] This fact holds even when inmates must be hospitalized on one or more occasions, because hospitalization usually provides only a brief respite from prison life, and the commitment process can involve abrupt discontinuities in service levels and environmental demands.[5] Moreover, inmates find eccentric peers unsettling, and prison staff often must respond to disturbed, disruptive behavior with punitive sanctions. These can exacerbate stress levels when maladaptation is already a product, or partially a product, of serious coping deficits.[6]

Among disturbed offenders who are sent to prison, we encounter a variety of problems that are not matched by a corresponding variety of responsive dispositions. Examples of career vignettes illustrate this fact and may help students of corrections understand the dilemma that the system faces in dealing with concrete and specific instances:

> An offender had broken into his neighbor's house. The police discovered that he had stolen a plate of chicken wings, a bottle of wine, and a yellow garbage can. The man was hospitalized because he was "grossly psychotic" and was diagnosed as suffering from paranoid schizophrenia. He was released from the hospital, found competent, and sentenced to prison.

*   *   *

> A man committed a burglary and was surprised in the act but did not flee, although he could have done so. He was

---

[4]Mental health-related adjustment problems of inmates are discussed in Toch, 1992a.

[5]H. Toch, "The Disturbed Disruptive Inmate: Where Does the Bus Stop?" *Journal of Psychiatry and Law,* Fall 1982, 327–349.

[6]For a study that shows that emotionally disturbed prisoners have relatively high rates of prison infractions, see H. Toch & K. Adams, "Pathology and Disruptiveness Among Prison Inmates," *Journal of Research in Crime and Delinquency,* 1986, 23, 7–21.

declared incompetent and hospitalized. He was subsequently released with the diagnosis "brief reactive psychosis in remission, adjustment disorder with emotional features, borderline intellectual functioning, possible mild organic brain syndrome, mixed personality disorder with histrionic and borderline features, history of head trauma," and was sent to prison.

\* \* \*

The offender (who had spent most of his life in institutions) snatched a woman's purse in a subway station. He was hospitalized for 2 years after his arrest, and diagnosed as suffering from schizophrenia, undifferentiated type, chronic. He was finally found competent to be tried, pled guilty to attempted robbery, and was sentenced to prison. In the prison reception center, staff observed that the man "became increasingly withdrawn . . . sat sideways in a chair and barely talked." Later, they recorded that "continued deterioration required transfer to [the hospital]."

Some cases do involve more serious offenses that pose at least the potential for violence at the time they take place. These offenses nonetheless raise the issue of the appropriateness of prison because the offenders' motives on the face of it appear to be clear products of their pathology:

The offender, a mentally disturbed alcoholic, had no history of violence, but threw a bottle at a parked police car, injuring a police officer. He could not account for his offense. While awaiting trial, the man spent 3 months in hospitals, where he was maintained on thorazine. Prison staff found him "lethargic, monosyllabic . . . preoccupied" and referred him for mental health assistance.

\* \* \*

The offender had been a resident of several hospitals. He had been diagnosed as suffering from paranoid schizophrenia and as having drug and alcohol problems. He also had shown a propensity to carry weapons. The offense for which he was imprisoned was one in which the police found him sitting on a curb stuffing a machete down a sewer. The man had a bag with drugs, ammunition, and a handgun, and warned the police, "Don't you put any bullets in the gun." Despite the man's strange obsession, he was found competent and convicted, though diagnosed as "probable mixed personality disorder with schizotype features."

\* \* \*

The offender walked into a store in which his nephew worked, carrying two knives and demanding money. In disarming him, the nephew was wounded. The offender was angry at his nephew, who had complained to the police because his uncle had become convinced that his family was trying to poison him. Unsurprisingly, the man was diagnosed as suffering from paranoid schizophrenia and was hospitalized for 9 months before he was declared competent and convicted. The man arrived in prison, "barely functional but taking his medication," and had to be transferred to the hospital.

The issue that is raised by such cases is not whether prison sentences can be legally justified. The offenders can be legitimately convicted and punished, because their culpability is usually not at issue[7] and they have been found competent. The question, rather, relates to the nature of constraints that impel judges to consider imprisonment as an option, though the record shows that the offender who is being sentenced has obvious mental health problems. In this connection, it is necessary to admit that (a) the dispositional options that are available to the judge may be limited and often (as with offenders

---

[7]We have already noted that the insanity defense does not come into play for the types of offenses with which we are concerned because the defense is, in practice, invoked primarily when a serious offender faces heavy penalties. Seymour Halleck writes that "in our current political climate, pressure is actually growing to avoid examining psychological issues related to culpability by narrowing the insanity defense or doing away with practices associated with the diminished capacity doctrine. . . . By providing a loophole for dealing with the worst possible cases, the insanity defense allows society to acknowledge that at least some offenders are different. This enables society to avoid the formidable problems that would arise if it were to adopt a more flexible approach in assessing the relationship of psychological disability to liability in the case of all offenders" (Halleck, 1986, p. 61).

who are subject to mandatory sentencing provisions) are non-existent, and (b) noncriminal justice alternatives may be sparse, because of the tendency we have noted for agencies to try to select their clients subject to restrictive definitions of eligibility.

Such considerations, however, do not account for the routine use of prison sentences for inmates who are disturbed, which suggests that sentencing rationales or other affirmative considerations must be at work. Closer scrutiny reveals at least two reasons that may inspire judges to consider prison as the milieu of choice for some disturbed persons.

## The Prison as Backup Structure

Prison sentences are sometimes invoked for persons whose distinguishing attribute is their demonstrated incapacity to negotiate life. This observation raises the possibility that prisons may be selected on humanitarian grounds because they furnish sustenance, shelter, and supervision.[8] The third ingredient (supervision) may be particularly prized because it ensures the availability of the client for supportive assistance around the clock. This fact may become a prime consideration when the person who is being sentenced looks particularly helpless or lost:

> The offender had held up a gas station, had "a blank stare on his face," and was incoherent. He was found incompetent to stand trial, and shuttled between jail and hospital for 3 years before he was convicted. He had been raped by

---

[8]The same issue arises for the parole board when it comes to releasing multiply disadvantaged offenders from prison. William McMahon, chairman of the New York State Commission of Correction, testified, for example, that developmentally disabled inmates are "less likely to receive parole, and are more likely to serve longer [prison] terms." He pointed out that "they are perceived as poor candidates, largely because the combination of community-based services considered essential for the success of these individuals are not available in most localities. Thus, the parole board believes that it is protecting the inmate and the community" (W. G. McMahon, *Testimony*, New York State Assembly Standing Committee on Correction; New York State Assembly Standing Committee on Mental Health, Mental Retardation, and Developmental Disabilities, December 9, 1987, p.11).

fellow inmates, both in the jail and the hospital. When interviewed in the prison "he felt there was an umbrella with falling rain over his head." The interviewer's impression was that "schizophrenia is draining all of [the man's] energy" and concluded that he "needs protection or state hospitalization."

\* \* \*

The offender mugged a used car salesman and was arrested. The victim described him as a bum "who was not all there." (The offender's history was that of a chronic hospital patient, who otherwise "leads a nomadic existence.") The man was twice declared incompetent to stand trial. After years of hospitalization he was convicted and sent to prison, where he had to be committed. Prison staff pointed out that the man "doesn't know why he is in prison . . . lies in his cell a lot. Finds it hard to get up or get started. . . . Impresses a man who is content with his psychological condition and has no interest in . . . participating actively in life."

The use of prisons as supervised, multiservice environments may become attractive in cases in which less structured interventions seem to have failed to engage the offender, who appears to require more compliance-oriented supervision, guidance, or support:

The offender had attempted to commit a burglary. He had been resentenced as a probation violator because he was not employed and refused to submit to vocational training. After he arrived in prison, he was referred to mental health classification "due to depression with suicidal ideation."

The probation officer described the offender as "a young man whose emotional problems have played a role in preventing him from complying with the terms and conditions of probation. . . . Curiously, he cooperated with his obligations such that he never missed a probation appointment and basically kept most of his mental health appointments as well. . . . This officer tried repeatedly to discover the source of the defendant's inhibition to look for work or accept vocational training. I can only conclude that the defendant lacks the motivation but also seems to have a genuine fear of academic/training situations which may be difficult for him to overcome. . . . He was told that probation did not exist to allow him to remain at home and do nothing with his life. The crux of the matter is that the defendant has been unwilling or unable to accept this basic premise of probation supervision."

\* \* \*

The offender had been diagnosed as suffering from schizophrenia, chronic, undifferentiated, with mental retardation (his IQ was 67). His offense consisted of a "tug of war" in which he tried to separate a lady from her handbag but failed. The offender had been paroled from prison (where he had spent most of his time hospitalized) to a civil hospital, from which he absconded. He was consequently resentenced to prison, where intake analysts pointed out that he "has a history of being unable to function in the community" and "has requested that the police arrest him simply so he will have somewhere to be cared for." At prison intake the man refused to take medication, requiring an emergency commitment (the man was "eager" to be transferred to the forensic hospital) with the recommendation that "long-term psychiatric residence be provided for him in the facility and upon discharge to the community."

The most direct incentive to imprisoning the offender may exist when he or she has evaded or rejected community services, whose staff cannot enforce their prescriptions. The prison serves as an inviting backup, particularly where backsliding by the offender makes him or her a nuisance or raises the presumption (admittedly often remote) that he or she may reoffend. In such instances the prison is seen not only as having the virtue of being escape-proof but also as serving to interdict trouble the offender seems headed for if left at large:

The man had grown up in foster homes and had graduated to psychiatric settings. He was arrested for a burglary and placed on probation. Within 3 months he violated probation by absconding from a halfway house and not responding to treatment: He had been dismissed from an alcohol program for showing up drunk and not attending group therapy sessions.

* * *

As a child the offender had been taken to a mental health clinic for punching a teacher in the mouth. He was convicted of stealing a motorcycle. He had done so after running away from his seventh foster home placement. He was put on probation and referred to a youth corrections program, from which he also absconded. He was placed in a residential substance abuse program, from which he again absconded, and was sentenced to prison.

* * *

Six years ago the man had committed a violent sex offense and was declared not guilty by reason of insanity. He had been committed to a hospital, from which he was released subject to conditions that included therapeutic involvements. The man's probation was revoked because he [was] "said to have not taken his medication on several occasions, to have missed two-thirds of his rehabilitation classes and about one-third of his therapy appointments." Prison officials found the man "distant, removed, unkempt" and "not always in touch with reality." They committed him to the forensic hospital.

* * *

The man arrived in prison 10 years after he had committed his offense. The offense was an assault. The man had been involved in a family fight and was ordered [by the police] to sleep in a hallway. He knifed a neighbor who objected to his presence, was placed on probation, and was later hospitalized. He was imprisoned after he rejected the hospital's discharge plan, indicating that he would prefer living in men's shelters. He arrived in prison actively psychotic and was transferred to the forensic hospital.

## Prison as a Secure Hospital

Some disturbed persons evoke worry about risks that relate to their self-care, including posing a danger to self; others spark concerns about the milieus in which they must function, which they can disrupt with noisy, unseemly, or destructive behavior. Such concerns are particularly inspired by offenders whose symptoms include a history of acting out, both in institutions and the community:

The offender was a patient who was prone to episodes of bizarre explosive outbursts. He had been hospitalized for behavior such as running through the street nude proclaiming that he was Jesus Christ. He had also been arrested for unprovoked assaults. Jail staff noted that "he goes nuts and throws things, sets fires and talks constantly. . . . He said he was a voodoo doctor and stood naked in his cell."

\* \* \*

The man was convicted for waking up residents of a house and shouting at their windows that he needed money for drugs. The victims instructed the man to come to their front door, where the police arrested him. After the man arrived in prison, prison staff complained that he was "hostile, verbally aggressive, and emotionally unstable."

\* \* \*

The man had been convicted for an incident that took place two years previously in which he set his apartment on fire. He spent much of the intervening time in a hospital, from which he was gratefully discharged with the diagnosis schizophrenia, chronic, in remission. As soon as he entered prison, the man proved disruptive, "disturbing the entire block and staff." He could not be processed because he "shouted throughout the [intake] interview" and refused to take medication. He had to be transferred to the hospital.

\* \* \*

The offender committed a mugging during which he "made stabbing motions to the shoulder of a female victim." The victim described the offender as "somewhat off." The man had a history of assaulting his mother, which had invited multiple hospital commitments. The diagnosis assigned to him was schizophrenia, paranoid type, chronic, with acute exacerbation. In the hospital he engaged in disruptive behavior, such as burning holes in sheets and setting his mattress on fire.

After the man arrived in the prison, staff wrote that "his adjustment is marked by continuous hallucinations with which he dialogues while in his cell, and extreme mood swings." The man sang, sometimes loudly, in his cell. Staff wrote, half facetiously, that "a significant feature of a positive nature is that he has a beautiful singing voice which impresses all who hear him."

The notion that prisons may be envisioned as secure hospitals or hospital-equivalents is, in the abstract, implausible. If one does not consider this possibility, however, it becomes hard to explain why hospital offenses with clear psychotic overtones result in imprisonment instead of in the upgrading of security arrangements within the hospital. The same point holds for disturbed persons who prove troublesome in community settings but are imprisoned rather than institutionalized in more treatment-relevant settings:

The man was convicted of a robbery after he was declared incompetent on five occasions, but later found competent. He served 6 years, mostly in prison hospital settings.

After leaving prison, the man was sent to a civil hospital for a 15-day evaluation. He became disgruntled when his release was delayed and assaulted a fellow patient who "said the wrong thing at the wrong time." He explained that "something snapped." The man was sent back to prison, where staff concluded that "he will need ongoing psychiatric care."

\* \* \*

The offender was a badly retarded young man who set his bed on fire because he was "angry at his brother." He was charged with committing arson but was hospitalized. While he was in the hospital, the man fondled a female patient and was again arrested. He was found fit to proceed and was convicted of his sex offense.

\* \* \*

The offender was a retarded schizophrenic. He had a long history of hospitalizations and brushes with the law. He had attempted suicide by choking himself and jumping out of a second-story window. In the hospital, he entered the rooms of other patients looking for money, took a wallet, and was caught. He was declared incompetent but was later sent to prison on a guilty plea for attempted burglary. The prison found that "obviously, he is a disturbed psychiatric patient" and committed him to the forensic hospital. Staff observed that "he prefers the role of patient and is a difficult client whose prognosis is bleak."

\* \* \*

The offender was a mentally retarded man who had been convicted of rape after engaging in intercourse with a 14-year-old agency client who "apparently [was] a willing participant." The man had sustained brain damage as the result of an accident in which he was involved as a child. He had subsequently experienced "nervous breakdowns," had attempted suicide, and had been diagnosed as suffering from a schizoid personality disorder.

A final category of imprisoned offenders enhances the plausibility of the "secure hospital" image of the prison, because the offenders at issue are persons who are imprisoned after becoming destructively refractory in other settings. These offenders are not only difficult to manage, but also react violently to efforts to manage them. The other side of the coin is that these persons are not premeditatedly violent but are clearly disturbed at the time they pose a danger to their treaters. The relevancy of this second fact to sentencing authorities recedes, however, given the safety concerns of treatment staff, which seem to underlie their urgent or plaintive demand that their clients be sent to prison.

The offender was a severely retarded man who had become convinced that staff of a mental health program were laughing at him. He set fire to the agency's building and tried to burn down its van. He threw bottles at agency staff and arrived there with a knife in his pocket announcing that he intended to stab someone. He also threatened to rape a social worker who was attached to the agency.

The man was sent to jail, where he was repeatedly raped. He was declared competent, pled guilty to Arson 2, and was sent to prison with a long sentence.

\* \* \*

The man was a former hospital patient who was imprisoned for arson after he set fire to a group therapy room in an outpatient clinic where he was treated. While he was being arrested the man was described as "rambling continuously." He made statements such as "it was a political arrest," "there is a question of constitutionality involved here; I didn't want to gain any more weight," "it was all after the fact, and there is defamation involved," "I got lonely and I wanted to be with my people at the clinic," and "I never got over the first hump." The man was subjected to competency examinations but was declared competent, convicted, and imprisoned. In the prison, according to staff, he "suddenly experienced a full psychotic breakdown."

\* \* \*

The offender had been sentenced to probation for assaulting his girlfriend. At the time he was diagnosed as experiencing a "depressive reaction with paranoid features." Six years later, the man had a psychotic breakdown after he was fired from his job and evicted from his room for "bizarre" behavior. While he was disturbed he entered his probation office and refused to leave. He ransacked the office, trapped the staff behind desks, and threatened to assault them. He was restrained and removed from the premises. His probation was revoked, and he was resentenced to prison, where he arrived medicated and was judged "friendly and cooperative."

\* \* \*

The man had a long career as a hospital patient. His offense took place in the hospital in which he was confined. There he assaulted a psychiatrist, breaking a chair over his head. He also destroyed windows at the nurses' station before he was subdued. In the past, he had assaulted a social worker and tried to choke an attendant. In jail, the man attacked a corrections supervisor, who lost two teeth. In prison, he threatened to "deck" correction officers at the reception center. Staff wrote that he "impressed as having limited intellect, horizons and mental sophistication."

# What Is to Be Done?

The illustrations we have provided document our impression that disturbed persons are sometimes adjudicated in surprisingly routine fashion as they are sentenced to imprisonment. We infer that the probability of such prison sentences is enhanced in cases in which offenders have failed to respond to community programs or have proved disruptive to community settings. In neither case can the concern of sentencing authorities be regarded as misplaced, but it is also not obvious that prison is the most appropriate solution to these concerns.

The difficulty lies in the fact that the hypothetical type of setting that does address concerns about the need for support and structure for disturbed persons does not at present exist, and public pressures are not being exerted to create such a setting.[9] This indifference is understandable because (a) the types of persons we have described are socially undesirable individuals who have no constituency, (b) they do not fit neatly

---

[9]This point is applicable to seriously retarded offenders, for whom new types of facilities may have to be envisaged. This point has been made by (among others) Beverly Rowan, in a position paper prepared for the President's Committee on Mental Retardation. Rowan wrote that "Special facilities should be created to handle mentally retarded offenders in a more intelligent, humane, and effective manner. These facilities should be more secure than state institutions for the retarded, but free from the perverse influences found in standard training schools or prisons. They should be located near institutions of higher learning so that students, professors, and qualified corrections people will be available to assist with habilitation problems" (Rowan, B. A., Principal Paper, Correction Section, in M. Kindred, et al. (eds.), *The Mentally Retarded Citizen and the Law* [New York: Free Press, 1976, p. 674).

into service-related classifications,[10] (c) once offenders are in prison, they are invisible to the public, as are the problems they experience, and (d) prisons are institutions of last resort; they have the obligation to deal with their inmates, even if they have proven to be inhospitable and thankless clients elsewhere. The dilemma is further compounded by the fact that a problem person can become a correctional client for life on the installment plan, because once he or she has been in prison his or her chances of being recycled into prison are enhanced.

Considering the problems created for the prison by nonserious disturbed offenders and the unimpressive, checkered careers that precede their imprisonment, must we accept their prevalence as prison inmates? Prison officials do not think so, for their agency's sake and that of their charges. Judges should probably not think so either, because the integrity of their profession is demeaned whenever they send a person to prison by default rather than because he or she belongs there.

Admittedly, it is easier to delineate the current situation than it is to envisage its resolution. The best we can hope for is that the future of forensic psychiatry and psychology may come to include more serious input into sentencing and involvement in the creation of programs that can divert offenders before or after they are sentenced.[11] There is an obvious need

---

[10]Commissioner Thomas Coughlin noted, for example, that "it is abundantly clear that a person suffering from mental retardation and some form of mental illness is the bain of everyone's existence. The retardation people point to the mental illness and throw their hands up. The mental health people point to the retardation and do the same. . . . The current practice of labelling everything just reinforces this process. I once proposed a State Department of Dual Diagnosis, so that no one could hide behind a label" (Coughlin, personal communication, December 29, 1987). McMahon (see note 8) concurred. He testified that "in the case of the dual diagnosed, it is difficult to access services because (agencies) have difficulty agreeing upon primary responsibility." He cited as an added problem the fact that "residential and treatment programs, in general, avoid persons with a criminal record." (McMahon, 1987, p. 9)

[11]The most modest possible arrangement that can address the problem of sentencing involves screening suspected arrestees before they are charged. E. Hochstedler described the work of a Mental Health Screening Unit operating out of a Wisconsin prosecutor's office ("Criminal Prosecution of the Mentally Disordered: A Descriptive Analysis," *Criminal Justice Review*, 1987, 12, 1–11). She observed that prosecutors may deliberately charge offenders

for arrangements or systems in the community that will willingly accommodate persons who now fall between the cracks, most notably those impaired, disabled, and disturbed men and women who inappropriately become correctional clients because we honestly do not know what else to do with them.

---

as a means of imposing treatment arrangements where such persons would not be civilly committable. She also noted that "judges show leniency at the final disposition to those who receive treatment, either as a condition of pretrial release or while being examined for competency to stand trial" (p. 10).

# The Extremely Disturbed and Extremely Violent Offender: The Problem of Programming

In a sense, the dictum "history is destiny" provides an empirically testable hypothesis in studying individual careers. Some individuals will be found to behave in patterned, redundant ways, and others will show the ability to change for the better (or worse) over time. Recidivism refers to one form of predestination—not escaping from a propensity to engage in undesirable conduct.

Whether people who have a history of emotional problems will remain "disturbed" is a crucial issue for those who deal with such people. Historically derived measures that describe continuing patterns of maladaptation carry substantial implications regarding the failure of prevention or the need for further treatment of chronic patients.

We have followed all of our disturbed offenders into the prison to ascertain whether they still require mental health services when they arrive there. The summary results of this inquiry (Table 9.1) show that only 4% of inmates who have not received mental health services in the community will require outpatient services or hospitalization in prison. This modest figure compares to 43% for the inmates who have mental health histories and 36% for inmates with "mixed" histories that include substance abuse services. Substance abuse histories alone yield a 10% service delivery figure.

Commitments to the prison psychiatric hospital, which presuppose very serious illness, are called for with 1 out of 7

**Table 9.1**

*Mental Health Services Required During First 2 Years of Incarceration by Offenders in Our Four Samples*

| The offender's mental health history | Mental health services provided | | | |
| --- | --- | --- | --- | --- |
| | Screening by staff | Outpatient services | Hospitalization Single | Multiple |
| No history (*n* = 544) | 16.9% | 3.7% | 0.02% | 0% |
| Substance abuse (*n* = 83) | 18.1 | 9.6 | 0 | 0 |
| Psychiatric (*n* = 540) | 20.4 | 29.3 | 7.2 | 6.3 |
| Combined substance abuse and psychiatric (*n* = 141) | 21.3 | 29.8 | 4.3 | 1.4 |

members of the psychiatric sample, but only 1 out of 20 inmates with "mixed" histories. One lone inmate in the comparison sample (out of the total group of 544) required hospitalization.

These results are quite surprising given that a large number of inmates in the four groups are screened, usually at intake and for the parole board. We also know that guards, who refer most inmates for service by mental health staff, have no access to mental health files.

Which are the disturbed inmates who need assistance in prison? Several clusters disproportionately account for mental health clients (Table 9.2). Heading the list are the Acute Disturbed Exploders, 39% of whom will be hospitalized. We recall that this group, on the average, has experienced extensive mental health involvements, particularly in the recent past. Its violence is often eccentric (see chapter 7) and is always extreme, though the offenders have no violence histories and low arrest records. In this respect these inmates differ from Chronic Disturbed Exploders, whom they otherwise resemble. This Exploder group—which we have described as one of extreme violent recidivists with long-term mental health difficulties—has less serious problems in prison, although half of the group (51%) needs hospital or other mental health services. The third most violent cluster in the sample is that of Disturbed Sex Offenders, 26% of whom are hospitalized. The group is one that recorded the third highest rate of eccentric

**Table 9.2**

*Mental Health Services Required During the First 2 Years of Incarceration by Offenders with Mental Health Histories*

|  | Mental health service provided | | | |
|---|---|---|---|---|
|  | Screening by staff | Outpatient services | Hospitalization Single | Multiple |
| Psychiatric history offenders |  |  |  |  |
| Impulsive burglar | 36% | 21% | 5% | 0% |
| Impulsive robber | 26 | 18 | 5 | 0 |
| Long-term explosive robber | 25 | 30 | 0 | 4 |
| Young explosive robber | 38 | 15 | 0 | 0 |
| Mature mugger | 9 | 32 | 5 | 5 |
| Acute disturbed exploder | 16 | 25 | 25 | 14 |
| Chronic disturbed exploder | 13 | 42 | 6 | 3 |
| Disturbed sex offender | 17 | 32 | 9 | 17 |
| Composite career offender | 17 | 25 | 7 | 8 |
| Compensatory offender | 21 | 37 | 11 | 0 |
| Combined substance abuse and psychiatric history offenders |  |  |  |  |
| Dependent burglar | 20% | 25% | 0% | 0% |
| Skid row robber | 44 | 22 | 0 | 0 |
| Skid row exploder | 14 | 31 | 9 | 3 |
| Compounded career offender | 14 | 32 | 3 | 0 |
| Multiproblem robber | 29 | 32 | 7 | 0 |

offenses, and its members have a substantial history of mental health involvements but a limited offense history.

Our findings are dramatic and consistent: Individuals who are disturbed in the prison after they offend tend to be disturbed before they offend, and when we look at the samples in more detail we discover that the most disturbed inmates have committed the most extreme violence and, mostly, the "craziest" violence. This trend continues on inspection: The fourth most disturbed group (the Compensatory Career Offenders) proves to be the fourth most violent group, and the most disturbed cluster in the mixed sample (Skid Row Exploders) is responsible for the most serious violence in the sample. We conclude that there exists a clear-cut type that we can call the Seriously Disturbed Violent Offender, meaning an offender who is extremely violent when he or she offends and is chronically disturbed. This chapter will deal with the question of what to do with such offenders.

# The Insanity Defense Revisited

If the insanity defense were more frequently invoked, fewer seriously disturbed violent offenders would be in prison because they could lay claim to being adjudged insane. This is so because their mental health problems are mostly contemporary with their crimes, which at least makes it reasonable for psychiatric testimony to be invited. The offenses the group commits are also consequential, which makes an expensive defense more cost-effective.

If the offenders we describe had offended in continental Europe, many would be acquitted of their crimes because continental insanity rules are at times broader than those that fall in the McNaghten tradition.[1] These European offenders would not walk free, of course, any more than they would if they were acquitted in the United States. Insanity acquittees everywhere tend to earn terms of hospitalization, which are less determinate than prison sentences. In practice this means that hospital terms may prove longer or shorter than prison terms, but one cannot predict whether they will be longer or shorter. Civil libertarians focus on the possibility that hospital terms can prove longer than the prison sentences offenders would otherwise serve. The average member of the public, on the other hand, worries that hospitalization may result in earlier release, with the double result that the offender will be insufficiently punished and will pose the danger of renewed predation. The public also does not trust hospital psychiatrists (who are presumed to have offender-centered concerns) to consider the interests of crime victims.

---

[1]In Norway an offender who is known to have been psychotic at the time of his or her offense is found not guilty even if there is no alleged connection between his or her psychosis and the offense. Other European countries use standards that approximate the Durham rule (see M. Roth & R. Bluglass, eds., *Psychiatry, Human Rights and the Law* (Cambridge, England: Cambridge University Press, 1985).

Less controversy would occur if the insanity defense were invoked primarily for nonserious offenses (see chapter 8), because in such offenses no victims have been hurt. The absence of injuries that cry out for redress would make it easier for the courts to center on the offenders' state of mind and to consider community treatment for them. At worst, offenders could always be subjected to short-term hospitalization, with discharge criteria uninflated by public concern, revulsion, and risk considerations. Because substantial penalties would not be at issue, it might also be possible to make the dispositional process, in practice, less adversarial, dispensing with battles of experts and working out solutions through plea bargains.

The atrophy over time of the insanity defense in trials of serious violent offenders has created a situation that accomplishes two results: It makes the amount of time the offender serves more predictable and reassures the public that offenders will "pay" for their crimes. On the other side of the ledger, the nonuse of insanity pleas has had consequences that muddy the waters of public policy. Among these are (a) the fact that persons are convicted who do not resemble the coldblooded offenders envisaged in statutes and thus could in theory be held nonresponsible for their crimes; (b) the fact that there are only evanescent differences between many persons who are convicted and insanity acquittees, which raises the specter of discrimination based on the availability of defense funds or other unfair considerations; and (c) the point we have already discussed, that the influx of disturbed offenders makes prisons repositories of inmates for whom prisons were not ideally designed.

In the long run, to be sure, the nonuse of the insanity defense makes little difference. Disturbed offenders need mental health services no matter where they are sent, and such services must be provided by mental health staff in one setting or the other. Unsurprisingly, most mental health staff prefer to work in hospitals, but close reflection might tell them that the prison may have some advantages as a place in which to treat violence-prone persons. Among these advantages are that prisons are unquestionably secure, which means that staff and fellow residents are protected from the violence of explosive inmates, and that the escape of such inmates is unlikely. Mental health staff in the prison also need not decide when to release potential troublemakers into the community, which is a "damned if you do, damned if you don't" type of assignment. On the other hand, a mental health staff member who works in the prison is a guest of prison officials, whose concerns must be respected.[2]

Mental health staff may also find the prison discomfitting because prisons are self-consciously nonrehabilitative. This is so despite the fact that corrections has not been able to stake out a positive mission other than keeping offenders off the streets.[3] Given the obvious ambiguity of the prison's goal, the mental health staff members, whose role is uncertain to begin with, have an even harder time defining a defensible mission for themselves.

The authors of a recent survey of prison mental health services wrote that

> strong disagreement still exists in a number of areas regarding what services are proper and appropriate for prisoners who desire or are in need of mental health services. Those with a client-centered perspective operate out of a totally different philosophy from those with an institution-centered perspective. One extreme regards the mentally disordered prisoner as entitled to the care and privacy one would enjoy in the private and civilian sector; the other, focused on maintaining order and discipline in a large cor-

---

[2]An example of mental health staff's concern with this issue is a prison standard proposed by the American Association of Correctional Psychologists, which reads, "The psychologists, and the staff activities for which these individuals are responsible, [must] have professional autonomy regarding psychological services, within the constraints of appropriate security regulations applicable to all institutional personnel, such regulations being in conformity with the written directives of institutions and or headquarters" (American Association of Correctional Psychologists, "Standards for Psychological Services in Adult Jails and Prison," *Criminal Justice and Behavior*, 1980, 7, 89.

[3]We have mentioned elsewhere that "though nature abhors a vacuum, corrections lives with one in disquietingly unnatural comfort. The rejection of rehabilitative goals has created a reluctance to define a new mission. The closest approximation we have makes prisons the handmaidens of dispassionately vengeful courts" (H. Toch, "Quo Vadis?" *Canadian Journal of Criminology*, 1984, 26, 511.

rectional setting, desires as little differentiation as possible in the administration of rules and sanctions. If we add to this the bureaucratic infighting endemic within and between agencies, it is hardly surprising that no one has come to total agreement on the subject. Without consensus on policy, however, and without the dollars to back up the policy, major conflicts break out among the personnel actually charged with prisoner management, and the disparity between service levels at different institutions grows.[4]

## The Disturbed Offender in Hospitals

The problems associated with mental health services in prisons may be serious, but one must recognize that mental hospitals have counterpart problems in dealing with serious violent offenders.

Mental hospitals, like prisons, are in a continuing state of transition. The transitions of prisons and hospitals, however, are opposite, or at least disparate. Prisons are expanding their purview and are holding convicts for longer periods of time. Hospitals are shrinking their in-house clientele and are releasing patients as quickly as they can, continuing to treat them (or referring them for treatment) on an outpatient basis. Today's resident hospital population is usually more seriously disturbed, and the hospital's aim is to "stabilize" the condition of patients so it can be dealt with—in theory at least—in the community.

The disturbed offender fits uncomfortably into the contemporary hospital's mission. For one, the serious offender cannot be quickly stabilized and released under medication because the community will not tolerate the risk this entails. As a consequence the disturbed offender has to remain on hospital wards for long periods of time, until he or she is certified as nondangerous as well as nondisturbed. In the past, this would have been par for the psychiatric course, but today it means

---

[4]K. H. Gohlke, "Executive Summary," in National Institute of Corrections, ed., *Source Book on the Mentally Disordered Prisoner* (Washington, DC: Department of Justice, 1985), p. 3.

that offenders may be surrounded by persons who are more disturbed than they are, while in the prison the offender's peers would be nondisturbed offenders serving sentences as long as (or longer than) the offender's own. In the hospital the offender also carries the stigma of his or her offense. Mental health staff who work in hospitals are apt to be intimidated by violence and may approach the offender uneasily and with fear.[5] This creates problems for staff morale, but it can also affect patient care because staff apprehension leads to over-medication as a reassuring "management" tool.[6]

---

[5]J. R. Lion & S. A. Pasternak, "Countertransference Reactions to Violent Patients," *American Journal of Psychiatry*, 1973, *130*, 207–210. The fears of mental health staff may sometimes be reinforced by the advice that these staff receive from correctional experts. A sample injunction is the following: "The psychiatrist should be keenly aware of his own safety. When unfamiliar with an inmate who has been recently violent, he should inquire into his present behavior before seeing him. If there is any uncertainty regarding the inmate's present state of control, he should not hesitate to interview the inmate in the doorway of his cell with an officer at arm's length." (U.S. Bureau of Prisons: *A Handbook of Correctional Psychiatry*, [Washington, DC: Department of Justice, 1968], vol. 1, p. 20).

The same source also tells its readers that "failure to face his fear and hostility will lead the psychiatrist to reject the violent inmate and withdraw from the focal activity of the prison. Facing these fears partially can lead to an over-identification with the inmate and diatribes against "inhumane" treatment. Facing his fears fully, however, will allow him to help the inmate and the staff" (U.S. Bureau of Prisons, 1968, p. 21).

[6]The author of a survey of mental health services points out that "many prison medical staff members admit that medication is used as much for custody purposes as for medical purposes" (R. Wilson, "Who Will Care for the 'Mad and Bad'?" *Corrections Magazine*, February 1980, p. 10). A similar impression prevails in other settings in which psychotropic medication is used. An authority on medication in civil hospitals, for example, records, "This author has often seen the "snow phenomenon" whereby a patient is viewed as exceedingly dangerous and assaultive, given large amounts of medication, and secluded and put in what is tantamount to sensory deprivation. Fearful of being in a locked room, the patient's behavior escalates and becomes loud and boisterous. Nursing staff become more frightened and ask the doctor to prescribe more medication. The medication is administered parenterally without any verbal discussion, the patient's condition worsens leading to more medication, and a vicious cycle ensues. This situation can be reversed both by taking the patient out of seclusion and lowering his medication" (J. R. Lion, "Special Aspects of Psychopharmacology," in J. R. Lion & W. H. Reid, *Assaults Within Psychiatric Facilities* [New York: Grune & Stratton, 1963], p. 290).

Medication is a key issue in hospitals because psychotropic drugs are the therapeutic modality of choice in most psychiatric settings. This is not in itself a problem, but it becomes a problem if treatment goals are envisioned for the offender other than reducing or deleting the symptoms of his or her psychosis. If there is a subsidiary concern with contributing to offender socialization, the hospital has some advantages over the prison—it can be more democratic, for instance—but it has particularly serious disadvantages, such as the fact that one cannot rehearse prosocial living in a place where the prevailing concern is with humane storage pending the elimination of florid symptomatology.

## The Disturbed Offender in Prison

The other side of the same coin is that prisons are not designed to accommodate psychotics, who are apt to behave in eccentric ways. Two features of prison pose particular problems for the disturbed inmate. The first is that prisons insist on at least a minimal amount of participation in prison routines, which include self-care, following instructions, and involvement in programs. Opting out of prison life results in an accumulation of write-ups or disciplinary infractions, which invite punishment no matter how "crazily" motivated the inmate's lapses may be.[7]

A second feature of prison is that it requires close cohabitation among individuals who must depend on each other not to increase the discomforts built into the prison experience or to pose risks of harm to their peers. Eccentricity—especially unpredictable eccentricity—creates discomfort for prison staff and inmates because it makes the environment less dependable. Disturbed offenders also invite predation from fellow inmates when they appear vulnerable, or pose risks to inmates and staff when they unpredictably explode.[8]

Another problem is one of logistics. Disturbed persons often

---

[7]H. Toch & K. Adams, with J. D. Grant, 1989.
[8]Toch & Adams, with Grant, 1989; see also Toch, 1975.

require gradations of mental health assistance. If one is serious about responding to changing needs of clients in any routinized setting this means that one must shuttle them from place to place, so as to adjust their regime and social milieu to accommodate the changes in their condition. This becomes a particularly serious issue when a prisoner needs hospitalization. Hospital commitments must usually be approved by the courts and require shifting jurisdiction from corrections to mental health staff. Among the typical squabbles this invites is that hospitals may regard some of the inmates referred to them as insufficiently disturbed, and prisons may view the inmates as insufficiently recovered when they return.[9]

Many prison systems do not have a range of options to accommodate offenders whose conditions fall short of meeting hospital commitment criteria. And later, when such inmates are moved from the hospital to a different setting, the sharp transition can undo whatever benefit hospitalization has offered because stabilization (the standard goal of inpatient treatment) presupposes aftercare, including outpatient services.[10] In the community the unavailability of lower-order mental health assistance contributes to homelessness and to vagrancy. In the prison, unrecovered patients can often become disciplinary problems, and this creates a vicious cycle if punishment exacerbates the mental health problems of some of the inmates.

Above all, prisons must decide to what extent they are in

---

[9]Wilson wrote that "a common criticism by psychiatrists of prison administrators is that they want the doctors to handle the problem cases, which are not always psychiatric problems" (Wilson, 1980, p. 14). The other side of the coin is that mental health staff may classify a disturbed offender as "not a psychiatric problem" if he or she appears overly threatening. Wilson quoted an official of the American Medical Association, for example, who admitted that "the mental health administrators don't want to monkey around with acting-out clients, so they send them back" (p. 8).

[10]Commuting between hospital and prison settings is referred to as "bus therapy," especially by observers who see the practice as detrimental. Freeman, Dinitz, and Conrad, for example, wrote that "until courts can establish rules to govern the disposition of such inmates their programming will be punctuated by bus movements which are clearly not intended for their benefit" (R. A. Freeman, S. Dinitz, & J. P. Conrad, "A Look at the Dangerous Offender and Society's Effort to Control Him," *American Journal of Correction*, January–February 1977, 25–31, p. 30).

the business of providing mental health assistance. Such a resolve, however, is not simple because the line between rehabilitation and mental health services is hard to draw. The courts have determined that inmates have a "right to treatment" to preserve health, but it is not clear how much "mental health" is included in the "health" that must be preserved in the prison. The legal formula implies that the goal of the therapy one must provide to inmates is to help them reduce symptoms that disable them and make them suffer.[11] But substandard mental health is a continuum of symptoms or suffering, and lines can be more or less generously drawn. Another problem is that there is an unascertainable connection between the offenses of inmates and their psychological handicaps, which obfuscates the line between correctional goals and treatment. Emotional problems can also affect prison adjustment, which is a concern of prison administrators. Even if a mental health staff member did not wish to assist the guards or the warden to preserve security in the prison, it is hard to envision successful therapy that would not improve prison behavior. Therapy translates into management because the inmate's difficulties are observed and addressed in encounters that arise in the prison. If the inmate becomes better adjusted, he or she should plausibly become a better functioning inmate.

Putting aside issues of mental health goals, we can consider what some of the choices would be for corrections if it wished

---

[11]In discussing the rights of disturbed prison inmates, F. Cohen points out that, "a constitutional right to treatment might be fashioned as a right to the most thorough diagnosis and the most skillful treatment available for the particular condition. A mentally retarded inmate might be entitled to such habilitative efforts as will maximize his human potential. On the other hand, such rights could be constructed to require only that some medical or professional judgment be brought to bear to identify and then to provide minimally acceptable care in order to avoid death or needless suffering. . . . The constitutional right to treatment is much closer to the second construction than the first. The most important point we must make here is that constitutional minima in this (or any other) area must not be confused with desirable governmental policy, desirable professional practices or standards, or desirable penal practices or standards" (F. Cohen, "Legal Issues and the Mentally Disordered Offender," in National Institute of Corrections, eds., Sourcebook on the Mentally Disordered Prisoner [Washington, DC: Department of Justice, 1985], p. 33).

to create a program that met the needs of the disturbed violent inmate, those of the prison, and those of the society to which the inmate must return.

# A Program for Disturbed Violent Offenders

Any program for disturbed violent offenders must recognize that this group of offenders will contain persons with chronic mental health problems. However, this does not mean that all offenders in high-risk groups have chronic problems or that chronic problems are problems that remain at the same level of seriousness all the time. The approach to the offender must, therefore, be open-ended, invoking mental health assistance as it is needed and when it is needed. Beyond this requisite there are some questions that any program designer must resolve, and the answers to these questions are less clear-cut.

## Homogeneity of the Population

There are advantages in working with a group of offenders who have similar problems, such as the members of any of our clusters. These advantages increase if one's task includes rehabilitative concerns, because homogeneity means that deficits are similar in kind. Other problems one may wish to address can also become more comparable if one's clients have reached a commensurate stage of life and if they share similarities of background. The most noteworthy advantages accrue if one envisions a therapeutic community in which pathology is confronted, peer interactions are important, and the compatibility of inmates matters.[12]

Homogeneity, however, reduces size, and where prisons are crowded few systems can afford small, specialized programs. A compromise structure involves combining clusters, which can be subdivided for certain purposes (such as treatment) and recombined for others. One advantage of this model is that an

---

[12]H. Toch, ed., *Therapeutic Communities in Corrections* (New York: Praeger, 1980).

offender may be assigned to a group concerned with violence (in which Sex Offender A may be paired with Sex Offenders B, C, and D because they share the same offense background) and to a different group concerned with mental health-related issues (in which Offender A might be paired with Offenders E, F, and G, who are schizophrenics in remission or have chronic substance abuse problems). More heterogeneous groups can also be formed around issues of living in a prison unit or for helping staff run a program or around activities such as academic self-study.

## Segregation of the Program Population

The inmates we have described often cause problems, and have problems, in the prison. The fact that the inmates are at times troublesome, disturbed, or both, argues for a separate setting—even a separate facility—which can be part of the system and at the same time have a measure of autonomy. One advantage of autonomy is that it introduces flexibility, if one wants or needs it. Some prison routines—such as the operation of the disciplinary process—could thus be relaxed if necessary.[13] More important, in a special setting one can afford tolerance of deviance, which is difficult in the prison. A special setting, however, must not be too special. If one assigns an inmate to a program known to contain eccentric or dangerous individuals one risks stigmatizing him or her or creating a ghetto from which it is difficult to escape.

---

[13]The administrators of an interdisciplinary program for disturbed offenders in Pennsylvania provide a case in point. They wrote, "At one point the Bureau of Corrections wished to implement a procedure whereby hospital staff would be required to formally report any infraction of the rules to the prison for inclusion on the patient's record. Treatment staff felt this procedure would be countertherapeutic in that such infractions, which are often a product of the patient's illness, if reported, would interfere with treatment processes aimed at eventual release via parole. An agreement was eventually reached whereby minor infractions would continue to be handled by the unit disciplinary committee and not entered on the record, while major infractions (serious fights, escapes, etc.) would require formal reporting to Corrections" (M. K. Cooke & G. Cooke, "An Integrated Program for Mentally Ill Offenders: Description and Evaluation," *International Journal of Offender Therapy and Comparative Criminology*, 1982, 26, pp. 53–54).

## Ingress and Egress in a Program

The problem of ghetto existence can be partly addressed by regarding program participation as time-bound and as a phase of the inmate's career defined by his or her progress. An offender can become a program resident at prison intake, or later, if staff feel that he or she can benefit from special placement. The presumption would be that the inmate can graduate from the program or be transferred to some other program when he or she is ready to make the transition.[14]

The virtue of this approach is that it expects and accommodates change. It permits "mainstreaming" of inmates whose problems dissipate over time but allows for formal mental health assistance, or more specialized services, for inmates who cannot adjust to a midrange program.

## Staff Teaming

Programs for inmates who are disturbed require involvement of mental health staff. Such staff may be invoked for individual inmates as needed, but this arrangement invites jurisdictional problems between types of staff and compartmentalizes services. A more integrated solution is to use teams that include mental health workers and correctional officers.[15] Staff of both kinds benefit from such teaming because it offers cross-fertilization and democratization of roles. The inmate also benefits because the stigma of labeling him or her as sick is reduced. Where all staff deal with all inmates no lines need to be drawn

---

[14]Fairweather and his colleagues emphasized that this requisite is essential to any mental health programs that play a transitional role between the hospital and the streets (G. W. Fairweather, D. H. Sanders, D. L. Cressler, & H. Maynard, *Community Life for the Mentally Ill* [Chicago: Aldine, 1969]).

[15]The Pennsylvania program referred to in note 13 described its staffing as follows: "[The program] was administered jointly by the Bureau of Corrections and the Department of Welfare. Correctional personnel included an on-site full-time project coordinator, as well as the security staff (correctional officers). Hospital personnel included psychiatric aides, nurses, psychiatrists, psychologists, social workers and auxiliary treatment personnel. Hospital and correctional personnel jointly comprised the treatment team" (Cooke & Cooke, 1982, p. 53. Also see Toch, 1980).

(or emphasized) that differentiate "disturbed" and "nondisturbed" inmates, which is in any event an artificial distinction.

## Building in a Research Component

We began by noting that disturbed violent offenders are a badly unexplored entity, and we admit that we have far from exhausted the topic as a subject of research. Any concentrated availability of a study population of such offenders provides an opportunity to add to our knowledge about this important subject. An officially designated research mission can enhance the role of a prison program because staff can see themselves serving a larger cause than the program itself. This sort of mission also underlines the importance of keeping records, such as of interview summaries (or transcripts) and the minutes of group meetings.[16] A research function can even appeal to inmates, who can rationalize that they are helping others by providing data (with appropriate assurance of confidentiality) when they share intimate problems and concerns.

## Providing Treatment

We have not said much about our program's treatment goals, but we can delineate some options. These options include attending to mental health problems and reducing violence recidivism (which entails studying violence), but one can also

---

[16]Such information can prove useful in extending knowledge about the causal connections between emotional problems and violent acts. One author concerned with such links, for example, concluded that "extensive accounts—both spontaneous and structured—from the subject and as many other sources as possible of a violent act, the mental state around the time of that act and states of both pre-act health and social adjustment are thus all important. Collection and integration of many such accounts, and comparison of these between schizophrenic and non-psychotic groups will clarify ways in which the illness has been important and, I believe, identify subgroups who are particularly violence prone, perhaps improving our predictions about the risks of violence. Only then can the role of psychiatrists and of available treatments in managing the violence, even of a psychotic group, be clarified. (P. Taylor, "Schizophrenia and Violence," in J. Gunn & D. P. Farrington, eds., *Abnormal Offenders, Delinquency and the Criminal Justice System* [London: Wiley, 1982], p. 281).

try to reach some more general goal, such as enhancing living skills, which encompasses narrower and more specific objectives.

Recidivism reduction is no doubt the riskiest goal one can claim, and the hardest to defend. For one, some would argue that mental health problems are not the most plausible concerns one should address if recidivism reduction is one's goal. Monahan and Steadman, for example, write,

> If the effectiveness of therapeutic techniques is to be measured against the criterion of reduced criminal recidivism, those techniques should be targeted directly against recidivism, not against mental disorder as an intervening variable. There may, for example, be a small group of "psychotic rapists" for whom the cure of their psychosis will result in the cessation of their raping. But there may also be a much larger group of nonpsychotic rapists—or rapists for whom psychosis and criminal tendencies coexist without being causally related—for whom psychological techniques aimed directly at reducing recidivism (e.g., training in self-control and socially appropriate forms of making sexual requests) would prove effective. The use of such techniques, of course, would leave any existing mental disorder intact.[17]

The example offered in the quote is somewhat misleading, because the criterion it proposes for the pairing of targets is their offense alone. If one pools disturbed and nondisturbed rapists, the assumption is that rapists are more similar to each other than are rapists and similarly motivated offenders (such as arsonists) who have comparable backgrounds and dispositions. With such pairing it is also implied that one can address the behavior (rape) without worrying about why it occurs. This presumption would in fact be particularly surprising with rape, which ranges from subcultural gang activity to sadistic, pathologically tinged rage.

On the other hand it would be shortsighted to work with offenders without considering the offenses they have com-

---

[17]Monahan & Steadman, 1983, p. 183.

mitted. Many crimes express broader behavior trends that we can hope to observe in nonoffense settings. This holds particularly true of violence, which reflects dispositions such as suspiciousness, explosiveness, egocentricity, and limited acumen. When one takes a closer look at violent offenses (as we have done in examples) thematic content can be seen that simultaneously emerges—usually in attenuated form—in everyday behavior.

Continuity of motive also operates in the other direction, and one can assume that improvements one can effect (enhanced competence, mental health, or interpersonal skill) may modulate some offense behavior. This does not justify defending treatment as a way to reduce recidivism, but one can postulate that there may be crime-related outcomes to across-the-board improvement, which can be documented with behavior that is observable. The behavior that needs attention will of course vary with the person and his or her level of pathology. It can range from keeping oneself clean and maintaining a respectful demeanor with authority figures to not losing one's cool, being predatory, and posturing toughness in compensatory ways.

Treatment goals that address observable deficits need not fall under the heading of mental health restoration or rehabilitation but can approximate such objectives, depending on the transfer or generalization that occurs. The intervening goal one must have in mind in working with disturbed violent individuals must be to incrementally improve mental health or reduce violence potential as coping capacity is enhanced.

The gains in most instances will be modest. The fact that they can also on occasion be dramatic need not be unduly exciting. Such results must be placed in the same hopper as the fact that on other occasions program graduates will revert to mental illness, or to crime. Neither development can be unambiguously ascribed to change agents whose jurisdiction ends once the offender is released or is placed in a different environment.

Recidivism would be more saliently at issue if aftercare extended into the community, which would be possible if halfway settings were available under parole auspices. We have noted that coping abilities in life cannot be challenged in institutions because the range of challenges that institutional settings offer—even of painful challenges—is narrow. What institutions can provide is a combination of constraint and support (staff call it structure) that reduces temptations and helps vulnerable people to survive. Individuals without support who need support and are offered sudden freedom use it to flounder and fail. Freed psychotics develop anxiety when they meet complexity. Absent constraints, they refuse medication and decompensate. Released addicts face an influx of choices they cannot handle. Given temptation, they revert to drug use and to crime. Such men and women need intermediate institutions until they evolve the resources to survive outside completely structured settings.

## What Sort of Hybrid?

The uniqueness of a setting of the kind that would be designed for disturbed offenders lies in a combination of hospital features and prison features that it needs in pursuit of its mission.[18] The offenders we are concerned with (disturbed violent offenders) must be placed in confinement because they have taken lives or injured people in the community; but they also require a mental health setting because they have long-standing psychological problems.

How can a setting be neither prison nor hospital, and yet be both? We have already discussed some criteria or requisites, but we could add some others that have to do with combinations of attributes of prison and hospital:

1. *One must make sure that clients qualify on all counts.* The kind of setting we would envision must contain clearly disturbed

---

[18]The art in designing a hybrid setting is to link the most desirable features of component settings. If one links the least admirable features (such as the way medication is used as treatment in hospitals and the emphasis on conformity in prisons) one can harm inmates and damage the system. This principle of designing composites was captured by Bernard Shaw, who was asked by an actress to father a child that could combine her appearance with his intelligence. "But madam," Shaw said (or words to that effect), "what if the child had my looks and your brains?"

offenders. The most plausible way to start might be to replicate our sampling design, which asks whether the offenders of concern have histories of mental health problems. The next step would be to find those offenders whose mental health problems are still alive or have resuscitated in prison. Mental health problems should be substantial but must fall short of requiring hospital commitment.

2. *One must make sure the clients match the setting.* One matching issue revolves around the severity of mental health problems with which a setting can deal. The more substantial the representation of mental health staff in a setting, the more serious the problems it can address. It does not matter in this connection whether the administrative umbrella of a program is corrections, mental health, or conjoint, but whether staffing levels are sufficiently rich. (For example, it is to be assumed that medication must be administered by nurses, under medical supervision). A second matching issue has to do with security concerns. Some disturbed offenders are dangerous, some are victim-prone, and others combine predatory and vulnerable features. A setting that contains such persons must be able to separate them so they pose no danger to each other, and it must provide sufficient coverage to prevent victimization.

3. *One must make sure clients get the benefit of helpful prison features.* We have noted that one advantage of prisons over hospitals lies in the educational, training, and work opportunities they often provide. This is a normalizing feature that can be adopted to good effect in hybrid settings. Programming is particularly helpful in providing respectable content around which inmates and staff (and inmates in groups) can relate to each other.

In a classic study of federal prisons, Glaser found that work supervisors had rehabilitative effects on inmates far out of proportion to their numbers.[19] These findings document a listing of requisites for constructive prison impact, which would include that

---

[19]D. Glaser, *The Effectiveness of a Prison and Parole System* (Indianapolis: Bobbs-Merrill, 1964).

- The place where change occurs has dominant or salient work to be done (such as plumbing, carpentry, running Sunday school, or clerking for a guard) which frames a relationship that is a vehicle for change.
- If possible, a legitimizing peer ingroup develops that approves of staff/inmate links, or
- The staff and inmate(s) are ecologically insulated from pressures that emanate from the prison-at-large.
- Staff–inmate links shift from instrumental task orientation to links featuring supportiveness, warmth and loyalty, permitting modeling, emulation, and spontaneous influence.[20]

A second feature of interest to us is that prisons are cafeterias of settings that can be used as substitutes or supplements in designing a well-rounded program. During the day an inmate could attend a specialized group or a regular shop setting. He could also be segregated or isolated if he needs time to be alone and regroup.

4. *One must make sure the inmate gets the benefit of hospital components.* We have alluded to the fact that prison regimes are rigid. Prisons treat a wide range of behavior lapses as rule violations. Dispositions—which are punitive—vary with the severity of the infraction, rather than with the expected impact of dispositions on future behavior. Hospital reactions to disruptive conduct are more personalized and more concerned with anticipated effects on the patient, including iatrogenic

---

[20]H. Toch, "Psychological Treatment of Imprisoned Offenders," in J. R. Hays, T. K. Roberts, & K. S. Solway, eds., *Violence and the Violent Individual* (New York: Spectrum, 1981), p. 230. See also, H. Toch, "Regenerating Prisoners Through Education," *Federal Probation*, 1987, *51*, 61–66. In referring to the therapeutic community inmate, Maxwell Jones observed, "If his interest can be obtained in some simple and familiar work, and particularly if the occupational therapist can enter into a supportive relationship with him, even the most elementary occupation may be therapeutic; it may bring out and direct constructively a variety of emotions which have been denied outlet, and it may do something to offset the restrictions of the mental hospital regime. . . . [an effectively used constructive work group] is capable of leading to better contact with reality, to behavior more in accordance with social standards, and to the foundations of self-esteem" (M. Jones, B. A. Pomryn, & E. Skellern, "Work Therapy," *Lancet*, March 31, 1956, p. 343).

effects (which make the patient sicker).[21] This more personalized approach can be used in prisons for disturbed inmates where standard dispositions make the least sense or where they can do the greatest harm. Another practice worth emulating is that of mental health case management, which includes treatment planning, conferences that review progress, and revised programming contingent on observed behavior.

5. *One must make sure the inmate gets the benefit of interdisciplinary cross-fertilization.* This last point is probably the most important, though it is the least obvious. Disturbed violent offenders are multiproblem offenders, not because they are disturbed and violent, but because their problems are longstanding and complex. The same circumstance holds for many other offenders (and many patients) but plays a limited role in how one deals with them. If future approaches are to be better approaches, the presumption is that they must be less monothematic than current strategies, using a wider range of interventions and expertise. The disturbed violent offender's needs are nonoptional in this regard because he or she demands interdisciplinary confluence, interagency collaboration, and teaming in delivering services. The necessity of experimenting with staff interface arrangements forces prisons to evolve flexible models for responding to multiproblem clients with multiservice approaches. This is an exciting frontier for experimentation and innovation. For those in corrections who might participate and become parties to extending this frontier, it may be a source of adventure.

---

[21]R. F. Morgan, *The Iatrogenics Handbook* (Toronto: IPI, 1983). Glaser is one of few students who argues that "let the punishment fit the crime" is an excessively rigid criterion for disciplining institutional transgressors (D. Glaser, 1964).

# 10

# Responding to the Checkered Careers of Multiproblem Offenders

O ur concern so far has been with the preprison careers of disturbed offenders, and the challenges they present for correctional policy. It should be obvious that there are offenders who arrive in prison because society has given up on them, or has run out of things that it can do for them. We have also noted that the typical disturbed violent offender is a composite of presenting problems, many of which have their inception early in life. Such problems coexist even among offenders who have had no contact with the mental health system before arriving in prison. Most seriously, multiproblem offenders are dealt with by the system one attribute at a time. This means that the inextricable humanity of offenders as clients can be lost in the service delivery shuffle.

Today, a man is arrested, and is a criminal. Tomorrow, he attempts suicide and is a patient. In prison, intake staff discover the man is a drug addict, and assign him to a substance abuse program. Tests show him to be illiterate, and this suggests remedial education. A guard observes the man hallucinating, and he is seen by psychiatrists. On parole, he becomes a homeless person, and is sheltered. He commits a misdemeanor, is jailed, and next transferred to the mental health tier of the jail. And so it goes. At each stage, the man's label changes. The services provided are congruent with his label du jour, or with the facts of current concern. Communication among service providers, or among officials, is minimal. In fact, communication would often be seen as wildly distracting. The remedial learning instructor cares less whether her student is a drug addict. The arresting officer and the judge would have little use for information that tells them that an offender may be illiterate, or even addicted and sporadically psychotic.

The closest to an overview the disturbed offender might get is from his counselor in prison, who updates his file but has no time (nor occasion) to read it. The man's parole officer will also keep track of him while he is on parole. But the parole agent has a limited array of resources and, on the average, has an indecently large case load.

If somewhere along the line the offender becomes a participant in a research study, he will have been selected for study because he currently demonstrates a problem that is of concern to the researcher. His other problems are "controlled for" in designing the study, provided the researcher knows of them and can accommodate them as data.

When research deals with multiple problems, the goal tends to be to demonstrate (or disprove) that people who have one problem are likely to manifest another. The closest to a multiproblem focus would be the assumption that two problems must at times be related because they are statistically correlated.[1]

Such has been state of the art in the research about the link between emotional problems and involvement in crime. One experienced student of the subject who reviewed the research has said that today there is evidence that a link exists. He wrote that

> The data that have recently become available, fairly read, suggest the one conclusion I did not want to reach: Whether the measure is the prevalence of violence among the disordered or the prevalence of disorder among the violent, whether the sample is people who are selected for treatment

---

[1] K. M. Abram & L. A.Teplin, "Co-Occurring Disorders Among Mentally Ill Jail Detainees: Implications for Public Policy," *American Psychologist*, 1991, *46*, 1036–1045.

as inmates or patients in institutions or people randomly chosen from the open community, and no matter how many social and demographic factors are statistically taken into account, there appears to be a relationship between mental disorder and violent behavior. Mental disorder may be a robust and significant risk factor for the occurrence of violence, as an increasing number of clinical researchers in recent years have averred.[2]

The currently popular research assignment is to outline studies that would increase the strength of statistical relationships between mental illness and violence so that we can predict which individuals who have mental health-related problems are most likely to develop offense-related problems. This concern is called "risk assessment" because it promises to help practitioners decide which individuals to target for services that might prevent the onset of a problem or to determine who ought to be sequestered to protect the public from danger the person might pose.[3] Incapacitation is a prominent corollary of this strategy because the term "risk" primarily denotes problems the person poses for others. In the case of disturbed violent offenders who have a problem (mental disorder) and pose a problem (violence to others) the desire is, therefore, to determine which disturbed individuals are likely to offend, rather than which offenders are likely to suffer emotional (or other) problems.

One can make weak predictions about future dangerousness of patients if one uses single predictors. For example, some disturbed persons who are extremely angry or impulsive are more likely to behave violently than other disturbed persons.[4]

---

[2]J. Monahan, "Mental Disorder and Violence: Another Look," in S. Hodgins, ed., *Mental Disorder and Crime* (Newberry Park, CA: Sage, 1993b), pp. 287–302.

[3]J. Monahan & H. J. Steadman, eds., *Violence and Mental Disorder: Developments in Risk Assessment* (Chicago: University of Chicago Press, 1994).

[4]For anger, see R. W. Novaco, "Anger as a Risk Factor for Violence Among the Mentally Disordered," in S. Monahan & H. J. Steadman, eds., *Violence and Mental Disorder: Developments in Risk Assessment* (Chicago: University of Chicago, 1994), pp. 21–60. For impulsivity, see E. S. Barrett, "Impulsiveness and Aggression," also in Monahan & Steadman, 1994, pp. 61–80.

So are some psychotics who respond to command hallucinations, or who suffer from other symptom constellations.[5] Most of these single predictors of violence have been hypothesized based on psychological theories about the nature of the link between clinical conditions and violence. In other words, some researchers have had notions about why certain types of impulses or feelings or states of mind might contribute to the fact that people could behave violently.

But single predictors tend to be useless, in isolation, for risk assessment, because too many other factors can affect the outcome. Risk assessment studies, therefore, try to make predictions more reliable by, among other things, combining several predictors in a single test battery.[6] This strategy is by its very nature eclectic. It works for statistical purposes, but can create a conceptual melange because the psychological process whereby one variable (say, impulsivity) predisposes to violence, is apt to be very different from the reason why another (say, hallucinations) makes patients more dangerous. The greater the diversity of predictors that are summated (and the more variance that is thus accounted for) the more this holds true.

In other words, as the person becomes a statistically more convincing source of danger, the more he or she tends to become an enigma. Armed with prediction equations, one can say with greater certitude that a given patient may become an offender, but one becomes less able to specify why this is so, and to spell out how the person's current problem relates to his or her future problem. Instead of describing a multiproblem person, one describes a one-problem-today-and-another-problem-tomorrow person. One can make a more convincing argument for the need to undertake an intervention designed to forestall impending destructive behavior, but this does not mean that one has clues about what to do. This is so because

---

[5]For psychotics who respond to command hallucinations, and those who suffer from other symptom constellations, see, respectively, D. E. McNiel, "Hallucinations and Violence," pp. 183–202, and B. G. Link & A. Stueve, "Psychotic Symptoms and the Violent/Illegal Behavior of Mental Patients Compared to Community Controls," pp. 137–160, both in Monahan & Steadman, 1994.

[6]Monahan & Steadman, 1994.

the more convincing the predictors become, the less apt they are to make coherent clinical sense.

## Assessment of Offenders

The prevention challenge is especially pressing with disturbed offenders because they are the objects of substantial public concern, which relates to the fact that their offenses seem senseless and unpredictable. One reaction of the public, or at least, the media, to unpredictable behavior is to deny its unpredictability. Faith in the predictability of violence goes hand in hand with a desire to blame the last professional who treated (or refused to treat) the perpetrator of violence. The assumption is that the expert must have ignored clues—of the kind that would be obvious to a moderately intelligent observer— that would have forewarned him or her of impending disaster.

At some junctures, to be sure, the public and the press modulate their censoriousness by admitting that the overall system within which professionals work may be partly at fault for their seeming ineptness. In the case of one offender, for example, the *New York Times* wrote that

> Government officials and advocates alike say the case of Mr. Battiste, who for years drifted among jails, psychiatric emergency rooms and homeless shelters, demonstrates the need for sweeping changes in three distinct, though clearly intertwined, areas.
>
> Many experts argue strongly for breaking down the traditional barriers between mental-health services and drug treatment—a separation that has left most people with combined psychiatric and drug problems adrift in a vast no-man's land. They are often rejected by mental-health clinics because of their drug abuse and by drug programs because of their mental illness.
>
> At the same time, the experts argue that the Battiste case underscores the need for much greater sharing of information among the fractured medical, social-service and criminal-justice bureaucracies.

And some also contend that psychiatrists must be given greater power to confine people for treatment.[7]

With regard to this offender, the *New York Times* pointed out that "doctors had no immediate way of getting a fuller account of his medical histories because of confidentiality laws . . . and because the city has no centralized system of record keeping."[8] This may have been crucial because "his medical records indicated he had exhibited violent behavior in the past," and "the police have said that [he] . . . had a criminal record dating back to 1977 that included arrests for robberies, assaults and attempted rape."[9]

The information whose absence is deplored in this case would be relevant on two counts. One use of the data, especially those related to past transgressions, would be for risk assessment. Decision makers would know that they would be advised to take the offender out of circulation or to restrict his freedom because of his past propensity to react violently. Given a long offense record, the professional who left the offender at large would be open to accusations of negligence if the offender committed a new offense.

The medical history would in turn be needed for an appreciation of the chronicity and complexity of the offender's disorder. The medical history would also be relevant because it provides information about past treatment, which might suggest which treatments had worked and which had not worked in the past. The chart might also illuminate relationships, if any, between symptoms, efforts to ameliorate symptoms, and violence.

Information, of course, can also be damaging. A decision maker's career and reputation could be affected by the way information is used, because he or she could be blamed for ignoring a person's shady past, no matter how irrelevant the

---

[7] J. B. Treaster with M. B. W. Tabor, "Little Help for Mentally Ill Addicts: The Two Treatment Bureaucracies Compete to Avoid Them," *New York Times*, February, 8, 1993.

[8] Treaster with Tabor, 1993.

[9] D. Gonzalez, "Homeless Man Was Treated Before Slaying, Visits to Hospital Were Not Followed Up," *New York Times*, January 21, 1993.

person's past might have been to his current condition. No comparable consequence accrues to the professional who errs in ways that are unrelated to risk assessment. This makes it unsurprising that practitioners may not urgently demand information that might help them decide what to do with patients who are not at presumed risk or those who are defined as having long-term problems. Moreover, such information is of no practical use if the resources needed to treat the person are unavailable to the clinician and to the setting in which he or she works.

The clinician could justifiably argue that some violence of disturbed persons is unpredictable, but the public will not accept this fact. The public is especially likely to assume that any patient who combines emotional problems with drug addiction is apt to behave violently. Therefore, the clinician who discharges such a patient into a resourceless community could be unfairly blamed for his or her offenses. This circumstance invites overprediction and the selective reinstitutionalization of multiproblem patients.

## Risk Management

The song line "what do you do with a drunken sailor?" describes the dilemmas of risk management. The point is that something must be done if a person poses a risk. John Monahan suggests that "for a patient flagged as *high risk*, it is important to explicitly consider preventive action."[10] But for a clinician who operates in a clinical setting, there is an additional consideration, beyond that of prevention: "Preventive action" must be clinically defensible as well as risk reducing, because the clinician is a person whose obligation it is to treat people. The clinician's dilemma is a different one from that of a probation officer, whose preventive action must strive to be fair and legal as well as risk reducing, but need not be clinically defensible. The probation officer must revoke an offender based

---

[10]J. Monahan, "Limiting Therapist Exposure to Tarasoff Liability: Guidelines for Risk Containment," *American Psychologist*, 1993a, *48*, 242–250.

on something he or she has done, but need not argue that jail is a beneficent environment, nor that it can helpfully address the problems that might underly the offender's offense.

Monahan lists three goals of strategies to reduce risk. The first is *incapacitation*, which is the strategy that probation officers would use. The clinician's version consists of commitment to hospital or "transferring the patient to a more secure ward until the level of risk is reduced."[11] But if one takes such action as a clinician, it ought not to reduce risk through physical confinement alone: One has to presume that committing or transferring one's patient offers treatment benefits, given that hospitals are not prisons, and that secure wards are not punitive segregation settings. The assumption governing involuntary hospital commitment is that the subject suffers from a disease or defect that makes him or her dangerous, and that a hospital is equipped to minister to the disease or defect, and to "cure" or ameliorate it. By the same token, one has to assume that a more secure ward provides more structure that the person needs, rather than being a place of purely physical sequestration.

The other goals that Monahan lists are *target hardening* and *intensified treatment*.[12] Target hardening (such as warning potential victims) is a civic obligation. Intensified treatment is clinically defensible provided that the suggested enriched regimen (frequent staff contacts, increased medication, etc.) is designed to address the psychological condition that is presumed to underly the person's diagnosed destructive potential. In theory, contacts would have to be for therapy, not just for surveillance. Medication as chemical restraint would not be clinically defensible, though it might reduce risk.

Ideally, a person should be retained in a setting in order to benefit from treatment modalities that the setting has available that can address the person's problems. The decision to retain should imply the availability of a treatment regime that is responsive and relevant. This, in turn, presupposes that the nature of the person's condition is understood, that the pre-

---

[11]Monahan, 1993a, p. 48.
[12]Monahan, 1993a.

scriptive implications of the diagnosis are clear, and that these implications are outlined as the rationale for retention. Risk assessment data of the sort we have described become unhelpful at this point because statistical compilations of risk factors can be a discordant melange of psychological apples and oranges.

Clinical prediction, which is the alternative to statistical prediction, has been castigated over the years for being less than accurate. But, clinical risk assessment had an overriding virtue: It was compatible with needs assessment, in that both had to be based on an effort to understand the offender's problem. The clinical prediction said, "What I think goes on inside this offender makes me think he or she is likely to explode." Needs assessment said "This offender requires medication (or some other intervention) to reduce the turmoil he or she is experiencing until other supports are in place." The reason for holding the person therefore was to address the problem for which the person was being held.

## Case Management

In hospitals, patient care tends to be coordinated by multidisciplinary treatment teams that invoke institutional resources as the patient needs them, but in the community arranging services for a patient can be a logistical nightmare. One solution to this problem has been that of case management teams. According to Smith et al.,

> Under earlier versions of this model, a case manager functioned primarily as a service broker, working actively to link clients with available resources. Later versions of the case management model involved a much broader spectrum of functions including (a) assessing the needs and resources of the client, (b) planning treatment for the client, (c) linking the client with resources, (d) monitoring the client and evaluating the effectiveness of treatment, and (e) advocating for the client. The range of functions necessary in comprehensive case management requires a variety of skills. Because

of the many functions required, a team approach is often used.[13]

The case management team becomes the keeper of the person's file, as well as the coordinator of services that will address the person's problems as they manifest themselves.

The file the case manager is supposed to maintain details in chronological order problems and diagnosed needs, services received, and actions taken to respond to offenses or misbehavior. This file is a repository of data from agencies that have dealt with the person. Such, at least, is the theory. In practice, files contain lacunae because some data sources (e.g., juvenile offense records) are sealed and others (e.g., mental health information) are classified as confidential. Case managers may have to make do with summarized information or details obtained through interviews.

Information subserves service coordination, and service coordination presupposes access to deliverers of services. Case managers must be able to mobilize networks of service providers to whom they can refer clients as the need for services arises. This, however, can be a sticking point because agencies that deliver services may have their own criteria for who qualifies for their service. Many offenders also deny that they have a problem or resist being referred to agencies that they regard as unhelpful or uncongenial.

Multiproblem persons who are not dangerous often end up in jails because police officers have discovered that mental health staff refuse to admit such persons for treatment. Teplin reports that

> arrest is often the only disposition available to the officer in four types of situations: (1) when the person is not sufficiently disturbed to be accepted by the hospital, but is too public in his or her deviance to ignore; (2) when the hospital staff anticipates that the person will become a management

---

[13]G. B. Smith, A. J. Schwebel, R. L. Dunn, & S. D. McIver, "The Role of Psychologists in the Treatment, Management, and Prevention of Chronic Mental Illness," *American Psychologist*, 1993, *48*, 969.

problem; (3) when the person is thought to be too dangerous to be treated in the hospital setting; and (4) when the person suffers from multiple problems (e.g., is both mentally ill and alcoholic) and is difficult to place. . . . If a person is rejected by the hospital, the only disposition available to police may be arrest.[14]

Torrey et al. point out that

most psychiatric emergency services have full waiting rooms and/or are understaffed. In many jurisdictions police officers bringing mentally ill people to such facilities are required by law to wait with the patients until they have been evaluated and a decision has been made whether to admit or release them. It is not uncommon for this wait to last two to four hours, thereby tying up the officers so that they are not available for other law enforcement duties. Even worse, sometimes the patient is released after the officers have waited for several hours.

Because of such factors police officers frequently decide to charge mentally ill individuals who are acting disruptively on the street with misdemeanors. They can then take them directly to jail rather than spending several hours in a psychiatric emergency facility where admission of the individual is not assured. . . . As a Dade County (Miami) police officer explained: "Look, I can take the sick person to jail and get him booked in 10 minutes and be on my way, or I can take him to the mental health center and sit there for four hours while some incompetent psychiatrist decides to release him and the next day he's back on my beat. Which would you do?"[15]

As previously indicated, multiproblem clients can be turned

---

[14]L. A. Teplin, "Policing the Mentally Ill: Styles, Strategies, and Implications," M. H. J. Steadman, ed., *Effectively Addressing the Mental Health Needs of Jail Detainees* (Boulder, CO: National Institute of Corrections, 1990a), pp. 10–34.

[15]E. F. Torrey et al., *Criminalizing the Seriously Mentally Ill: The Abuse of Jails as Mental Hospitals* (Washington, DC/Arlington, VA: Citizens Health Research Group/National Alliance for the Mentally Ill, 1992), p. 85.

down for service simply because they are multiproblem clients. A mental health clinic may reject a referral because "the client is addicted, and we don't deal with addicts." A substance abuse program staff member may, in turn, indicate that "the man you sent us appears to be disturbed, and we are not equipped to treat addicts with emotional problems, and we do not allow our clients to take psychotropic medication."

Any criminal record compounds this problem because deliverers of service tend to be understandably wary of disruptive and dangerous persons. Webster and Menzies have pointed out that "case management principles to date have not been well applied to forensic psychiatric patients. Some programs specifically debar persons with criminal records. Many hospitals, having achieved 'deinstitutionalization,' understandably shudder at the thought of erecting new secure forensic psychiatric facilities on their premises."[16]

# Hybrid Approaches

In theory, the solution to the challenge posed by multiproblem clients is to create "one-stop shopping" programs that address multiple needs. Webster and Menzies note, for example, that

> although it may not actually make sense to establish separate forensic psychiatric services, this may well be the only realistic course. Integration of forensic psychiatric patients into the ordinary remedial and support stream may be more easily possible once they have been given the chance to establish something of a crime-free record."[17]

Hybrid programs of various kinds would be programs that see themselves as serving multiproblem clients, such as emotionally disturbed homeless persons or drug addicts with men-

---

[16]C. A. Webster & R. J. Menzies, "Supervision in the Deinstitutionalized Community," in S. Hodgins, ed., *Mental Disorder and Crime* (Newbury Park, CA: Sage, 1993), p. 35.
[17]Webster & Menzies, 1993, p. 35.

tal health problems or forensic mental health patients. Hybrid programs would be by definition multimodal and offer a variety of services under one roof. Such programs would have the advantage of being attuned to the interconnectedness of multiple problems such as mental disorder, retardation, poverty, drug abuse, homelessness, joblessness, and violent behavior. They would thus come closer to dealing with the whole person, or approximations of the whole person, than conventional approaches. They would also have a better chance of dealing with core conditions, such as the coping problems that are associated with pathology which may cause an individual to lead a rootless existence (become a homeless vagrant) or to engage in socially inept demonstrative behavior (become a misdemeanant).

The need for hybrid programs is illustrated by the experiences of parents who have advocated for their disturbed family members who have ended up homeless or in jail. Many relatives of multiproblem individuals see a disjuncture between the needs of their loved ones and the way mental health and criminal justice agencies respond to them. In considering alternatives, these relatives, as activists, tend to become attracted to a medical perspective that sees relief for the suffering of young people in the administration of psychotropic drugs.[18] The perspective is attractive because it implies a consistent explanation and offers a tangible solution, but it undersells the complexity and obduracy of the challenges posed in the tangled lives of multiproblem clients. Given the deeply felt needs of patients and relatives, it may be difficult for people who care to accept the fact that compounded problems call for compounded solutions to address them.

Of course, this does not mean that multimodal approaches are needed at every point in time, and that there are not junctures at which the need for medication or housing preempts other needs the offender might have. Some offenders, in fact, may sometimes need jail. They may need the sort of structure that only an institution provides. Such may at times be the

---

[18] E. F. Torrey, *Nowhere to Go: The Tragic Odyssey of the Homeless Mentally Ill* (New York: Harper & Row, 1988).

case for addicts or others who find themselves unable to control runaway impulses.

For some offenders, long periods of parole may be desirable, with strategic interventions as needed. Even revocations may be in order, provided that they are based on violations of parole conditions that have been imposed on the offender to reduce his or her chances of offending, given what we know about his or her offense pattern. These violations could include, for example, refusals to take essential medication or failure to participate in mandated drug treatment, or involvement in interpersonal conflicts that threaten to escalate into violence. When the offender's behavior poses a threat to other persons and suggests short-term dangerousness that is not sufficiently associated with a mental disorder to justify a psychiatric commitment, a jail cell or its equivalent may be the most appropriate setting in which the offender can "cool off," or undergo crisis-related counseling, if such is available.

Hybrid arrangements are especially helpful because they can orchestrate varying approaches as the offender's needs change over time. They can also take into account the fact that a problem can get complicated because of the intrusion of other problems. An offender may need housing, for instance, but might require supervision, or supportive services, as part of his or her living arrangement. He or she might need treatment, and assistance with problems of living between treatment sessions. By centering on all (or most) aspects of an offender's life, service providers can be attuned to the environment in which the person functions. This matters with violent offenders, whose dangerousness often resides in situational transactions between offender and environment.[19] The more one knows about the circumstances under which the person has offended, as well as about the circumstances that face him or her now, the better one can assess—and possibly neutralize—the person's potential for violence.

---

[19]See J. Monahan, *Predicting Violent Behavior: An Assessment of Clinical Techniques* (Beverly Hills, CA: Sage, 1981); H. Toch, *Violent Men: An Inquiry Into the Psychology of Violence* (Washington, DC: American Psychological Association).

# Career Typologies and Career Junctures

When clinicians see a disturbed offender, they need to know what type of multiproblem constellation he or she represents. To quote Webster and Menzies, they "must discern workable typologies that may incorporate psychiatric diagnoses, but that must also go beyond clinical classification as the exclusive or main focus of attention."[20] This generous view of the information that must be at hand is most applicable when there is a network of service providers who could be invoked to address the client's diverse and multifarious needs. But even when this is not so, one must determine whether treatment is the most pressing need, or whether other interventions must take precedence in order for treatment to make sense. A homeless drug-addicted mother, for example, may have problems of living that transcend the need for mood-modulating medication or psychological counseling.

An encounter with a patient must also be viewed in a temporal context, as a juncture in his or her multiproblem career. The patient may have spent most of his or her life in *ad seriatim* institutional settings or have a history of failure on parole, or may have repeatedly discontinued medication, decompensated, and ended up in jail. If career patterns are ignored, this can give rise to sagas such as those of the disturbed and addicted derelicts in New York who terrorized neighborhoods between short-term hospital stays.[21] Contingencies such as these can be avoided if clinical dispositions are arrived at with due regard to patterns of behavior, instead of as responses to episodes or cross-sectional symptom clusters.

If an intervention is seen as career-related, its result can be assessed in career-related terms. In other words, one can see what effect one has had on the person's subsequent life as a

---

[20]Webster & Menzies, 1993, p. 36.

[21]J. P. Fried, "Court Orders Confinement of Drug User. Larry Hogue is Called Threat to Neighborhood," *New York Times*, March 3, 1993; R. Perez-Pena, "Mentally Ill Man Who Abused Drugs Is Freed," *New York Times*, February 5, 1993; M. B. W. Tabor, "Hearing Held on Freeing Drug Abuser," *New York Times*, February 18, 1993.

result of what one has done. Successful impacts can inform future decisions whenever one encounters comparable careers, building experience with career-oriented interventions.

Research can help by isolating and describing the typical careers of disturbed offenders. Studying the pre-prison careers of disturbed inmates is one approach to this task. A different approach would be to track the difficulties that are encountered by a cohort of prison graduates.

Career research that describes the lives of offenders in the community must not only inventory extreme problems, but also those of day-to-day existence. Parole officers know a good deal about maladaptive behavior that falls short of offending and can gather impressions from employers and relatives through routine periodic reviews. Mental health providers also have a great deal of information, and may be able to share it with the permission of their clients.

The problems encountered by offenders include offense-related problems, mental health problems, and problems of daily living. If careers are segmented or subdivided in time (e.g., into an early postincarceration stage, a middle period, and a late period) one can preliminarily obtain four "pure" or consistent career types (offenders who over time have mental health problems, offense-related problems, coping problems, or no problems) and many "mixed" types. One can describe persons who experience shifts from one problem category to another, or sequences involving mixed or compounded stages. An offender could start with a mixture of coping and mental health problems, move on to experiencing problems of daily living, and end up with a stage of offense-related and coping problems. Another parolee may start off with coping problems and minor offenses, develop mental health problems, but achieve a relatively problem-free status over time.

Ideally, one ought to interview offenders with empathetic care to get their perception of their problems as they unfold. Corresponding interviews ought also to be conducted with parole officers and other service providers to elicit their versions of the offenders' problems. Focused interviews could explore perceptions of the services delivered to the offender. In each case, the similarities and differences between perceptions of clients and service providers could be explored, because if clients think they have different needs than those seen by their service providers they are unlikely to be grateful consumers of services that they receive.

Perceptions could be elicited without predefinitions, by having difficulties described in a step-by-step fashion. Scales could be developed to allow interviewers to rate the seriousness or complexity of problems. Services might also be rated as to effectiveness and relevance. One could similarly explore the impact of services, as the providers and clients see them. Objectively favorable impact would consist of the amelioration of the problem at which services are targeted, but subjective impact (perceived amelioration) is also relevant, because one is dealing with human beings who ought to be mindful consumers of services.

The case for comprehensive interviews has been convincingly made by Humphreys and Rappaport in discussing research about service delivery to substance abusers. Humphreys and Rappaport wrote that social scientists ought to "do intensive research with (not on) people who seek services from public substance abuse agencies. By intensive, we mean research that attempts to find out about the real lives of poor substance abusers in context."[22] They also pointed out that

> in studying substance abusers of lower socioeconomic status who are treated in public agencies, it is important that social scientists let these persons tell their own story rather than shape it for them. Rather than assuming we understand the lives of poor, disenfranchised substance abusers, we could give voice to their definitions of reality."[23]

Humphreys and Rappaport further recognize that studying clients uncovers only part of the service equation, because problem definitions are influenced by the shape of service delivery systems. "What is so special (about) substance abuse

---

[22]K. Humphreys & J. Rappaport, "From the Community Mental Health Movement to the War on Drugs; A Study in the Definition of Social Problems," *American Psychologist*, 1993, *48*, p. 899.

[23]Humphreys & Rappaport, 1993, p. 899.

as a problem," Humphreys and Rappaport ask, "that makes it the admission ticket to resources such as shelter, food, counseling, job placement, and social support?"[24] To answer such questions one must study the process by which client needs can be defined in terms of service modalities that are available and affordable. Humphreys and Rappaport suggested that "rather than simply studying individual substance abusers, we could also study treatment agencies, granting bodies, and social policy."[25]

Data from client interviews and information about clients obtained from agency files can be compared. This comparison would be helpful in assessing the adequacy of the information that is available to various agencies that deal with the offender. It would also place labels (e.g., diagnoses) and decisions (e.g., revocations, arrests, and convictions) in client-centered contexts.

Clinical inquiries that focus on offender careers can flesh out portraits provided by statistical clustering, and attach human meanings to them. Major statistical types gain life if they are illustrated by narrative case studies that track problems, responses to problems, and subsequent problems and responses in some detail. The juxtaposition can help improve the adequacy of service delivery to groups of offenders, once the most sensible career groupings are determined.

# The Criminalization of Deinstitutionalized Patients

During the period that preceded the deinstitutionalization movement of the 1960s and 1970s, hospitals kept psychiatric patients for appreciable periods of time. This practice represented overkill, because research was beginning to show that hospital treatment carried no advantage when its results were

---

[24]Humphreys & Rappaport, 1993, p. 892.
[25]Humphreys & Rappaport, 1993, p. 899.

compared with those of alternative care.[26] The studies that were being done suggested that "the technology exists to treat people more effectively, probably even less expensively, outside a hospital setting."[27]

The application of what was known about alternative care at this time, however, had not been widely implemented, and this meant that the alternative to hospital treatment was often no treatment at all. Released patients were left to their own devices, trying, unsuccessfully, to adjust to life in the community, while the community attempted, unsuccessfully, to cope with confused and sometimes disruptive individuals.

One result of this failure was that many former patients became veterans of the criminal justice system, ending up in jails and detention facilities. Torrey et al. found that "most jails in the nation have one or more mental health "regulars" who rotate through the jail on a regular and predictable basis, knowing and known to jail officials on a first name basis."[28] Torrey et al. concluded that

> In reviewing the accounts of mentally ill individuals who are repeatedly jailed, two characteristics of such individuals consistently recur. The first is that these people are non-compliant in taking the medications that they need to prevent a relapse of their illness. Typically they take medications as long as they are in the jail or hospital, but stop taking them when they are released. The other characteristic is that many of these individuals also abuse alcohol or drugs.[29]

A number of studies found sad and impressive correlations between rates of release of mental patients and rates of admission to adjoining jails. The author of one such study, Marc Abrahamson, coined the phrase "criminalization of the mentally ill" to describe the process whereby patients in San Mateo

---

[26]C. A. Kiesler & A. E. Sibulkin, *Mental Hospitalization: Myths and Facts About a National Crisis* (Newbury Park, CA: Sage, 1987).

[27]Kiesler & Sibulkin, 1987, p. 276.

[28]Torrey et al., 1992, p. 82.

[29]Torrey et al., 1992, p. 83.

county ended up in the San Mateo jail.[30] Nearby locations experienced concurrent increments in admissions, sometimes in the order of 300%.[31] In Los Angeles, the detention system gained the label "the nation's largest mental hospital," because of the number of disturbed inmates it acquired.

Estimates of how many jail residents are disturbed range widely, but start at over 6% in large municipal jails, if extremely conservative definitions of mental illness are used.[32] Disproportions are also found when problem indexes other than mental illness are inventoried. Moreover, studies have demonstrated that such problem categories overlap. In one study, for example, 31% of disturbed jail inmates were discovered to be homeless at the time of arrest.[33] Another study conducted in the New York correction system showed that 22% of detainees were homeless when they were arrested and that there were high correlations between homelessness and past hospitalization or outpatient treatment.[34]

Disturbed detainees in jail settings are not usually offenders who have committed serious offenses, but this does not mean that such prisoners are altogether nonviolent. In their survey of jails, Torrey et al. found that the most commonly cited offense with which disturbed offenders had been charged (41% of the total) was assault or battery. Other frequently mentioned charges, however (theft, disorderly conduct, intoxication, drugs, and trespassing), referred to relatively innocuous behavior. The authors indicated that

---

[30]M. F. Abrahamson, "A Comparison of Referrals by Police and Other Sources to a Psychiatric Emergency Service," *Hospital and Community Psychiatry*, 1972, 23, 13–17.

[31]Torrey et al., 1992.

[32]L. A. Teplin, "The Prevalence of Severe Mental Disorder Among Male Urban Jail Detainees: Comparison With Epidemiologic Catchment Area Program," *American Journal of Public Health*, 1990b, 80, 663–669.

[33]P. L. Solomon, J. N. Draine, M. O. Marcenko, & A. J. Meyerson, "Homelessness in a Mentally Ill Urban Population," *Hospital and Community Psychiatry*, 1992, 43, 169–171.

[34]D. Michaels, S. R. Zoloth, P. M. Alcabes, C. A. Braslow, & S. Sofyer, "Homelessness and Indicators of Mental Illness in New York City's Correction System," *Hospital and Community Psychiatry*, 1992, 43, 150–155.

one of the most surprising findings in our survey was the number of instances in which police arrest mentally ill individuals as 'mercy bookings' to protect them. This is especially true for severely mentally ill women who are easily victimized, even raped, on the streets."[35]

One informant who was quoted by Torrey et al. was a Los Angeles police officer who reported "frequent arrests of seriously mentally ill homeless persons whom he described as 'suffering from malnutrition, with dirt-encrusted skin and hair or bleeding from open wounds. . . . It's really, really pitiful,' he said."[36]

On the other side of the ledger, Torrey et al. pointed out that "a small subgroup of seriously mentally ill individuals can and do become dangerous and are in jails because of very serious offenses."[37] Such offenses include murder, felony assault, armed robbery, arson, and sex offenses. Torrey et al. also observed that "the most striking impression in reading the case histories of these individuals is how frequently the crimes are directly the product of the person's untreated mental illness."[38]

## Diversion, Care, and Aftercare

There is agreement among police, jail officials, prosecutors, and others in the criminal justice system about two related points: The first is that extremely disturbed persons should not be routinely processed by the system, except as a last resort. The second point is that to the extent to which mentally ill and other multiproblem individuals find themselves relegated to the system, provision must be made to accommodate their needs and to arrange for continuity of care after the offenders leave the system.

---

[35]Torrey et al., 1992, p. 47.
[36]Torrey et al., 1992, p. 49.
[37]Torrey et al., 1992, p. 50.
[38]Torrey et al., 1992, p. 48.

The first point favors the creation of systematic diversion programs, a few of which have been implemented in progressive communities. In some programs, diversion starts with the police, who invoke networks of service providers in their community.[39] Where such programs exist, the police start by training a small group of officers as specialists who can respond with sensitivity to the mentally ill and to other persons with problems. Members of networks that the police work with are on call to assist officers on the street, and to consult with them at other times. Contractual arrangements are made between police and some service providers to ensure the rapid referral and expedited commitment of persons deemed to be in need of intramural care. Services that become available to the police through network membership can range from shelter and detoxification through placement of mentally retarded or emotionally disturbed individuals.

Other arrangements involve interdisciplinary teams that operate at the point of entry into detention settings and are attached to courts, prosecutors' offices, and jails. The teams may include paraprofessionals as well as professionals, and their assignment is to move seriously disturbed offenders from the criminal justice system into the mental health system before the offenders are charged or convicted.

Some large jails have diagnostic classification professionals who are attached to a mental health tier.[40] Treatment providers from the community are invoked to offer therapy to inmates. Before the prisoners are released, they are screened to see whether they need aftercare services and to arrange for continuity of care. Prisoners who need help are sometimes referred to a consortium of service providers, who farm them out to sources of assistance. Griffin pointed out that

> the most explicit and far-reaching articulation of aftercare linkage standards for jail mental health programs is outlined in the 1989 American Psychiatric Association Task Force

---

[39]L. A. Teplin, 1990a.

[40]H. J. Steadman, D. W. McCarty, & J. P. Morrissey, *The Mentally Ill in Jail: Planning for Essential Services* (New York: Guilford Press, 1990).

Report on 'Psychiatric Services in Jails and Prisons.'. . . . More specifically, the APA guidelines define discharge/transfer planning to include 'all procedures through which inmates in need of mental health care at time of release from jail to the community are linked with appropriate community agencies capable of providing on-going treatment.[41]

Ideally, police-operated diversion efforts intersect with programs that are attached to jails; in turn, jail programs should have links to community networks that undertake to provide continuing assistance. Some examples of such arrangements exist. In Memphis, police teams refer mentally ill persons to an emergency psychiatric unit. If a disturbed offender is arrested, the officers notify a jail liaison person who works with local mental health centers. In Seattle, mentally ill inmates have case managers assigned to them from a mental health center. These case managers coordinate programs in the jail and arrange for services after offenders are released. Nonviolent offenders are not arrested, but instead are taken by the police to a facility run by a community psychiatric clinic, which in turn works with a detoxification center. In Madison, Wisconsin, an interdisciplinary Community Treatment Alternatives (ACT) team works to obtain bail or modification of sentence for disturbed offenders, and places those who are released in an intensive aftercare program.[42]

Community networks, where they exist, take the form of coordinating groups. These groups meet for case conferences to discuss multiproblem clients. One such program is that of the Whatcom County (Washington) jail, which has a model mental health program. According to Jemelka

The county sheriff and jail administrator had initiated and sustained other efforts in the community which fostered the sense of a "common client" among law enforcement, mental

---

[41]P. A. Griffin, "The Back Door of the Jail: Linking Mentally Ill Offenders to Community Mental Health Services," in H. J. Steadman, ed., *Effectively Addressing the Mental Health Needs of Jail Detainees* (Boulder, CO: National Institute of Corrections, 1990), p. 95.

[42]Torrey et al., 1992.

health, health care, and substance abuse professionals in the county. One was the creation of the "Critical Client Network," in which representatives of these professional groups meet every two weeks to discuss specific cases, work out problems with system boundaries, and brainstorm solutions to community problems. These efforts have fostered the development of strategies for dealing with specific cases. Agency responsibilities are discussed and coordinated plans for interventions by appropriate agencies in the community are developed for each case.[43]

Griffin pointed up the need for "continuity agents" in such systems, that is, people who can "continually develop a widening network of community resources."[44] The role entails serving as advocates for multiproblem persons and as catalysts who can goad agencies into providing services for those who ordinarily would not be served. Such linkage involves delicate but persistent diplomacy. It also presupposes that information about clients and their needs is compiled and disseminated. Griffin suggested that

"Continuity Agents" must ensure that relevant information reaches the right people. Much fragmentation occurs because information is not shared in the most effective fashion. Frequently, clients "fall through the cracks" between jails and community mental health centers because appropriate information about an individual's needs for continuing mental health care is not transmitted accurately or in a timely fashion to those who need it. Likely recipients include judges, attorneys, jail staff, family, and local providers of mental health services. Jail mental health programs must see beyond the reaches of their immediate treatment settings and

[43]R. Jemelka, "The Mentally Ill in Local Jails: Issues in Admission and Booking," in H. J. Steadman, ed., *Effectively Addressing the Mental Health Needs of Jail Detainees* (Boulder, CO: National Institute of Corrections, 1990), p. 53.

[44]P. A. Griffin, "The Back Door of the Jail: Linking Mentally Ill Offenders to Community Mental Health Services," in H. J. Steadman ed., *Effectively Addressing the Mental Health Needs of Jail Detainees* (Boulder, CO: National Institute of Corrections, 1990), p. 98.

find ways to share their valuable information to the benefit of the individuals they serve.[45]

# The Personal Equation

One important contribution continuity agents or case managers can make is to neutralize the impersonality of bureaucracies with which their clients must deal. Clients whose motivation is low to begin with, whose coping skills are limited, and whose trust in officialdom may be nonexistent are apt to not show up when referred to intimidating sources of assistance, or to drop out along the way. A continuity agent can prevent these contingencies by establishing a personal relationship with his or her client that is close and intimate, and puts a congenial face on an otherwise faceless system.

Dvoskin and Steadman have noted that

> two of the most important reasons for low case loads for intensive case managers are that it takes a good deal of individualized time and attention to develop a personal relationship with a client and, further, most of this work does not take place in offices, but in the streets where the clients live and hang out.[46]

They wrote that

> another advantage of having a personal relationship with a case manager is that it provides a less stressful way of increasing the intensity of help. . . . If the case manager is perceived as an agent of the state, whose sole intention is to make the client 'toe the line,' the client will be unlikely to invest an effort into the relationship. Thus it is important that the case manager be seen as an advocate for the client even if other (e.g., criminal justice) agencies are concurrently

---

[45]Griffin, 1990, p. 99.
[46]J. A. Dvoskin & H. J. Steadman, "Reducing the Risk of Living With Mental Illness: Managing Violence in the Community," *Hospital and Community Psychiatry*, in press.

dealing with the client in more coercive or authoritarian ways.[47]

Case managers can make their clients partners and participants in change, and "the presence of a case manager can be a mechanism for enlisting the client's intelligence and 'street survival' skills."[48] The client in such encounters comes to be viewed as someone with whom information can be shared and options discussed, so that he or she can make mindful decisions. If it is at all possible, clients can be afforded choices of services, and can be involved in periodic reviews of the adequacy of the services they receive.

Continuity agents must enjoy the trust of clients, but they must also be seen as credible by professionals in various agencies. Dvoskin and Steadman wrote that "when a client is placed on a case management load, it is imperative that the case manager be viewed as a member of any treatment team that interacts with a client."[49] The linkage must be an intimate one, with the client feeling close to the agent, who is in turn collegially accepted by a wide range of service providers. This prescription calls for an agent who is a "mensch," a concerned and charismatic human being, whose academic qualifications are less important than the dedication, experience, and interpersonal competence he or she brings to the job. It is also an argument for cultural sensitivity among continuity agents who deal with a variety of clients.

In larger case management teams, different members can take responsibility for different aspects of the job. Some members of teams ought to be paraprofessionals, who "should ideally be of cultures similar to the clients they will serve."[50] They can even be ex-offenders or mental patients who "have succeeded in learning to gain control of their life circumstances."[51] Other members can be professionals who are steeped

---

[47]Dvoskin & Steadman, in press.
[48]Dvoskin & Steadman, in press.
[49]Dvoskin & Steadman, in press.
[50]Dvoskin & Steadman, in press, p. 14.
[51]Dvoskin & Steadman, in press, p. 15.

in the discourse and practices of disciplines other than their own, so that they can serve multifarious bridging functions.

## From Diversion to Multiversion

Diversion programs get people out of jails who don't belong in jail. In the process, they make the jails easier to run, and spare some inmates excruciatingly painful experiences involving callous peers and obdurate regimes.[52] Other programs assist jail graduates by acting as brokers, obtaining services for them they would not otherwise obtain. This permits some persons to survive who otherwise would not have survived and could have gravitated back into confinement.

But to get the benefit of diversion, one must first be a candidate for arrest or detention, and one must be disturbed tangibly enough to invoke a "cop card" or to be flagged by screening teams. One becomes eligible if one shows florid psychotic symptoms, or if one has been hospitalized in the past. Failing this, one must be despondent enough (and extrovert enough) to talk of thoughts of suicide.

Offenders are divertible before they have been sentenced, but offense seriousness (and especially, violence) often calls for incapacitation or punishment. Many disturbed individuals have not been eligible for diversion at critical junctures of their careers. Moreover, the precocious start of many multiproblem careers makes jail a point too late in the sequence of offenses committed by young offenders to make diversion possible.

If violent offenders are to benefit from continuity agents— from brokerage and case management—they must ideally be identified before they become chronic multiproblem offenders. This means that one may have to think of schools rather than jails as staging points for diversion programs. One may also have to think of diversion in other than mental health terms. Toby pointed out that "special education" (intraschool diver-

---

[52]J. A. Dvoskin, "Jail-Based Mental Health Services," in H. J. Steadman, ed., *Effectively Addressing the Mental Health Needs of Jail Detainees* (Boulder, CO: National Institute of Corrections, 1990), pp. 178–197.

sion) is sometimes deployed for "behavior problems from which emotional handicaps are inferred without independent psychiatric justification."[53] He wrote that

> 'Special education' students placed in that category because of supposed emotional disturbance may have violence-prone personalities. On the other hand, they may only be assumed to have such personalities because they have engaged in inexplicably violent behavior. They might be able to control their behavior if they had incentives to do so."[54]

According to a recent *New York Times* article, New York's special education system "deploys legions of psychologists and social workers."[55] These professionals have been charged with providing "endless evaluations of marginal worth at tremendous cost." Diagnoses are easier to come by than services. Special education was created by law to ensure instruction for students with tangible psychological deficits. However, most students "are labelled either 'learning disabled' or 'emotionally handicapped,' classifications that many academics say were vaguely defined by statute and have been even more loosely applied."[56] The system is said to be nurtured by a variety of incentives. For each special education student, schools receive federal funds to help support his or her education. Youngsters who are referred tend to present behavior problems (very much including aggressivity) that make them a liability to their teachers. The referrals ease the teacher's task of managing his or her classrooms, but the students acquire a designation that may be an "educational fiction."

Another argument against classifying juveniles as mentally ill is that such a label can be attached to virtually every youngster who is brought to official attention. According to Melton and Pagliocca,

---

[53]J. Toby, "Everyday School Violence: How Disorder Fuels It," *American Educator*, 1993, 17(4), 45.

[54]Toby, 1993, p. 45.

[55]S. Dillon, "Special Education Absorbs School Resources," *New York Times*, April 7, 1994.

[56]Dillon, 1994.

youth in the juvenile justice system are not very different from delinquent and status offending youth in general. At the same time, they are not very different from emotionally disturbed youth in other public-sector service systems (e.g., mental health, child welfare).[57]

The problem is that if every troubled juvenile qualifies as emotionally disturbed, the diagnosis is at best nondiscriminating and at worst discriminatory. Being dubbed mentally ill means that one is selected out of a pool of age-mates for differential treatment. The diagnosis subserves the desired disposition, rather than the other way around.

The reason why kids can invite labeling is because clinical taxonomies have pathologized destructive behavior that is very prevalent among young offenders. Melton and Pagliocca refer to diagnostic criteria, and note that

> it is difficult to imagine a youth whose behavior is sufficiently objectionable to remain in the juvenile justice system who would not meet the *DSM–IIIR* criteria for conduct disorder. Any three of the following list of behaviors is enough to obtain the diagnosis: stealing, running away, lying, arson, truancy, breaking and entering, cruelty to animals, rape, fighting, fighting with a weapon, and armed robbery or extortion. Accordingly, a thief who sometimes lies and initiates fights would fit the criteria. When one considers the possibility of other behavior disturbances (e.g., oppositional disorders), it seems even more likely that most delinquents would fit a diagnosable condition.

> Taking the point a step further, it is difficult to imagine that such a youth would not be classified as seriously emotionally disturbed. The National Institute on Mental Health criteria for classification as SED require only a diagnosable condition (e.g., conduct disorder), involvement in two or more service systems (e.g., education and juvenile justice), and evidence

---

[57]G. B. Melton & P. M. Pagliocca, Treatment in the Juvenile Justice System: Directions for Policy and Practice, in J. J. Cocozza, ed., *Responding to the Mental Health Needs of Youth in the Juvenile Justice System* (Seattle, WA: National Coalition for the Mentally Ill in the Juvenile Justice System, 1992), p. 108.

of persistent problems. Because the latter two criteria are generally satisfied by involvement in the juvenile justice system itself, the fact that most delinquent and status offending youth could be diagnosed as having a mental disorder means that virtually all youth who are more than transient clients of the juvenile justice system are SED. In short, the definitional criteria for conduct disorder and SED are such that the identification of emotionally disturbed youth in juvenile justice is virtually a search for a tautology![58]

The other problem, which is discussed in chapter 1, lies in the connotations of diagnoses that focus on character disorder. As Vicky Agee has put it,

Character disorders are unpleasant types who are generally thought of as having no consciences, little if any human emotions such as warmth and caring, an inability to profit from experience, illogical thinking, and a deep resistance to treatment. In fact, in many settings a diagnosis of some type of character disorder is tantamount to a diagnosis of untreatable. . . . Many mental health professionals feel that the place for all character disorders is some sort of correctional setting. . . . This implication can be couched in very sophisticated mental-health-ese. . . . (This) differentiation can be carried to the absurd to the point that youths who act out or have behavior problems are excluded from treatment because they have no "underlying emotional disturbance"—which would presumably indicate that their behavior is more or less motivated by an empty organism, with no feelings or thought processes.[59]

Labeling youths as emotionally disturbed can be unnecessary and can undersell other problems the youths have by preempting their salience. The point we have repeatedly made for adult disturbed offenders applies with added force to aggressive delinquents: Troubled youths are walking case his-

---

[58]Melton & Pagliocca, 1992, pp. 109–110.
[59]V. L. Agee, *Treatment of the Violent Incorrigible Adolescent* (Lexington, MA: D.C. Heath, 1979), pp. 15–16.

tories, and invitations to multimodality. To the coexisting problems we find frequently among adults they reliably add others, such as dysfunctional families, learning disabilities, gang membership, chronic truancy, and school failure. No intervention that is based on a simple problem definition is apt to do the job. As Melton and Pagliocca put it,

> metaphorically, walls ought to come tumbling down between disciplines. . . . Those services that have the best track record with the 'multiproblem' clients who remain in the juvenile justice system are highly integrated and individualized. Such service models combine educational, social, family and psychological interventions in a single treatment."[60]

One source of open-ended intervention (at least, in theory) has been the juvenile court, an institution that was created at the turn of the century to serve as a case manager or continuity agent for multiproblem youths. Unfortunately, for some time, juvenile courts have been under crossfire from the left (for not observing legal niceties and dealing harshly with status offenders) and from the right (for being too lenient). This sustained onslaught has begun to heavily erode the power of the courts to invoke a range of services, from counseling or enriched probation, to detention. Revitalizing the substantial discretion of the juvenile courts may in the short run not be in the offing, but it could arguably be a positive step, because it would allow society to intervene and intercept violent (and disturbed violent) careers at their inception.

To accomplish this goal, the courts would not only have to have their power restored to them, but would have to have more treatment options than are now funded and available, plus the power to order service providers to provide services. The courts would have to dispose of more intermediate sanctions (short of reformatory confinement) to back up their referrals, in case of noncompliance. This prospect is admittedly uncongenial to reformers who are concerned about the unfet-

---

[60]Melton & Pagliocca, 1992, p. 114.

tered exercise of arbitrary discretion. However, there is no other way to link reluctant service providers with clients who are unconvinced that they need help.

One must similarly provide for continuity of service over time. It is difficult to envision such continuity—or to imagine sensible risk assessment and management—as long as juvenile records are routinely sealed and remain inaccessible to persons who work with youths after they have graduated from the system. The prospect of compromises of confidentiality strikes some as objectionable, but such observers forget that the danger lies in how information is used, rather than in the information itself. This sort of problem can be addressed by limiting access to the information and by providing safeguards against its inappropriate use.[61]

At the adult end, a greater variety of services must be envisioned for the criminal justice system. Attention now centers on jails because deinstitutionalized patients gravitated to them in large numbers, and because jails have come to contain many disturbed persons in obvious need of service. However, most seriously violent offenders are not found in jails and therefore, are not candidates for conventional diversion programs. Most violent offenders must be dealt with after they have been sentenced to prison. The strategy must be one of building service modalities into the system in which offenders must remain, rather than diverting offenders from one system (the criminal justice system) to another (the mental health system), or vice versa.

One must be able to respond to a variety of needs and offer a variety of services to offenders on probation, on parole, or even (as we have suggested) in prisons. The offenders who are clients of such service must be consulted about their needs and desired responses to their needs. And criminal justice personnel other than police must be involved in what is done. Whenever possible, such personnel must be converted into continuity agents, case managers, and brokers. The involvement of hospitals in case management must also be increased

---

[61]J. F. Sullivan, "Whitman Calls for Less Secrecy Surrounding Juvenile Offenses," *New York Times*, March 18, 1994.

beyond the preparation of discharge plans, which run the risk of leaving follow up to chance.

Integration presupposes the creation of hybrid approaches and composite systems. There is nothing new in this notion. Some schools now act as multiservice agencies for children who come from multiproblem homes.[62] Prisons provide remedial services, such as literacy training. Prisons have also increasingly become the sources of substance abuse treatment that is less-than-available in the communities from which offenders originate. And parole officers in progressive agencies try hard to continue the process. They deal daily, for example, with parolees for whom mental health services are mandated as a condition of release from the prison.

If jails are hospitals by default, the rest of the system—also by default—serves multiproblem offenders. It is a delusion to think of the criminal justice system as being able to exist for punishment alone. If the system is an engine of retribution, it perpetuates rather than reduces crime. Crime is associated with personal deficits, and with disjunctures between personal needs and societal options. If the system does not attend to the deficits and needs of offenders while they serve time for their offenses, antisocial careers will inevitably be renewed when the offenders are released. To try to prevent this contingency the system must work with offenders, and intercede with the community as necessary, to ameliorate the personal problems of the offenders and to promote their reintegration, so that the preconditions of their criminal behavior are addressed.

---

[62]R. H. Price, E. L. Cowen, R. P. Lorion, & J. M. Ramos-McKay, eds., *Fourteen Ounces of Prevention: A Casebook for Practitioners* (Washington, DC: American Psychological Association, 1988).

# References

A killer in St. Patrick's: Hospital to jail to death. (1988, September 23). *New York Times.*

Abrahamson, D. (1973). *The murdering mind.* New York: Harper & Row.

Abrahamson, M. F. (1972). A comparison of referrals by police and other sources to a psychiatric emergency service. *Hospital and Community Psychiatry, 23,* 13–17.

Abram, K. M., & Teplin, L. A. (1991). Co-occurring disorders among mentally ill jail detainees: Implications for public policy. *American Psychologist, 46,* 1036–1045.

Agee, V. L. (1979). *Treatment of the violent incorrigible adolescent.* Lexington, MA: D. C. Heath.

Alexander, F., & Healy, W. (1935). *Roots of crime.* New York: Knopf.

Alexander, F. G., & Selesnick, S. T. (1966). *The history of psychiatry.* New York: Harper & Row.

Allport, G. W. (1961). *Pattern and growth in personality.* New York: Holt, Rinehart & Winston.

American Association of Correctional Psychologists (1980). Standards for psychological services in adult jails and prison. *Criminal Justice and Behavior, 7,* 81–127.

American Law Institute (1962). Proposed official draft. *Model Penal Code.* Philadelphia, PA: American Law Institute.

Anderberg, M. (1973). *Cluster analysis for applications.* New York: Harcourt Brace Jovanovich.

Ashley, M. C. (1922). Outcome of 1,000 cases paroled from the Middletown state homeopathic hospital. *State Hospital Quarterly, 8,* 64–70.

Barratt, E. S. (1994). Impulsiveness and aggression. In J. Monahan & J. J. Steadman (Eds.), *Violence and mental disorder: Developments in risk assessment* (pp. 61–80). Chicago: University of Chicago Press.

Brill, H., & Malzberg, B. (1954). *Statistical report of the arrest record of male ex-patients, age 16 and over, released from New York state mental hospitals during the period 1946–48.* Albany, NY: New York State Department of Mental Hygiene.

Cather, J. (1987, December 10). Judge cites loopholes for mentally disturbed. *Albany Knickerbocker News.*

Cocozza, J., Melick, M., & Steadman, H. (1978). Trends in violent crime among ex-mental patients. *Criminology, 16,* 317–334.

Cohen, F. (1985). Legal issues and the mentally disordered offender. In National Institute of Corrections (Ed.), *Sourcebook on the mentally disordered prisoner* (pp. 31–90). Washington, DC: Department of Justice.

Cohen, L. H., & Freeman, H. (1945). How dangerous to the community are state hospital patients? *Connecticut State Medicine Journal, 9,* 697–700.

Cooke, M. K., & Cooke, G. (1982). An integrated program for mentally ill offenders: Description and evaluation. *International Journal of Offender Therapy and Comparative Criminology, 26,* 53–61.

231

Coughlin, J. A. (1987, December 9). Testimony before the Assembly Standing Committees on Correction and Mental Health, Mental Retardation and Developmental Disabilities. *Public hearing on persons with developmental disabilities and the criminal justice system.* Albany, NY: Department of Correctional Services.

Dillon, S. (1994, April 7). Special education absorbs school resources. *New York Times.*

Durbin, J. R., Pasewark, R. A., & Alberts, D. (1977). Criminality and mental illness: A study of arrest rates in a rural state. *American Journal of Psychiatry, 134,* 80–83.

Dvoskin, J. A. (1990). Jail-based mental health services. In H. J. Steadman (Ed.), *Effectively addressing the mental health needs of jail detainees* (pp. 178–197). Boulder, CO: National Institute of Corrections.

Dvoskin, J. A., & Steadman, H. J. (in press). Reducing the risk of living with mental illness: Managing violence in the community. *Hospital and Community Psychiatry.*

Everitt, B. (1974). *Cluster analysis.* New York: Wiley.

Fairweather, G. W., Sanders, D. H., Cressler, D. L., & Maynard, H. (1969). *Community life for the mentally ill.* Chicago: Aldine.

Farrington, D. P., Ohlin, L. E., & Wilson, J. Q. (1986). *Understanding and controlling crime.* New York: Springer.

Finch, J. R., & Smith, J. P. (1970). *Psychiatric and legal aspects of automobile fatalities.* Springfield, IL: Charles C Thomas.

Fogel, D. (1979). *We are the living proof.* Cincinnati, OH: Anderson.

Freeman, R. A., Dinitz, S., & Conrad, J. P. (1977, January–February). A look at the dangerous offender and society's effort to control him. *American Journal of Correction,* 25–31.

Fried, J. P. (1993, March 3). Court orders confinement of drug user. Larry Hogue is called threat to neighborhood. *New York Times.*

Giovannoni, J. M., & Gurel, L. (1967). Socially disruptive behavior of ex-mental patients. *Archives of General Psychiatry, 17,* 146–153.

Glaser, D. (1964). *The effectiveness of a prison and parole system.* Indianapolis: Bobbs-Merrill.

Glueck, S. S. (1925). *Mental disorder and the criminal law: A study in medicosociological jurisprudence.* Boston: Little, Brown.

Gohlke, K. H. (1985). Executive summary. In National Institute of Corrections (Ed.), *Sourcebook on the mentally disordered prisoner* (p. 3). Washington, DC: Department of Justice.

Gonzalez, D. (1993, January 21). Homeless man was treated before slaying. Visits to hospital were not followed up. *New York Times.*

Griffin, P. A. (1990). The back door of the jail: Linking mentally ill offenders to community mental health services. In H. J. Steadman (Ed.), *Effectively addressing the mental health needs of jail detainees* (pp. 91–107). Boulder, CO: National Institute of Corrections.

Groth, A. N. (1979). *Men who rape.* New York: Plenum.

Group for the Advancement of Psychiatry, Committee on Psychiatry and

Law (1954). *Criminal responsibility and psychiatric expert testimony* (Report No. 26). Topeka, KS: Author.

Guze, S. (1976). *Criminality and psychiatric disorder.* New York: Oxford University Press.

Halleck, S. L. (1969). *Psychiatry and the dilemmas of crime.* New York: Harper & Row.

Halleck, S. L. (1986). *The mentally disordered offender.* Washington, DC: National Institute of Mental Health.

Healy, W. (1914). *The individual delinquent.* Boston: Little, Brown.

Healy, W., & Bronner, A. (1936). *New light on delinquency and its treatment.* New Haven, CT: Yale University Press.

Hochstedler, E. (1987). Criminal prosecution of the mentally disordered: A descriptive analysis. *Criminal Justice Review, 12,* 1–11.

Humphreys, K., & Rappaport, J. (1993). From the community mental health movement to the war on drugs: A study in the definition of social problems. *American Psychologist, 48,* 892–901.

Jemelka, R. (1990). The mentally ill in local jails: Issues in admission and booking. In H. J. Steadman (Ed.), *Effectively addressing the mental health needs of jail detainees* (pp. 35–63). Boulder, CO: National Institute of Corrections.

Jones, M., Pomryn, B. A., & Skellern, E. (1956, March 31). Work therapy. *Lancet,* 343–344.

Kassebaum, G., Ward, D., & Wilner, D. (1971). *Prison and parole survival: An empirical assessment.* New York: Wiley.

Kiesler, C. A., & Sibulkin, A. E. (1987). *Mental hospitalization: Myths and facts about a national crisis.* Newbury Park, CA: Sage.

Levin, J., & Fox, J. A. (1985). *Mass murder: America's growing menace.* New York: Plenum.

Link, B. G., & Stueve, A. (1994). Psychotic symptoms and the violent/illegal behavior of mental patients compared to community controls. In J. Monahan & H. J. Steadman (Eds.), *Violence and mental disorder: Developments in risk assessment* (pp. 137–160). Chicago: University of Chicago Press.

Lion, J. R. (1963). Special aspects of psychopharmacology. In J. R. Lion & W. H. Reid (Eds.), *Assaults within psychiatric facilities* (pp. 287–296). New York: Grune & Stratton.

Lion, J. R., & Pasternak, S. A. (1973). Countertransference reactions to violent patients. *American Journal of Psychiatry, 130,* 207–210.

Lynch, D. (1994, April 10). Crime and stupidity. *Albany Times Union.*

Maguire, K., & Pastore, A. L. (Eds.). (1994). *Sourcebook of criminal justice statistics, 1993.* Washington, DC: U.S. Government Printing Office.

Martinson, R. (1974). What works?—Questions and answers about prison reform. *Public Interest, 35,* 22–54.

McMahon, W. G. (1987, December 9). Testimony before New York State Assembly Standing Committee on Correction. New York State Assembly Standing Committee on Mental Health, Mental Retardation, and Developmental Disabilities.

McNiel, D. E. (1994). Hallucinations and violence. In J. Monahan & H. J. Steadman (Eds.), *Violence and mental disorder: Developments in risk assessment* (pp. 183–202). Chicago: University of Chicago Press.

McQuitty, L. M. (1987). *Pattern-analytic clustering: Theory, method, research and configural findings.* New York: University Press of America.

Melton, G. B., & Pagliocca, P. M. (1992). Treatment in the juvenile justice system: Directions for policy and practice. In J. J. Cocozza (Ed.), *Responding to the mental health needs of youth in the juvenile justice system* (pp. 107–140). Seattle, WA: National Coalition for the Mentally Ill in the Juvenile Justice System.

Mental health system fails alcoholics, drug abusers. (1988, March 13). *Albany Times Union.*

Michaels, D., Zoloth, S. R., Alcabes, P. M., Braslow, C. A., & Safyer, S. (1992). Homelessness and indicators of mental illness in New York City's correction system. *Hospital and Community Psychiatry, 43*, 150–155.

Millon, T. (1981). *Disorders of personality DSM–III Axis I.* New York: Wiley.

Monahan, J. (1981). *Predicting violent behavior. An assessment of clinical techniques.* Beverly Hills, CA: Sage.

Monahan, J. (1993a). Limiting therapist exposure to Tarasoff liability: Guidelines for risk containment. *American Psychologist, 48*, 242–250.

Monahan, J. (1993b). Mental disorder and violence: Another look. In S. Hodgins (Ed.), *Mental disorder and crime* (pp. 287–302). Newbury Park, CA: Sage.

Monahan, J., & Steadman, H. J. (1983). Crime and mental illness: An epidemiological approach. In N. Morris & M. Tonry (Eds.), *Crime and justice: An annual review of research* (vol. 4, pp. 145–189). Chicago: University of Chicago Press.

Monahan, J., & Steadman, H. J. (Eds.). (1994). *Violence and mental disorder: Developments in risk assessment.* Chicago: University of Chicago Press.

*Monte W. Durham v. United States*, 214, F.2d 862 (D.C. Cir., 1954).

Morgan, R. F. (1983). *The iatrogenics handbook.* Toronto: IPI.

Morrow, W., & Peterson, D. (1966). Follow up of discharged psychiatric offender. *Journal of Criminal Law, Criminology and Police Science, 57*, 33–34.

Mulvihill, D. J., & Tumin, M. M., with Curtis, L. A. (Eds.). (1969). *Crimes of violence. A staff report to the National Commission on the Causes and Prevention of Violence.* Washington, DC: Government Printing Office, 12:459.

Novaco, R. W. (1994). Anger as a risk factor for violence among the mentally disordered. In J. Monahan & H. J. Steadman (Eds.), *Violence and mental disorder: Developments in risk assessment* (pp. 21–60). Chicago: University of Chicago Press.

N.Y. Penal Law §§ 140.20–140.35 (McKinney 1988).

O'Leary, V., & Glaser, D. (1972). The assessment of risk in parole decision making. In D. West (Ed.), *The future of parole* (pp. 135–199). London: Duckworth.

Overholser, W. (1973). Isaac Ray, 1807–1881. In H. Mannheim (Ed.), *Pioneers in criminology* (pp. 177–198). Montclair, NJ: Patterson Smith.

Perez-Pena, R. (1993, February 5). Mentally ill man who abused drugs is freed. *New York Times*.

Perkins, R. M. (1957). *Criminal law*. New York: Foundation Press.

Pollock, H. M. (1938). Is the paroled patient a menace to the community? *Psychiatric Quarterly, 12*, 236–244.

Price, R. M., Cowen, E. L., Lorion, R. P., & Ramos-McKay, J. (Eds.). (1988). *Fourteen Ounces of Prevention: A Casebook for Practitioners*. Washington, DC: American Psychological Association.

Rappeport, J. R., & Lassen, G. (1965). Dangerousness—Arrest rate comparisons of discharged mental patients and the general population. *American Journal of Psychiatry, 121*, 776–783.

Rappeport, J. R., & Lassen, G. (1966). The dangerousness of female patients: A comparison of arrest rates of discharged psychiatric patients and the general population. *American Journal of Psychiatry, 123*, 413–419.

Ray, I. (1835). Lecture on the criminal law of insanity. *The American Jurist, 14*, 253.

Redl, F., & Wineman, D. (1962). *Children who hate: The disorganization and breakdown of behavior controls*. New York: Collier.

Robins, L. N., Helzer, J. E., Weissman, M., Orvaschel, H., Gruenburg, E., Burke, J. D., & Regier, D. A. (1984). Lifetime prevalence of specific psychiatric disorders in three sites. *Archives of General Psychiatry, 41*, 949–958.

Roth, M., & Bluglass, R. (Eds.). (1985). *Psychiatry, human rights and the law*. Cambridge, England: Cambridge University Press.

Rothman, D. (1980). *Conscience and convenience*. Boston: Little, Brown.

Rowan, B. (1976). Principal Paper, Correction Section. In M. Kindred, J. Cohen, D. Penrod, & T. Shaffer (Eds.), *The mentally retarded citizen and the law*. New York: Free Press.

Schofeld, W., Hathaway, S., Hastings, D., & Bell, D. (1954). Prognostic features in schizophrenia. *Journal of Consulting Psychology, 18*, 155–166.

Sechrest, L., White, S. O., & Brown, E. D. (Eds.). (1979). *The rehabilitation of criminal offenders: Problems and prospects*. Washington, DC: National Academy of Sciences.

Shah, S. A. (1981). Dangerousness: Conceptual, prediction and public policy issues. In J. R. Hays, T. K. Roberts, & K. S. Solway (Eds.), *Violence and the violent individual* (pp. 151–178). New York: Spectrum.

Shaw, C. R., & McKay, H. D. (1942, reprint 1972). *Juvenile delinquency and urban areas*. Chicago: University of Chicago Press.

Silberman, C. E. (1980). *Criminal violence, criminal justice*. New York: Random House.

Solomon, P. L., Draine, J. N., Marcenko, M. O., & Meyerson, A. J. (1992). Homelessness in a mentally ill urban population. *Hospital and Community Psychiatry, 43*, 169–171.

Smith, G. B., Schwebel, A. I., Dunn, R. L., & McIver, S. D. (1993). The role of psychologists in the treatment, management, and prevention of chronic mental illness. *American Psychologist, 48*, 966–971.

Steadman, H. J., & Cocozza, J. J. (1974). *Careers of the criminally insane.* Lexington, MA: D. C. Heath.

Steadman, H. J., Cocozza, J. J., & Melick, M. E. (1978). Explaining the increased arrest rate among mental patients: The changing clientele of state hospitals. *American Journal of Psychiatry, 135,* 816–820.

Steadman, H. J., McCarty, D. W., & Morrissey, J. P. (1986). *Developing jail mental health services: Practice and principles.* Washington, DC: National Institute of Mental Health.

Steadman, H. J., McCarty, D. W., & Morrissey, J. P. (1990). *The mentally ill in jail: Planning for essential services.* New York: Guilford Press.

Steadman, H. J., McGreevy, M. A., Morrissey, J. P., Callahan, L. A., Robbins, P. C., & Cirincione, C. (1993). *Before and after Hinckley: Evaluating insanity defense reform.* New York: Guilford Press.

Stevens, G. F. (1994). Prison clinicians' perceptions of antisocial personality disorder as a formal diagnosis. *Journal of Offender Rehabilitation, 20,* 159–185.

Sullivan, J. F. (1994, March 18). Whitman calls for less secrecy surrounding juvenile offenses. *New York Times.*

Szasz, T. S. (1974). *The age of madness.* Northvale, NJ: Jason Aronson.

Szasz, T. (1961). Criminal responsibility and psychiatry. In H. Toch (Ed.), *Legal and criminal psychology* (pp. 162–163). New York: Holt, Rinehart & Winston.

Szasz, T. (1979). Insanity and irresponsibility: Psychiatric diversion in the criminal justice system. In H. Toch (Ed.), *Psychology of crime and criminal justice* (pp. 139–141). New York: Holt, Rinehart & Winston.

Tabor, M. B. W. (1993, February 18). Hearing held on freeing drug abuser. *New York Times.*

Taylor, P. (1982). Schizophrenia and violence. In J. Gunn & D. P. Farrington (Eds.), *Abnormal offenders, delinquency and the criminal justice system.* New York: Wiley.

Teplin, L. A. (1984a). Criminalizing mental disorder: The comparative arrest rate of the mentally ill. *American Psychologist, 39,* 794–803.

Teplin, L. A. (1984b). Managing disorder: Police handling of the mentally ill. In L. A. Teplin (Ed.), *Mental health and criminal justice* (pp. 157–175). Beverly Hills, CA: Sage.

Teplin, L. A. (1990a). Policing the mentally ill: Styles, strategies and implications. In H. J. Steadman (Ed.), *Effectively addressing the mental health needs of jail detainees* (pp. 10–34). Boulder, CO: National Institute of Corrections.

Teplin, L. A. (1990b). The prevalence of severe mental disorder among male urban jail detainees: Comparison with epidemiologic catchment area program. *American Journal of Public Health, 80,* 663–669.

Thornberry, T. P. (1987). Toward an interactional theory of delinquency. *Criminology, 25,* 863–891.

Thornberry, T. P., & Jacoby, J. E. (1979). *The criminally insane.* Chicago: University of Chicago Press.

Toby, J. (1993). Everyday school violence: How disorder fuels it. *American Educator, 17*(4), 4–9, 44–48.

Toch, H. (1975). *Men in crisis: Human breakdowns in prison.* Chicago: Aldine.

Toch, H. (Ed.). (1980). *Therapeutic communities in corrections.* New York: Praeger.

Toch, H. (1981). Psychological treatment of imprisoned offenders. In J. R. Hays, T. K. Roberts, & K. S. Solway (Eds.), *Violence and the violent individual* (pp. 325–342). New York: Spectrum.

Toch, H. (1982, Fall). The disturbed disruptive inmate: Where does the bus stop? *Journal of Psychiatry and Law,* 327–349.

Toch, H. (1984). Quo vadis? *Canadian Journal of Criminology, 26,* 511–516.

Toch, H. (1987). Regenerating prisoners through education. *Federal Probation, 51,* 61–66.

Toch, H. (1992a). *Mosaic of despair: Human breakdowns in prison,* Washington, DC: American Psychological Association.

Toch, H. (1992b). *Violent men: An inquiry into the psychology of violence.* Washington, DC: American Psychological Association.

Toch, H., & Adams, K. (1986). Pathology and disruptiveness among prison inmates. *Journal of Research in Crime and Delinquency, 23,* 7–21.

Toch, H., & Adams, K. (1987). The prison as dumping ground: Mainlining disturbed offenders. *Journal of Psychiatry and Law, 15,* 539–553.

Toch, H., & Adams, K., with Grant, J. D. (1989). *Coping: Maladaptation in prisons.* New Brunswick, NJ: Transaction.

Torrey, E. F. (1988). *Nowhere to go: The tragic odyssey of the homeless mentally ill.* New York: Harper & Row.

Torrey, E. F., Stieber, J., Ezekiel, J., Wolfe, S. M., Sharfstein, J., Noble, J. H., & Flynn, L. M. (1992). *Criminalizing the seriously mentally ill: The abuse of jails as mental hospitals.* Washington, DC/Arlington, VA: Citizens Health Research Group/National Alliance for the Mentally Ill.

Treaster, J. B., with Tabor, M. B. W. (1993, February 8). Little help for mentally ill addicts: The two treatment bureaucracies compete to avoid them. *New York Times.*

Twain, M. (1893). *Sketches new and old.* Hartford, CT: American.

*United States v. Brawner* (471 F.2d 969, D.C. Cir., 1972).

U.S. Bureau of Prisons. (1968). *A handbook of correctional psychiatry* (Vol. 1). Washington, DC: Department of Justice.

von Krafft-Ebbing, R. (1904). *Textbook of insanity.* Philadelphia, PA: F. A. Davis.

Webster, C. A., & Menzies, R. J. (1993). Supervision in the deinstitutionalized community. In S. Hodgins (Ed.), *Mental disorder and crime* (pp. 22–38). Newbury Park, CA: Sage.

Weihofen, H. (1933). *Insanity as a defense in criminal law.* New York: The Commonwealth Fund.

Wertham, F. (1969). *A sign for Cain.* New York: Paperback Library, Coronet.

Wilson, R. (1980, February). Who will care for the "mad and bad"? *Corrections Magazine,* p. 10.

Wolfgang, M. E., Figlio, R. M., & Sellin, T. (1972). *Delinquency in a birth cohort*. Chicago: University of Chicago Press.

Wulach, J. S. (1983). Diagnosing the *DSM—III* antisocial personality disorder. *Professional Psychology: Research and Practice, 14*, 330–340.

Zigler, E., & Phillips, L. (1981). Social competence and outcome in psychiatric disorder. *Journal of Abnormal and Social Psychology, 63*, 254–271.

Zitrin, A., Hardesty, A. S., & Burdock, E. T. (1976). Crime and violence among mental patients. *American Journal of Psychiatry, 133*, 142–149.

# Author Index

# Subject Index

# About the Authors

Hans Toch is distinguished professor at the University at Albany of the State University of New York, where he is affiliated with the School of Criminal Justice. He obtained his PhD at Princeton University and has taught at Michigan State University and Harvard. Toch is a Fellow of the American Psychological Association and the American Society of Criminology. He is a recipient of the Hadley Cantril Memorial Award and has served as a Fulbright Fellow in Norway.

Among Toch's recent books are *Coping: Maladaptation in Prisons* (1989) with Ken Adams and *Police as Problem Solvers* (1991) with J. Douglas Grant, as well as *Violent Men: An Inquiry Into the Psychology of Violence* (1992), *Mosaic of Despair: Human Breakdowns in Prison* (1992), and *Living in Prison: The Ecology of Survival* (1992), three revised books published by the American Psychological Association. One of Toch's early works was *The Social Psychology of Social Movements* (1965); his first interests included problems of public opinion, perception and social perception, and violence. Toch has described himself as an applied social psychologist with a "serendipitous specialization" in criminal justice and criminology. The area of specialty evolved during decades of research in California and New York State prisons and in metropolitan police departments. Toch says that his crime-related concerns have made him "an unwitting pioneer" in a "now established interdisciplinary endeavor that has become a growth industry."

Kenneth Adams is associate professor and assistant dean for graduate programs in the College of Criminal Justice at Sam Houston State University. He received his PhD at the State University of New York at Albany. His earliest research, carried out while a Fellow at the Nelson A. Rockefeller Institute of Government, focused on the delivery of mental health services to prison inmates. Subsequently, he has directed several large-scale research projects, variously supported by the National Institute of Mental Health, the National Institute of Justice, and the John D. and Catherine T. MacArthur Foundation.

These projects have centered on the relation of mental health problems to violence and to prison adjustment and on developmental aspects of criminal behavior across the life span. He is also coauthor, with Hans Toch, of *Coping: Maladaptation in Prisons*. Most recently, his research interests have turned to issues of police violence.